About the Author

If you love reading about sport, there's likely to be at least one 'Ken Piesse' title, cricket or football in your collection. *Favourite Footy Yarns* is the 72nd book Ken has written, edited or published.

In a lifetime of sportswriting, Ken has collaborated in the auto-biographies of some of the biggest names in the game, from Dermott Brereton and Jason Dunstall through to Tony Lockett and Paul Salmon. He edited *Football Fan* magazine, *Football Australia* and wrote for *Inside Football* for years. His biggest 'scoop' story made the front pages of every News Limited Sunday paper Australia-wide when Sydney's Darren Jolly told him he was intending to be with wife Deanne at the birth of their first child rather than play in the 2006 Grand Final. Baby Scarlett was induced on the Friday night before the game!

Ken says there's never been a more exciting kick or a bigger roar than the day Jezza (Alex Jesaulenko) bounced through the sealer in time-on of the 1970 Grand Final or two more supercharged solos than produced by ex-Hawk Lance 'Buddy' Franklin one cold June Friday night at the 'G in 2010 when he kicked two extraordinary matchclinching goals from the boundary line to sink Essendon.

Ken and his artist wife Susan live on the Mornington Peninsula. They have five children, the youngest of whom, Bec, is a former Junior Olympian and plays AFL footy in Canberra.

· FAVOURITE ·
FOOTY YARNS

FROM LAUGHS & LARRIKINS TO BUSH LEGENDS & BAD BOYS

KEN PIESSE

echo

echo

Echo Publishing
A division of Bonnier Publishing Australia
534 Church Street, Richmond
Victoria Australia 3121
www.echopublishing.com.au

First published 2015
This edition published 2016

Edited by Kyla Petrilli
Cover design by Luke Causby, Blue Cork
Page design and typesetting by Shaun Jury
Cartoons © Paul Harvey

Printed and bound in China

National Library of Australia Cataloguing-in-Publication entry
     Piesse, Ken, author.
     Favourite footy yarns: from laughs and larrikins to bush legends and
     bad boys / Ken Piesse; an introduction by Robert Harvey.
     ISBN: 9781760404246 (paperback)
     ISBN: 9781760065737 (epub)
     ISBN: 9781760065720 (mobi)
     Includes bibliographical references and index.
     Australian football—Anecdotes.
     Australian football—Miscellanea.
     Other Creators/Contributors: Harvey, Robert, 1971– writer of
     introduction.
     796.336

Twitter/Instagram: @echo_publishing
facebook.com/echopublishingAU

Contents

Foreword by Robert Harvey   vii

Author's Introduction   1

1   Amazing & Mostly True   13

2   Bloopers, Gaffes & Pranks   35

3   Bush Royalty   49

4   Goals & Goalmen   79

5   Interviews   89

6   Larrikins   103

7   Laughs   125

8   Legends   157

9   Loves   191

10   Matches   201

11   Memories   221

12   Quotes   239

13   Snippets   255

14   Stats   279

15   Superstitions   289

Acknowledgements   295

Bibliography   297

Index   301

TEENAGER: Eighteen-year-old Robert Harvey with Demon Alan Johnson, MCG, mid-season, 1990
Ian Kenins/Inside Football

Foreword

By Robert Harvey

I was blessed to be born a footballer. When Darrel 'the Doc' Baldock first picked me (to play for St Kilda), I was 16 and still in fourth form at John Paul College in Frankston. I was skinny, underweight and overawed. But the Doc came to me and said no matter what happened, I was going to play the final four games of the season and he was true to his word. This was 1988. I'd gone from playing my first game in a back pocket in the Under 19s to a forward flank in the firsts – all in six months. To have emulated the longevity of Ted Whitten and Michael Tuck and play 20 League seasons was way beyond my rainbow. I just wish I could have played in premierships like them. But strange as it may seem, I don't regret anything about my career. To play on the biggest stages of all for two decades with and against some of the game's legends was an ongoing challenge and privilege. Sure, the final half of the 1997 Grand Final when Adelaide came from behind to beat us was a low point, but we had our chances that day and simply weren't good enough to take them. The premiership was there for us, but we fell away when it counted. I don't know if we could have done anything differently. But that's football. The highs can be incredible but so are the lows.

As a teenager, walking into Moorabbin and seeing the big stand enveloping almost half the ground is something that will always stay with me. Tingles would run up and down my spine. Our champions then like Tony Lockett, Stewie Loewe, Trevor

Barker and Danny Frawley were all heroes in my eyes. Yet they all had time to chat and make a young kid more comfortable. Fast forward a decade and blokes like Burkey (Nathan Burke), Fraser Gehrig, Lenny Hayes and Nick Riewoldt – still going strong – were every bit as important in helping us win respect and play off in finals.

My attitude to footy never changed over those 21 seasons. I wanted to succeed and do everything possible to help me be the best player I could be. My way was to train hard and then harder again. I don't know how many pairs of cross trainers I've worn out over the years, but it would have to be hundreds. Training was always an obsession with me. It was one of the reasons why I stopped playing cricket, a game very much in the Harvey blood and one I'd loved since I was a little tyke in the backyard at Seaford. I'd taken five wickets for my team Frankston Peninsula in the Premier first XI grade the day before, but was too sore to do weights the following day. I was young at the time and maybe some celebrating with mates that night had a little to do with it as well, but our coach Stan Alves was adamant: 'That's it, Harvs. No more cricket.'

It proved to be a blessing as football was fast becoming totally professional and juggling training and practice for two sports even in November and December was simply too complicated. By concentrating solely on footy, I was able to bring a new consistency to my game – and incidentally, provide a few extra dollars for my Dad, Jeff, family and mates who backed me at 70-1 preseason to win the Brownlow Medal in 1997. They did it again nice and early in 1998, got 33s and won big again. In those years, I may not have been as dynamic a player as earlier, but I had good balance to my game, had plenty of rest and physio and stretching sessions and didn't miss a beat. Looking back now, I was at my absolute top during those two years. To be able to play another 10 years after that was an ongoing bonus.

I'm certainly glad that I remained a one-club player. I would never have been able to forgive myself if I had ever left St Kilda and the club had made the finals without me. You can have all

UP FROM SEAFORD: Sixteen-year-old Robert Harvey, pictured squatting at the very front on the far left, first played in a back pocket for the St Kilda Under 19s in 1987. Also in the squad, sitting in the front row, far right, is Shane Warne

the comforts in the world, but if you're not at home, what's the point?

I'd like to thank Ken Piesse for the opportunity to contribute to his latest book. People say I had stamina but so does Ken. Maybe that's why he's known as 'the Master'. He loves footy and cricket. He tells me this is the 72nd book he has written or edited. More than 20 are on football. That's an amazing record. My Mum kept newspaper cuttings in scrapbooks over the years and Ken's stories figure prominently throughout, from my introduction to the club via recruiting officer John Beveridge right through to my 300th League game on preliminary final day, 2004. Ken is passionate, expert, loyal and caring. He's at the top of the tree – among the best and most knowledgeable sportswriters. We were cricket teammates at Frankston and for years have been near-neighbours at Mt Eliza. Years ago he got me out first ball at Port Melbourne, but my old man got runs against him that day, so I always say we're square.

I like the mix of his favourite stories and punchlines and love Paul Harvey's cartoons – particularly the one of 'Plugger' (Tony Lockett) picking up Mark Graham and squeezing him like a sponge. I was always glad Plugger was on our side. When he went off to Sydney it was like dancing with your sister.

It's my pleasure to endorse *Favourite Footy Yarns* and wish Ken every success with it. He deserves it.

ROBERT HARVEY
Mt Eliza

Author's Introduction

It's a red-letter day when a new book you've written arrives. I immediately rang Allan 'Yabbie' Jeans and said, 'Our book is here, Yab.' It wasn't his life story – years earlier he'd told me the truth and nothing but the truth would affect too many. Instead, he had written a foreword to my book *Football Legends of the Bush*. Hailing from Tocumwal, high up on the Murray, where he first ran the local pub as a teenager, Jeans was an old bushie at heart who loved to yarn and reminisce.

His autobiography would have been fascinating and full-frontal. Contributing a foreword to someone else's book was less demanding and hurtful. He'd been thrown into League coaching at 27, still the youngest-ever. Some of those he suddenly had a responsibility to had been his idols. Some resented a kid telling them what to do. His peers like Len Smith were all-embracing and encouraging. Jeans was at the coalface when St Kilda vacated the Junction Oval. He always reckoned the cricketers had too much power. Coaching champions like Baldock, Stewart, Howell and Ditterich had been incredibly rewarding – but stressful. He trusted me enough to elaborate – but not for the record.

'Coaching,' he'd say, 'is the art of surviving.' Every now and again I'd playfully suggest that he had a good story to tell – and how it would be something for the grandchildren ... 'You know why I can't do it, mate,' he'd say.

Every visit without fail, Mary Jeans would prepare morning tea, with percolated coffee and homemade cakes. It was country

1

hospitality in the city. 'You didn't need to do all this, Mary,' I said once.

'Oh yes I do, Ken.'

While Jeans was uncomfortable with penning a warts-and-all autobiography – one he'd just read had somehow neglected to mention the hero's long-time illicit lover, making it a less-than-true account – he had no problem in dictating 3000 words or so on his bush upbringings – especially as it also involved Mary, his wife for more than 50 years. She was a nurse completing her training in Melbourne and Jeans wanted to be closer to her. Initially he'd knocked back the advances of Les Foote and St Kilda, saying he was a country boy and had responsibilities to his mother. His father had disappeared to goodness-knows-where during the war and Mrs Jeans had to raise the family herself. She worked three different jobs to feed and clothe them all. Jeans had been promised 500 pounds, a small fortune back then, to come to the Big Smoke and play six games. On the night of the sixth, back he was at home again, with an envelope.

'Here you are, Mum, this [money] is yours,' he said.

'What are you doing here, Allan?' she said. 'You're supposed to be in Melbourne [playing football].'

'Mum, I've played my six games. They gave me all this money … 500 pounds … this is for you.'

'Allan,' she said, 'you can always come home, but you can't always move forward.'

I faithfully transcribed his foreword, including the anecdote on how he got his nickname: 'I used to follow my big brother around,' said Jeans. 'He was pretty red in the face and was known as "Lobby" – short for lobster. They asked him one day who the little tyke tagging around with him was? "Oh that's just a little yabbie," he said.'

I dropped the deluxe version around for his approval and as I was leaving, he called, 'Mate [he always called you "mate"], you don't want me to come to the launch [of the book] do you?'

'You'll be right, Al, you're fine.' But even then his lungs were shutting down.

COUNTRY BOYS: Tocumwal's Allan Jeans and Latrobe's Darrel Baldock piloted St Kilda's one-and-only premiership in 1966

Six or so months later, when the first copies of the book arrived, I rang him again. This time he was in the Allan Jeans Wing at a nursing home in Cranbourne. He was seriously ill. 'Come around ... now,' he said.

He'd lost an alarming amount of weight and was hooked up to an extra air supply. He couldn't even get out of his chair without assistance. As he'd confided a year earlier, he was stuffed.

'Hello, Al ... thought you'd like some copies for the family,' I said.

We had the best hour together, chatting about his coaching, his mates and Mary.

'What I'll never forget,' I said to him, 'were the feasts Mary would prepare when you knew I was coming over. It was so very kind.'

Jeans looked across the room to Mary and grinned. It was a true love match, that one.

'How's the cricket going?' he asked with a mischievous smile.

He'd never let me forget the time he provided a character reference following my one-and-only umpire's report in a District game at North Melbourne. I'd been given out lbw and told the umpire he was guessing, repeated it afterwards and he put me on report. I was a captain and should have been more diplomatic. Jeans loved that one. 'Fancy me giving a reference for you … a member of the mee-dya,' as he liked to pronounce it.

He signed some books and photographs in his impeccable hand, including one of him with Cameron Schwab at Richmond in 1992. I'd never asked him why he'd coached the Tigers. They were debt-ridden, had a poor list and in a decade hadn't finished higher than eighth. 'Alan Schwab [Cameron's dad] refused to take no for an answer,' he said. 'He kept on saying I had to help.' From the corner of the room, Mary spoke up: 'Ken … do you know why he did it? Poverty … we needed the money.'

They'd lost whatever savings they had in the Pyramid collapse. Jeans had also been one of the many creditors at St Kilda who were paid peanuts via a scheme of arrangement, despite his status as the club's only premiership coach. With four children to raise and care for, times were tough.

We shook hands and I wished him well. A day later the nursing home cut off all access to visitors other than the family and within a week he was gone. More than 5000 attended his funeral at the MCG. For so many of us it was like losing a father all over again. Dermott Brereton was particularly cut. He'd been to see Yab earlier that week and also knew he'd never see him again.

For Jeans, his players were his extended family. Ever since Dermott was 16 and first training at Glenferrie, Jeans had always provided wise consul. Dermott was often accused of being self-centred and lairy but he was also a matchwinner – and had raw courage and a team ethic matched by few. At the time he was driving a red Ferrari and had a bad back. 'Dermie,'

Jeans asked him once, 'have you ever thought about getting a more comfortable car – one where you don't have to be a contortionist to get into?'

'No, Yab … never.'

Teddy Whitten had fashioned a lime green set of adidas boots for Dermott and with his long blond hair and earring, he was quite a sight. 'Dermie,' said Jeans, 'all this flashiness … what happens if you need to go to a bank manager and ask him for a home loan? Do you think you need to be just a little more conservative?'

'Yab,' said Dermott, 'what happens if I don't have to go to a bank manager?!'

Brereton's on-field swagger and Irish temper could be a lethal cocktail. Once Jeans sent out his runner George Stone to deliver Brereton a message: 'Tell that blond poofta if he doesn't do what he's told, he's coming straight off.'

Brereton saw Stone racing towards him and told him to back off – for his own good. Wanting to stay healthy, Stone kept running to another blond – Russell Morris – and dashed back to the bench. 'Wadda he say?' demanded Jeans on his return.

'Nothin' Yab, nothin' at all.'

In one run into a late '80s finals campaign, the Hawks were playing St Kilda at Waverley and so certain was Jeans that a hyped-up Brereton was on the verge of losing his temper and going on report, he had Stone hovering 30 or so metres away from him for much of the last quarter, constantly calling to him to 'stay cool' and 'the finals start in a fortnight'.

Away from the game, Dermott was amiable, laidback and loud. At his 21st, he and his Dad, Dermott snr, both wore brand new matching singlets. One was lime green and the other bright pink. They both loved dogs. 'KD', the family's St Bernard, grew so tall, Mr Brereton removed the front seat of his old car so the pup could fit and still go on his favourite walks at Frankston beach. One day Dermott saw a bloke mistreating his dog at the beach, saw red and ended up in court. Once we visited on the way down to our holiday home and Mrs Brereton

LAIRY: Summer training at Glenferrie Oval and
Dermott Brereton was a standout with his pink
spotted legionaire's cap and lime green singlet, 1990
*Tony Greenberg/*Inside Football

was making vegetable soup, complete with croutons. The aroma
was magnificent.

'Gee, what are you making, Jean?' I asked, hoping we'd be
asked to take a seat.

'Ken, it's for the dog!'

Dermott and Trevor Barker were good mates and Dermott
would often stay at Trevor's place when he was out on the tear
at a weekend. Trevor was forever receiving chocolate boxes from
his many lady admirers and was always too polite to say he didn't
eat chocolate. He'd pack them one on top of another into his
tallest kitchen cupboard. Dermott discovered them one day and
had no problem devouring the lot – even the out-of-date ones.

When Dermott was cleaned up by Geelong's Mark Yeates at
the first bounce in the 1989 Grand Final, he writhed in agony
as Gary Ablett snr took the first shot at goal 60 metres away. A
rib was broken and he had kidney damage. He tried to stand up
but couldn't. Stone came out to get him off. Dermott refused.
Stone was insistent: 'Yab says you've got to come off.'

'No.'

Grimacing in pain, he was helped by the club's fitness advisor

John Kilpatrick into a forward pocket. Watching on, four rows back, Tony Jewell, a Richmond premiership player and coach, said Dermie looked positively green. Yet minutes later, when Hawthorn attacked, Brereton drove himself to get in front of the pack, somehow reached for the sky, took a crucial mark and kicked truly. It was one of eight for the term as Hawthorn opened a 40-point break.

In an instant Stone was again side-by-side. 'Yab says well done. Stay on.'

It was the most physical Grand Final since the 1971 donnybrook between Hawthorn and St Kilda. At the first break on his way to the Hawthorn huddle, Brereton walked past Yeates, winked and said, 'I'm still here.'

By half-time Hawthorn's lead had been cut to six goals. The rooms looked like a battle front. John Platten with his head bandaged was in Ga-Ga Land having been knocked out in the opening minutes, Robert Di Pierdomenico had a broken rib and a pierced lung, Brereton was passing blood and Gary Ayres had a bad corky. Despite its enviable run of Grand Final appearances, Hawthorn had never won back-to-back premierships. Already it was down to 16 fit men.

Jeans was known for his inspiring oratory. The only one who could possibly rival him was the club's first premiership coach, the iconic John Kennedy snr.

Jeans' ability to raise his voice and add emphasis to a word or a phrase just at the right time was uncanny. He would have made a remarkable general. He could see the hurt in his players' eyes and gradually, ever so gradually, worked himself into the most celebrated and inspiring Grand Final speech of all.

Jeans' messages were always simple and relevant. He started with a story. A teenage boy was at the shops buying a new pair of shoes. He had a choice: a really good pair which were more expensive, or a cheaper pair that didn't fit quite as well.

Sweeping his eyes around the group, he asked, 'What will we all be saying tomorrow? Will we be saying: I wish I HAD paid the price?

'Are you prepared to pay the price? Today … right here … now.

'ARE YOU?' his voice rising.

'To win today, to create history for the club, to go back to back, to achieve our goal, all of us … we must pay the price.

'We must. We must. Today. NOW.'

The 'now' was delivered quickly and with venom. This was a 'no-tomorrow' situation. The eyes of every player were on Jeans, who slowly and deliberately walked from player to player, looking directly at them and demanding, 'Are you prepared to pay the price?

'ARE YOU?'

Minutes later as the players ran down the race again with Jeans still booming, 'PAY THE PRICE, PAY THE PRICE,' Peter Curran was one of several with tears running down their faces, so charged was the atmosphere. Jeans had had a brain aneurism less than two years earlier. Mary Jeans scolded him later, saying the tremendous effort in trying to motivate his players that day could have triggered more issues.

Geelong kept on coming, reducing the gap further at the final change. Had the game gone even 30 seconds longer, Malcolm Blight was sure his Cats would have won. There was just a kick in it at the end. Somehow, despite nine goals from Ablett, Hawthorn survived. It remains the most remembered Grand Final since my first in 1963, right up there with the 1970 Carlton comeback against Collingwood and the titanic finish to the 2005 decider when Sydney's leaping Leo Barry took one of the great marks of all deep in defence with just seconds to play.

That night at the Hilton hotel, in between the speeches, the players spent much of their time together on couches out of the ballroom. Ayres, the toughest Hawk of all, told me how his mate Brereton had stood up like never before. He was like a proud big brother. 'He didn't want the Geelong boys to see that he was hurt, but he was … to take that early mark and provide the inspiration he did … it's something none of us will ever, ever forget,' he said.

FIERY: Tony Lockett's strong-arm sleeper hold on Essendon's Brad Fox was a talking point for weeks as the 1992 season opened furiously
Inside Football

In my 30-odd years of covering games each Saturday, the only others to corner as many headlines as 'the Kid' were Tony Lockett, Wayne Carey and Gary Ablett snr.

I penned Lockett's St Kilda autobiography, which Trevor Barker launched at Moorabbin. He didn't change even one sentence of the 50000-word manuscript. At the launch the big fellow was humble and softly spoken. He would much rather have been around his barbecue at Devon Meadows with his mates sharing a beer and a few snags. Late in 2014, I was in Bowral for a Don Bradman function and Plugger rang, apologising that he wouldn't be able to make it. 'Wednesday's my busiest day,' he said. 'Not only am I looking after my cows, but the fella next door's as well.'

The sports editor at the *Sunday Press* Scotty Palmer would always have me at St Kilda games as he knew Plugger trusted me and would always talk. But you had to wait for the right moment, until he was ready. The only full-forward to win a Brownlow, Plugger's idea of a perfect day was to kick six, flatten a few, have half a dozen pots in the social club and be back home in Ballarat by nine. He craved anonymity and distrusted the media. His shift to Sydney was a godsend, both for club and player.

Wayne Carey won more matches single-handedly than any other player I've seen. He was unstoppable, especially on Friday nights and the big games that really counted. He *was* North Melbourne and to see his life spinning out of control after his sudden exit from the club was extraordinarily sad. We'd met at Arden Street on his very first day in Melbourne in the late '80s. Under 19s coach Denis Pagan said he'd seen him down at training and Wayne had said, 'No, I'm here to play seniors.' Carey was incredibly athletic and took a remarkable number of screamers running straight at oncoming traffic à la Jonathan Brown. It was one reason why Pagan created 'Pagan's Paddock', so Carey could run into open space without the complication of opposition defenders jumping into him. 'He was our biggest asset. We needed to keep him fit,' Pagan said. With his tan and imposing Chesty Bond physique, Carey was the apple of everyone's eye. Once he did a fashion shoot as part of a players' fundraiser, wearing a pair of leather pants on the catwalk and nothing else. The girls squealed and whistled and the pictures were excellent. When I suggested to him that one would make a good front cover for the next *North News*, he said, 'Do you mind if you don't? Sally [his long-time girlfriend] won't like it.'

Ablett was also an amazing footballer who could kick staggering distances with either foot and mark the ball seemingly five storeys high. He'd take the ball in front of us on the wing at the old Waverley pressbox and my mate Daryl Timms and I would say, 'Have a shot.' His nine goals in that epic '89 Grand Final won him the Norm Smith, and *The Age* cartoonist depicted him walking on water back to Geelong that night. The great man almost became involved in a biography I was writing. He rang one Friday night and asked to meet. The book was virtually finished and at the printers. More than 60 had contributed from coaches and teammates from Hawthorn and Geelong to Drouin and Myrtleford. In the end, the publisher reckoned he wanted too much so the book went ahead as an 'unauthorised biography' and was a bestseller.

Many of my football books have been written on behalf

MATCHWINNER: Wayne Carey was the ultimate matchwinner, the finest of my time
*Ken Rainsbury/*North News

of a celebrity player, from Brereton and Lockett through to Tony Liberatore and Paul Salmon. In one taping session with 'Libba', young Tom Liberatore, now also a champion Bulldog, was playing balloon football up and down the corridor with the full Rex Hunt-type commentary: 'And Wynd knocks it down to Romero ... Romero to little Libba ... Libba sees a leading Chris Grant ... he marks it and ... it's another goal ... the Doggies lead!' Tony suggested to Tom to keep the noise down a little, only for Tom to say, 'It's okay Dad, it's almost orange [quarter] time.'

So significant a contribution did Salmon make in his five years at Hawthorn that he was named in the club's Team of the Century. Accorded the regular rucking role he'd craved at Essendon, he mixed his height and sheer skill with brainpower. This particular year North Melbourne's Corey McKernan was the outstanding follower in the game, his centre-bounce leaping his signature. There was a photo in the *Herald Sun* from the previous weekend's game with McKernan jumping into an opponent and using the opponent's body for extra elevation. We were in the early stages of taping and interviewing for

Salmon's autobiography *The Big Fish*, the first of a two-book deal I'd arranged for Paul with Bob Sessions, one of the great Australian publishers. In the lead-up to the North match and his meeting with McKernan, I suggested to Paul that he faced a huge challenge trying to combat McKernan who was almost 10 years younger and more athletic. Had he thought about doing something a little different at the bounces? Maybe coming in sideways at an angle ... anything to stop him jumping into him à la Simon Madden ...

Come game day, at the very first bounce Salmon faced McKernan and ran at him, as per normal, only to baulk at the very last moment and watch McKernan disappear over his shoulder, without having touched him or the ball. Salmon grabbed the ball and started a Hawthorn attack. Minutes later, the pair were opposed on a wing and McKernan was bolting towards free space at half-forward. Instead of following him, intent on manning-up, Salmon ran the other way, making his own space. Seeing Salmon bolting in the opposition direction, McKernan stopped and sprinted back to where Salmon was. Suddenly Salmon was doing all the dictating and Hawthorn had a big win. Paul was gracious enough later in the year to inscribe a copy of *The Big Fish* for me with a special message: 'Thanks, Master ... for everything.'

It was my privilege to work with him and so many others in 30-plus years of being paid to go to the footy. From being threatened by one ruckman who promised to 'come and get' me if my story wasn't to his taste to marvelling at the leapers like McKernan and Nick Naitanui and the bravery of Jonno Brown, Luke Hodge, Carey and Nick Riewoldt, it has been an amazing adventure. I trust you will enjoy the stories that follow.

KEN PIESSE
Mt Eliza

1

Amazing & Mostly True

'And by the way,' said Miller. 'There's another kid called Carey who is in the same boat. I'll give you $10 000 for him …'

ALL-SPORTSMAN

A teenage Dustin Fletcher once defeated a just-as-young Mark Philippoussis in boys' singles. Teaming with basketball-star-to-be Chris Anstey, he also won the Victorian Doubles Championships. Fletcher played his 22nd and final AFL season in 2015, joining an elite and ever-so-distinguished band to reach 400 games.

SURPRISE, SURPRISE, SURPRISE

It was Ricky Olarenshaw's first night at North Melbourne, home of the Shinboner of the Century Glenn Archer. Eyeing Archer with reverence and awe, as if he was some sort of footballing god, Olarenshaw followed the celebrated defender out into the Arden Street car park thinking he'd be hopping into a '67 Charger or something equally loud and brutal. Instead, Archer unlocked his Ford Festiva and headed home to play with his kids …

&$#@ THIS ...

Part of Darryl White's indoctrination at Brisbane FC in 1992 included an eight-kilometre bike ride up a mountain. Objecting to the Tour de France-type fitness test, White stopped halfway up and threw his bike off a cliff saying he'd arrived from Alice Springs to play football, not ride &$#@ing bikes.

Despite kicking Goal of the Year in his first month, White was keener on the Alice than Brisbane. When coach Robert Walls called to ask him when he'd be ready to start his new pre-season, White said he was very busy and call him back in a couple of weeks ...

FOOTBALL CRAZY

Australia's victorious 1989 Ashes cricket team did a lap of honour before the bounce in the 1989 Grand Final, captain Allan Border having rejected an offer of a $10 000 complimentary family holiday to Harare so he could attend his first Grand Final.

THE MAGICAL MILE

Glenn Archer admits to being headstrong at 17 and 18, and preferring his mates at Noble Park to anything North Melbourne FC could offer. Finally agreeing to turn up at a summer session for North's Under 19s, Archer had to join in with

the rest of the hopefuls for North's 'magical mile' – four starting laps of Kensington's Holland Park at top pace. 'It was a race and hard work,'

RELUCTANT: It took some talking to finally convince Glenn Archer to leave his mates at Noble Park and return to Arden Street. He's pictured in 1994 against Hawthorn
Ken Rainsbury/North News

14

said coach Denis Pagan. '"Arch" did it but then told me he was going back to Noble Park. It was another year before we could convince him to come down again.'

SNOOZING HAPPILY . . .

It was about midday one winter Saturday in 1980 when the phone rang at the Madden household. Big brother Simon was just about to leave for the game. The team's No. 1 ruckman Peter Keenan had a back complaint and was in doubt. Could Justin play – if needed? And was he at home? Checking his little brother's bedroom, Simon came back to the phone: 'Yes he's here ... he's in bed asleep.' Due to play the next day in the reserves, big Juzz was resting up as 18-year-olds tend to do. He certainly had no time to develop first-game nerves and within two hours was running out with the seniors for the first time.

DERMIE VERSUS EJ

High-profile Dermott Brereton was late for his plane from Tullamarine and joined his Big V teammates later. Waiting outside the team's Adelaide hotel for the latecomer was selection chairman Ted Whitten. In front of the media pack, Whitten stuck his chest out and gave Brereton a most public dressing-down for missing his plane, before ushering him inside and winking: 'It's all theatre, son ... just theatre.'

VIENI QUA (GET OVER HERE)

Big Bomber Steve Alessio's centre-bounce pairing with Peter Filandia was unique: they'd talk to each other in Italian. Their strategies worked swimmingly against most teams ... except for multicultural Carlton!

A STEAL

Steve Silvagni's reward for signing with Carlton, the team his father Sergio had represented, was a cheque for $100. He still has it, framed at home. In 2016, Steve's son and Sergio's grandson Jack became a Blue.

RUTHLESS RONNIE

Ron Barassi just had to win, no matter what. He and his artist wife Cherryl were playing pool very late one night for $10 a ball. Cherryl says she ended up owing Ron 'something like $64000!'

Cherryl and Ron sometimes played a social game of tennis with John and Rasa Bertrand at their house in Brighton. 'It was really Ron and John slugging it out and the women hiding up at the net,' Cherryl said. 'Once Ron yelled "mine" and stepped on my foot and bent my earring. Until then, I'd never thought of tennis as a contact sport! Later that same game, Ron ran for a return and went straight through their mesh fence and John had to take him to hospital. Back in an hour with stitches in his hand, Ron remembered the exact score and insisted on finishing. We won.'

'PRINT THAT AND I'll GET YOU'

A new AFL boss was about to be anointed: the frontrunners were Alan Schwab and Ron Cook, who had both had a lifetime in football. Then out of the blue, late one afternoon, *The Herald*'s chief football writer Greg Hobbs received a tip-off from a well-positioned mate: 'Forget Schwabby and Cooky,' he said. 'Ross Oakley has the job.'

Hobbs had heard little of Oakley since he'd been forced out of football early with a knee injury at St Kilda in the mid-'60s. But he knew he was the boss of Royal Insurance and also a board member at Hawthorn. 'It'll be a good story if it's right,' said Hobbs to himself.

He rang Oakley at his home the following morning at 7.30 and introduced himself.

NEWSBREAKER: Greg Hobbs broke one of the biggest stories of all in the Melbourne *Herald* when Ross Oakley was appointed the AFL's new CEO, despite Oakley telling Hobbs 48 hours earlier that the story wasn't on and if he wrote it he'd 'get him'
Ray Jamieson

'Ross, It's Greg Hobbs from *The Herald*,' he said. 'I'm writing that you're going to be the new boss of the VFL ...'

'Bullshit ... you've got to be kidding,' said Oakley, 'where did you get that from? I'm the boss at Royal Insurance. I've got my boss coming over today from England. I'm about to have a shower ... it's just not right ...'

'My source is impeccable.'

'Well, Greg,' said Oakley, 'print that and I'll get you.' And promptly hung up.

The call had lasted barely a minute.

Hobbs paced around the old reporter's room at *The Herald* weighing up his options. Half the back page had been reserved for his 'scoop'. There were 20 minutes to the first edition ... he kept pacing and pondering.

'Bugger it,' he said. 'I'm going to write it' – and he did. It was the back-page lead and a front-page banner: 'OAKLEY NEW FOOTY BOSS'.

Within 48 hours, Oakley *had* been appointed.

The following Saturday, Hobbs was in the president's room at VFL Park. Oakley was there with a bunch of blokes. Seeing Hobbs, he summoned him over. 'Greg,' he said, 'I'm sorry. I just couldn't tell you [at the time]. My boss was over and ...'

Hobbs' exclusive won the VFL's best news story – ironically, Oakley presented him with his award – and the following year Oakley hired him as his new communications manager and editor of the *Football Record* ...

BARGAIN BASEMENT ROOS

Greg Miller's 'CV' of big-name recruits to League football is unparalleled in the modern generation. From Riverina quartet Dennis Carroll, Greg Smith, Wayne Carey and John Longmire, through to the likes of Glenn Archer, Corey McKernan, Wayne Schwass and Mark Bayes, he unearthed a chain of champions.

He also signed elite teenager Nathan Buckley as a 17-year-old, only to lose his hold on him once he turned 18. 'Recruiting was a hard school,' he said. 'You could go to bed one night thinking you'd got someone, only to lose them the next day. There were no rules back then [in the '80s]. It was a matter of how clever you were and how persistent you were. I shifted blokes and shifted families from one area to another so they could be in Sydney or later North's [residential] zone. It's just what you did, within the going rules of the time.'

Several of his most-noted signings were flukes. Miller was in Wagga Wagga for a Saturday game and on the Sunday, drove to Albury to see a young player who had been highly recommended. 'By quarter-time I was pretty sure the kid I had been told about wasn't going to make it, but during the break I was walking past the North Albury huddle. Dennis Carroll tapped me on the shoulder and said hello. He was playing only his third game in the seniors. Apparently the year before he was one of many I'd brought down for a junior trial game the day after the Grand Final. I said, "Yeahhh ..." but didn't really know who he was, but stayed and watched him for the last three quarters. He convinced me that he'd play a lot of League footy – and he did, captaining the Swans for seven years. He was a superstar.'

Miller had switched allegiances to North Melbourne in the summer of '85 and was in Adelaide for a school's match, the Adelaide government schools versus the private schools at Unley Oval.

'There were a whole host of kids I was interested in, but one stood out above everyone else. He was playing at centre half-back

COUNTRY BOY: Corowa-Rutherglen's John Longmire became one of North Melbourne's finest in its golden era in the late '90s

and taking powerhouse marks and kicking it virtually from one end of the ground to the other. I rang his school [in North Adelaide] to find out more about him and they said his name was Wayne Carey and he was from Wagga. Bingo! I'd seen him years earlier in a primary school match in Wagga. John Longmire had played in the very same game. Wayne was still residentially tied to Sydney as he'd been in Adelaide only 16 or so months. Even then he had a presence about him. You could see he was going to be a star.'

At the same time Miller was tracking the progress of another key position forward, Corowa-Rutherglen's John Longmire. He lived on the family farm just outside Corowa, deep in Sydney's Riverina stronghold. But the club had shifted from the Coreen to the higher-profiled Ovens and Murray League, North Melbourne's zone. The Swans' hold on him would eventually expire.

Miller knew that both teenagers could be the makings of North. He met Sydney's Ron Thomas at VFL House in Jolimont and offered him $60 000 for Longmire, saying that Sydney would lose him anyway once the three-year residential 'embargo' was up.

'And by the way,' said Miller. 'There's another kid called Carey who is the same boat. I'll give you $10 000 for him.'

Thomas agreed and as it was right on the deadline for registrations, Miller hi-tailed it back to North where he finally convinced the club's treasurer Jimmy Hannan to release the funds and made it back to VFL House just before the 5 p.m. deadline. Longmire and Carey were *officially* North players.

NEVER AGAIN

Subiaco teenager Gary Buckenara was waiting for two of his mates to arrive for a dawn weights session demanded by the club's fitness expert Brian Douge.

His mates were late so Buckenara let himself in and got stuck in.

Looking at his card he read 'Bench-press, 120 pounds' and proceeded to put 120 pounds on one side and 120 on the other ...

'On the very first lift I got it straight up there before my arms collapsed and it came straight down on my chest pinning me to the bench,' said Bucky.

'I couldn't move no matter how much I wriggled. I was stuck. "Helpppp!" I started yelling.'

WEIGHTY ISSUE: Gary Buckenara

After five minutes he realised he could be in a bit of trouble and was beginning to imagine the worst when in rolled teammate Tim Gepp, who saw what had happened and started rolling around on the floor in hysterical laughter. Finally, having composed himself, he lifted the weight and Buckenara bolted. 'I never did go back to the gymnasium – anywhere – anytime again,' he said.

LEAVING NOTHING IN THE TANK

Wayne Schimmelbusch's extraordinary ability to be running as fast at the last bounce as he was at the first made him one of the most legendary and loved Kangaroos of them all.

His daily backyard competitions with teen brother Daryl were pivotal in his 'gut-running' abilities. 'Daryl was always

DYNAMIC: Wayne Schimmelbusch

chasing me around the backyard and throwing things at me, sticks and stones and all sorts of things. He'd chase me up the street wanting to "kill" me. You had to keep running as he wouldn't stop. We competed at everything, all day, every day. Even though he was younger, it was "take no prisoners".'

Once in a training drill, on the eve of the '77 finals, Wayne threw Daryl to the ground and broke his leg.

DANGEROUS PLACE, THE SHOWERS . . .

Few took defeat as hard as Jimmy 'Jock' Edmond. His Doggies had been beaten this particular day and Jock was stewing for ages. Finally he took himself off to the showers still pondering the injustice of it all when in walked Ian 'Mocca' Dunstan. Jimmy immediately demanded to know why Mocca hadn't handballed to him in the last quarter. Dunstan didn't answer so Jimmy belted him.

HITTING THEM WHERE IT HURTS

So irate was Fitzroy legend Bill Stephen at his team's lamentable 118-point loss to Richmond early in 1980 that he fined each player $100 ... big money back then.

THANKS GEORGE ...

Tall Tasmanian Peter 'Perc' Jones had been guaranteed a job as part of the deal to bring him across Bass Strait. Carlton president George Harris personally guaranteed him a job – and on Day 1 in Melbourne, big Perc found himself hard at it cleaning up the floors at the abattoirs at Newmarket! He didn't last even half the day.

THANKS BUT NO THANKS: Perc Jones lasted less than a day in his first job on the mainland

DIPLOMACY ON THE RUN

Notorious hardman Neil 'Knuckles' Kerley was coaching Torrens against West Torrens at Richmond Oval when opposition defender Ray Hayes crashed lightly built winger Kevin McSporran headfirst into the muddy goalsquare ... and for good measure dug his knees into his kidneys on landing.

McSporran was in agony and Kerley livid. Turning to his runner Wayne Jackson, he said, 'Go tell Hayes that's the most cowardly fuckin' act I've ever seen and I'll meet him outside the rooms after the game.'

Jackson rushed off in a straight line at the far goals, only for Hayes to glare straight at him as he approached. A future AFL boss, known for his diplomacy under fire, Jackson made an immediate life decision and veered left to talk to one of his own players, leaving Kerley's message undelivered.

Back in the box, he was asked by Kerley, 'You told 'im?'

'Yeah.'

'Wadda he say?'

'Not a thing.'

After the game, Kerley and Jackson took their time and

THE ULTIMATE GLADIATOR

According to his mates, pretty much every story you've heard about 'Knuckles' Kerley is true.

Early in one game for Glenelg he had his jaw broken. At half-time he ordered one of his players to chew a couple of packs of gum and then had him spit the wad out so he could use it to reinforce his jaw and resume the game.

After losing a Grand Final by three points and seeing a last-gasp shot from a teammate hit the goalpost, he returned that night in darkness, chopped down the post and burnt it on a bonfire.

An icon of the South Australian game, he lived by his mother Lil's ethics: 'Do things right the first time, don't cheat, be determined and never, ever give in.'

Plenty of times he was injured in a game. But never once in more than 250 games did he go off. He was the ultimate gladiator.

diplomatically allowed everyone else to leave, Kerley preparing himself for the showdown. Jackson paced nervously. He dared not tell Knuckles that he hadn't delivered the message.

'Okay, it's time,' said Kerley.

Jackson opened the back door nervously. What if Hayes had lingered in the rooms ... what if he'd been last into the showers and was only walking past now ... what if ...

'No one's here Kerls ...'

'That figures,' said Kerley. 'I knew he was a coward.'

LIVING HIS DREAMS

Just before releasing his Hawthorn players to take the field in the 1978 Grand Final, David Parkin made each of them lie on their backs in the dressing room, with their eyes shut, visualising the opening minutes of the game. In a cool, calm voice, he talked his players through a routine where they relaxed every muscle in their bodies, from forehead to feet, before outlining how the

ICONIC: Having been instrumental as co-coach beside John Kennedy in Hawthorn's 1976 premiership, David Parkin led Hawthorn to the first of his five League flags as outright senior coach in 1978. Two of those flags were at Hawthorn and three at Carlton
*Geoff Poulter/*Inside Football

game would unfold. 'Scotty [Don Scott] will get it to Leigh [Matthews], he'll kick long and "Gladys" [Michael Moncrieff] will mark it. It'll be just like a training drill.'

And so it occurred. Twice Moncrieff marked in the first five minutes and kicked goals, courtesy not of Matthews, but from hurried kicks downfield from Alan Martello and Robert Di Pierdomenico.

'It was like I was still in that dream,' said Moncrieff afterwards. 'It was only later I realised it all was actually happening.'

A PARTING SPRAY

Dismayed at Carlton's ineptitude during a must-win round 22 game at the Western Oval in 1977, coach Ian Thorogood's half-time speech was power-packed. His Blues trailed by a point and against a team ranked well below them.

He accused his players of playing reactive rather than proactive football.

'You're playing like a pack of sheep,' he said, 'just following everyone around the place.' The players left the rooms to sounds of 'Baaaa, baaaa, baaaa' from a still-disgruntled Thorogood. The Blues lost by three goals and missed the finals. Thorogood never coached the club again.

ALMOST FOOLED HIM, MICK

Mick Porter was under a fitness cloud approaching an important match but was desperate to play and at the final training session wore a protective guard around his forearm. As was his habit, Hawthorn's iconic coach John 'Kanga' Kennedy liked to conduct his own form of fitness test and with the players in a small circle, he grabbed Mick's arm, bent it, shook it and extended it and did it all again, waiting for a reaction. 'It's fine, John,' said Mick. 'I'm ready to go.'

'Good, Mick, good,' said Kanga, walking off. 'Let's hope your bad arm is just as good ...'

KENNY THE CARTWHEELER

Kanga Kennedy didn't have too many favourites, but beanpole ruckman Ken Beck was definitely one. Hawthorn was playing St Kilda in a typical rough-house in ankle-deep mud at Moorabbin and Kennedy was all about team involvement and doing everything possible to assist each other.

'Involve yourself in everything,' he said. 'When a bloke is shooting at goal and you're on the mark, just don't stand there all limp and listless. Do something. Wave your arms. Jump up and down. Anything which might put the bloke off his kick ...'

This day, Beck took it to heart and as a Saint lined-up from close range he completed a couple of picture-perfect cartwheels. As Beck was in mid-air on the second, the St Kilda player ran around the mark and from point-blank range kicked truly, in what proved to be a crucial goal.

Seeing a crestfallen Beck afterwards in the rooms, even Kennedy didn't have the heart to rebuke him.

WHOOPS, WRONG CLUB . . .

A teenage Merv Keane was down from Wycheproof for his first training run with Richmond. The boys were doing some circuits in leafy Yarra Park. So were the players from Richmond's MCG neighbour and co-tenant Melbourne. It was nearly dark when the two teams met, and somehow country kid Keane linked up with the Demons and jogged back into their rooms. It was only when he asked for Tiger secretary Alan Schwab that a Melbourne player pointed him in the direction of Punt Road.

CHAMPION KICK (1)

Having kicked two late goals to edge fast-finishing reigning premiers North Melbourne to within just a point of Carlton at Princes Park in 1976, Malcolm Blight took a chest mark 70 yards (64 metres) from goal when the siren sounded and clutching his head, said out loud, 'What should I do here?'

Keith Greig was next to him and said, 'How about you kick the bloody thing.'

Blight wasn't worried about the responsibility, more the debate within himself of going with either a drop-punt or a torpedo – which wasn't as accurate but potentially would travel further.

'Thankfully I got onto a torp,' he said. 'It hit the sweet spot just like hitting your driver straight down the fairway or lifting a six right out of the screws in cricket. It seemed like I'd hardly touched it but it went on and on, post-high through. It was a big finish. Like all goals after the siren, the distance tends to be embellished as the years roll by. Think it's up to about 85 yards now … but that's minimum …'

CHAMPION KICK (2)

Footballers played for peanuts in the old days. John Bahen made more from winning Channel 7's Champion Kick in 1965 than he grossed for his entire senior career at Fitzroy.

A teenage champion at Assumption College – where he never once played in a losing side – Bahen always punted above his weight, 70-yard (64-metre) torpedoes his speciality. He edged his way past some higher-profiled players in the competition and met Geelong's Paul Vinar and Carlton's John Nicholls in the final. The Junction Oval was a little greasy this morning and after 'Big Nick' dropped out, it came down to the last kick of the morning.

'What are you going to kick, John?' asked Vinar.

'Gotta be a drop,' said Bahen, who had no intention of kicking anything but a torpedo.

At his best Vinar could land his famed drop-kicks in the centre circle at Kardinia Park. This time with the wind getting up a little and the ground still a little damp, he slipped slightly on impact and shanked it right.

Bahen contacted a torp nicely without quite hitting it right in the middle. It flew 67 yards (61 metres). He'd won the rich first prize of 500 pounds – enough to buy wife-to-be Gerry a diamond sparkler.

'Thought you were going to kick a drop?' said Vinar.

'Nah, Paul … changed me mind.'

Everything had been pre-recorded for *World of Sport*. Bahen's father, Chris, an old-time bookmaker, found out that young Johnny had won it, mounted a betting plunge and cleaned up nicely. It was a win-win for everyone, except John never did get a slice of Dad's winnings … and is still talking about it today!

LUCRATIVE: John Bahen was the new hero of Brunswick Street after winning Channel 7's Champion Kick in 1965
John Bahen Collection

DON'T SPEND IT ALL AT ONCE, KID!

It was the opening game of the '66 season: an Under 19s match between Carlton and Richmond at Punt Road. The Tigers included a couple of handy stars-in-the-making in Royce Hart and Rex Hunt. Carlton fielded a 15-year-old Robert Walls, then in fourth form at Coburg High.

After the game, Walls was approached by one of the Carlton officials and asked if he was amateur or professional?

'Dunno,' said Walls, 'what's the difference?'

Told that amateurs received no match payments, but professionals did, Walls needed no more prompting. 'Definitely professional,' he said – and was handed $1!

HI-JINX AT YARRAVILLE

There was no way reigning VFL powerhouse Melbourne was going to lose to Footscray in the 1961 preliminary final – or so Lou Richards reckoned. So certain was 'Louie the Lip' of Melbourne entering an eighth consecutive Grand Final that in his breezy preview to the game in the *Sun News-Pictorial* he promised to trim Ted Whitten's front lawn with a pair of nail scissors if the unthinkable occurred and the Dogs caused an upset.

'That Saturday afternoon, I was walking into the MCG for the final alongside 86 000 others and who should I run into but the Prime Minister of Australia, Mr Menzies. "G'day young Richards," he said, with a chuckle. "All I want to see is Melbourne get beaten here this afternoon so you can cut that lawn!"'

Footscray won by almost five goals and first thing Monday morning, Lou and photographer Lloyd Brown ventured out to Whitten's home in Yarraville to be met by hundreds of Doggie fans, all decked out in jumpers, scarves and duffle coats waiting for Lou.

'There must have been 3000 there,' said Lou. 'Down on my hands and knees I went with these bloody nail clippers, clipping away until the crowd had its fun and Lloyd had his photographs. Teddy hadn't mowed his lawn for about six months. It was hard work.'

BARASS v THE DEES

Melbourne giant John Lord was centre half-forward against Carlton's Wes Lofts at Princes Park. It was the first game for Demon great Ron Barassi *against* his old side. The game was tight, with only a few goals in at the last change. So voluble was 'Barass' at three-quarter time that his voice could all but be heard in the Melbourne camp 75 yards (69 metres) away. He wanted Carlton to get the first score in the last quarter – no matter what. 'Let's get the jump on them …'

Instead Melbourne scored first, a point. On the kick-off, Lofts led for Graeme Donaldson, but his kick hung a little in the air allowing Lord, who was taller, to take a fine mark. 'Ron immediately raced over to Wes, thrust his jaw in front of him and pointing to me shouted, "I told you not to take your eyes off that bastard." It was the only compliment I think I ever got from Ron. But he was a brilliant player, one of the very best of my time. The game? We won by six goals ...'

A NEW ERA

So successful was St Kilda's Alan Killigrew with his summertime recruiting that the recruits defeated the senior players by eight goals in the last practice game of 1956. 'We dropped 26 of the 1955 listed players and all hell broke loose,' said 'Killer'. 'But at the time St Kilda were losers. It was the beginning of a new era for us.'

A NOT-SO-SECRET PREMIERSHIP

Brian Dixon was dropped from Melbourne's 1955 Grand Final team after defying the wishes of Melbourne coach Norm Smith and playing in a mid-week University Faculty Grand Final. A commerce student, Dixon had originally intended to only be coach but was talked into playing and hoped Smith wouldn't find out. The next day after the Melbourne *Age* reported that Dixon had been best afield in a premiership team, Smith dumped him and come Grand Final day he was demoted to second emergency, despite having played 16 of the 18 home-and-away matches.

Dixon soon rose again and went on to play in five Grand Finals with Melbourne. He also won Melbourne's best and fairest in 1960.

FRIENDLY FIRE

Phillip Gibbs was keen to use the much-heralded 'Captain Blood' Jack Dyer on radio and even after a terrible trial at Arden Street, Gibbs remained convinced that the Richmond legend would improve and the ratings would follow.

Dyer wasn't as convinced, so Gibbs promised to teach him the finer points of radio, if Dyer would teach Gibbs the finer points of footy.

'The lesson started at a social match at Keilor,' Gibbs told my colleague Geoff Slattery. 'All the old stars were playing. Jack told me to play in the ruck with him. We were waiting for the game to start and Jack told me to take the knockout. Up I went and I felt this whack across my ear. It all but knocked me out. Jack had hit me a beauty. I couldn't believe it.

'"What was that for?" I asked.

'"Now you know what it feels like," he said.'

'THIS IS IT, KID!'

Seventeen-year-old Ted Whitten was feeling pretty happy with life having kicked a goal with his first kick in his first game within the first minute of Footscray's opening-round clash with Richmond at Punt Road in 1951. As he re-took his position he was joined by his opponent, Richmond's rough-and-tough centre half-back Don 'Mopsy' Fraser. 'That's the biggest mistake you've ever made, Kid,' said Fraser. 'You won't see out the game.'

Having been kicked in the ankle by Fraser before the first bounce when he went to shake his hand, Whitten realised he was on a madman, capable of anything. 'I wasn't just frightened of Mopsy that day, I was terrified,' said Whitten. 'And he was right. Just after half-time I was backing back for a mark only to hear a voice: "This is it, Kid!" The lights went out and they carried me off.'

CLOSE, BUT NO CIGAR . . .

Having finished runner-up in the 1931 Sandover Medal count, Claremont-Cottesloe teenager Ron Cooper found himself in high demand among Victorian clubs. Geelong was particularly keen and arranged for Cooper to travel by ship to Corio where they planned to sign him. They even had him rowed to the boat at midnight so as not to alert anyone. But someone talked and when the boat berthed temporarily in Adelaide, Carlton FC officials were there to meet Cooper. He signed and was to play more than 150 games. His nickname was 'Socks' – he always wore them at ankle height.

SOMETHING'S ON THE GO . . .

Bruce Andrew thought something was 'up' late in the year in 1928 when Collingwood reserves coach Hughie Thomas sent him up the other end of Victoria Park to train with the seniors. He was just 19 and in his first year from local club Abbotsford.

'Hughie told me Jock [McHale] was looking for a winger. I'd come as a full-forward but was never going to play there in the firsts, not ahead of Gordon Coventry.'

The next day he was working at his clerical job at the Melbourne *Herald* when the telephone rang. It was Collingwood's tailor. He wanted to know Andrew's measurements for some white shorts.

'I wondered what was going on as the reserves always wore black shorts,' Andrew said. 'My mate and I got a ruler and a piece of string and measured me around the middle. Then we took another look at the morning's paper. They'd named a bloke called Andrews [rather than Andrew] on the wing. The penny dropped. I was going to play my first game.'

That night he made his way to the club and after prolonged discussions with the gateman, who'd never heard of him and initially wasn't going to let him in, was finally allowed into the rooms where he found the property room and was handed a jumper and a number 28 with the orders to 'ask your mother to sew it on tonight'.

It was the first time Andrew had ever been in Collingwood's senior training rooms; the reserves changed elsewhere.

He was to be flattened in his first game, at Fitzroy's Brunswick Street Oval, but did well enough to play in the finals and be a part of Collingwood's 1928 'machine', which was to win the second of four flags in a row.

A two-time premiership player, Andrew wore Collingwood's No. 1 guernsey for much of his career, jumper numbers being handed out alphabetically in those days. Known for his slicked-back hair, neatly parted in the middle, he became a renowned ambassador for football and among many media roles was one of the founding panellists and a judge on the popular long-kicking competition on Channel 7's iconic World of Sport.

MAGPIE STALWART: Jock McHale, who coached Collingwood for more than three decades, with Phonse Kyne (standing), Jack Green and Bernie Shannon
Francis Doherty collection

2

Bloopers, Gaffes
& Pranks

'Where do you want me to stand, Denis?'
'Just keep out of my bloody way, Ronny.'

SEEING RED AT KOKODA

This pre-season, among the Hawks experiencing the Kokoda Trail for the first time was a 17-year-old Lance Franklin. During a break, Franklin's backpack fell open and teammate Trent Croad noticed a framed photograph of his then girlfriend.

'He got it out and showed about 44 others,' said Franklin. 'Never have I been more embarrassed in my life.'

Welcome to League football, Buddy.

DAVID WHO?

David Parkin was at Vicroads having his driver's licence updated. A fellow in the queue just in front of him turned and recognising him said, 'Excuse me, Kevin, but shouldn't you be coaching Western Sydney?'

The girl serving was a rabid Carlton supporter and she quickly let the fellow know that standing behind him was in fact David Parkin and *not* Kevin Sheedy.

Having had his identity mistaken, Parkin continued on to Princes Park for a meeting with long-time official Shane

COACH OF THE CENTURY

O'Sullivan. Cheryl, the normal receptionist was away from her desk and instead a young man, dressed in a suit and tie, came to the counter and asked very politely, 'Can I help you, sir?'

'Yes please. Tell Shane O'Sullivan that I'm here for the meeting.'

'Oh ... and ... umm ... who should I say is calling please?'

'Tell him it's the coach of the century.'

The young man looked at him quizzically, and then spotting the receptionist at the end of the corridor, bustled up to her and said, 'There's some old Geeza here who says he's the coach of the century!'

All was soon resolved, but not before the now very red-faced young man had received an immediate history lesson.

HOME TRUTHS

The Melbourne boys had had a big night out and it wasn't until 4 a.m. that a worse-for-wear David Schwarz and David Neitz returned to Neitz's house to find the front door wide open.

Not thinking too much of it, the pair headed straight for the fridge looking for the two boxes of chocolate bars Neitz had taken home from *World of Sport* the previous weekend. 'We were starving,' said Schwarz, 'and ready to eat the lot.'

But they were gone. Gear was strewn all around the lounge room, but that was nothing unusual for Neitz, then living solo. They went to turn on the television but couldn't find the remote control. Only then did they realise that the TV, too, was gone, and that Neitz had in fact been burgled.

The police arrived and saw all the mess around the lounge room. 'Gee, they really ransacked the place,' said one.

'No,' said Schwarz. 'All that crap was already there. They just pinched the TV and our bloody chocolate bars ...'

Neitz and Schwarz might have been best mates but they were forever playing pranks on each other. One of the best was when Schwarz arranged for a load of firewood to be dumped on Neitz's front nature strip very early one Sunday morning, with a sign: 'FREE FIREWOOD, PLEASE KNOCK ON THE DOOR BEFORE TAKING IT'.

Neitz's Sunday slumber time was dramatically interrupted that morning …

GOT YA

Collingwood was on a 'get to know you' weekend at Traralgon in 1993. Star forward Peter Daicos had a wedding the night before and didn't arrive until Sunday morning. Seeing everyone was at breakfast, he joined in. 'I'm famished,' he said, dipping into everything from the hot food to lashings of toast. 'Gee this is good,' he said. 'Might have to double up I reckon.'

'Wouldn't if I was you,' said teammate Mick McGuane.

'Why's that, Micky?'

'Didn't they tell ya?'

'Tell me what?'

'You'll find out, Daics.'

Gary Pert was passing and said, 'Yeah, it's a killer, Daics. Even Shawrey [Tony Shaw] had a chuck at the end of it …'

'Come on boys, what's going on?'

'The obstacle course, mate, the obstacle course. They sprung it on us. It's a shocker,' said McGuane. 'The 60-degree hill climb got me … none of us could do it …'

Enter Mark McKeon, Collingwood's fitness coach. Seeing Daicos, he marched straight over. 'Good, you're here, Daics, follow me … let's get it over with.'

Daicos felt like a man going to his last supper. Suddenly he wished he hadn't tucked into quite as much food. Leaving his second helping of bacon and eggs alone, out he trudged looking all forlorn. Suddenly McKeon stopped. It was too much for him. He broke into gusts of laughter. 'Mate, there is no obstacle course,' he said.

The guys had followed them out and were near tears. 'Got ya, Daics,' laughed McGuane, 'good and proper.'

WORLD TRAVELLERS

The celebrations for the victorious first-time premiers the West Coast Eagles took them to the Greek Islands in the spring of '92. On returning home, teenage Adonis Glen Jakovich was asked how he liked the local sights: for example, had he gone to the Acropolis?

'Mate,' said Glen, 'we went to *all* the night clubs.'

THANKS BUT NO THANKS

When the Adelaide Crows arrived at Windy Hill to play Essendon early in their inaugural season of AFL in 1991, coach Graham Cornes found the coaching box was filthy, the ground's wind sock had been removed and they were sharing dingy, messy dressing rooms with one of the reserves teams.

Eyeing the viewing windows of the box which looked as though it hadn't been cleaned since the previous season, Cornes ordered team manager Barrie Downs to clean them with Windex.

'We haven't got any …'

'Well get some … and make sure it's Windex.'

There was just half an hour to go before the game. Downs wondered down Fogarty Street looking for an appropriate shop, but everyone had closed early for the footy.

Finally he came to a small seven-days-a-week supermarket and on asking the lass where the Windex was kept, he found to his chagrin that the last bottle had been sold just that morning. Buying something else instead, Downs hurried back to the ground and dashed into the rooms to be confronted by Cornes who immediately complained, 'It's not Windex.'

Downs went to the box and feverishly did his best to clean the windows, working himself into a lather of sweat in the process. By match time he was quite satisfied with his handiwork when Cornes and his coaching staff appeared. Nodding to Downs on a job well done, Cornes slowly opened the window. 'I always like to have the window open. You can hear more of the crowd ...'

Downs' reaction was unprintable.

OUT OF THIS GALAXY

It was Fitzroy's traditional dinner and team meeting night where coach Robert Walls would read out the side and detail everyone's role.

Coming to the rucks, Walls said captain Matt Rendell would change with rookie Glenn 'Galaxy' Coleman. They were to have equal time on the ball and in a forward pocket. 'But,' he said, looking at Coleman, 'if Matty is running hot he'll stay on the ball.'

Coleman looked a little puzzled and interrupted. 'But Rob,' he said, 'what if I'm running hot?'

'Galaxy,' said Walls smiling, 'that's something I've never considered.'

ROD THE RING-IN

Had Australian international Roger Woolley not slipped while taking a throw-in from substitute fieldsman and Hawthorn premiership winger Rodney Eade, Eade could easily have had his name in the illustrious pages of *Wisden Cricketers' Almanack* ...

Tasmania was playing Victoria at Carlton's Princes Park and with two players off the field, Eade was called in as a substitute and all but ran out Australian rebel batsman Mick Taylor with a quick throw that had Taylor scrambling short of his ground – but for Woolley's slip.

Using a cricket shirt borrowed from his old Newtown team-mate, Eade had a ball, running and fetching. He even enjoyed the abuse. 'One bloke kept giving me the raspberry,' he said, 'saying how he hoped I played cricket better than I played footy.'

Before his football commitments took priority, Eade played sub-district firsts alongside Gary Buckenara at Balwyn. As a 14-year-old he played first-grade club cricket in Hobart and back in the late '70s, he was a member, alongside David Boon, of Tasmania's Under 19 team.

WHOOPS

It remains among the '70s classic bargain buys: the untried champion-on-the-rise Terry Wallace in exchange for Gerry McCarthy and $15 000. Wallace was to play 196 games in nine years with the Hawks, win two club championships and play in three premiership teams. He'd initially been tied to Fitzroy and trained with the Lions only to be told that he was too slow and the club possessed many similar types. Gerry McCarthy? He had 75 games.

PORNO FOOTY

Among many weird and wonderful jobs before becoming the star of the long-running *The Footy Show*, Sam Newman worked for years as a specialist ruck's coach at a variety of clubs. Andrew Purser had just joined Footscray and Sam was showing him some of the ruck moves he should best employ as a VFL ruckman. Also present at this particular time were Andrew's parents.

Sam slotted a cassette into his VHS machine and began explaining the finer details of ruck positioning. But suddenly there was an interruption … instead of the best of Polly Farmer, it suddenly became the best of porn queen Linda Lovelace.

'Terribly sorry about that,' said Sam, fumbling for the eject button. 'Fancy that getting onto this ...'

SORRY JOHN, WE TOOK THE PIC YESTERDAY ...

John Sharrock says it simply wasn't his fault that he was absent from Geelong's 1963 official team premiership photograph.

A week after the club's greatest-ever season – the seniors and the reserves both won the premiership – the team was set to continue celebrations in Honolulu and San Francisco where exhibition games against Melbourne FC had been arranged.

Geelong secretary Leo O'Brien told Sharrock to be at the club on the Monday by 11 a.m. Everyone was flying out on the Tuesday.

'I got there at 10.30 a.m. and they'd taken the picture on the Sunday,' said Sharrock. 'My best mate Daryl Barker had stood in for me.'

Later, when the official photos were distributed to the premiership 20, Sharrock's 'headshot' had been superimposed on Barker's body. 'I always thought I was a bit wider across the shoulders than Daryl!' said Sharrock. 'Had I known they'd take the picture on the Sunday I would have come down a day earlier, but whenever I could I'd always go back and help on the farm [at Tooleybuc]. Dad and Mum had no money. They'd be lucky to get 10 shillings for a case of oranges. There was 40 acres [16 hectares] to work of citrus and vineyard. It was tough.'

A left-footer who could kick the ball further than just about anybody, Sharrock was the apple of Geelong coach Bob Davis's eye from the time he ventured to the tiny Murray River town late in 1962. Young John had kicked 87 goals and won the club and competition best and fairest.

'Mum and Dad played golf to relax and during a break at lunchtime they were outside in the paddock, chipping a ball to one another,' said Sharrock.

'This big Ford LTD rolled up and out hopped Bobby and Leo. I knew who they were but Mum and Dad had no idea.

STAND-IN: Geelong used a stand-in player in Daryl Barker when it was decided to take the 1963 premiership team picture team a day early without star first-year player John Sharrock. The winning squad was, back row, left to right: Colin Rice, Barker, John Watts, John Yeates, Geoff Rosenow, Roy West and Tony Polinelli. Standing: Gordon Hynes, John Brown, Paul Vinar, Doug Wade, Ken Goodland, Peter Walker, Ian Scott and Hugh Routley. Front: Graham Farmer, Alistair Lord, John Devine (vice-captain), Bob Davis (coach), Fred Wooller (captain), Stuart Lord and Billy Goggin

Dad thought they might be policemen. "What have you done, John?" Dad asked me.'

Saying he'd been called a lot of things but never a copper before, Davis asked if he could have a swing and proceeded to middle a seven iron and send it 150 yards (137 metres) into the groves way beyond before throwing Wally Sharrock a pound. 'That'll cover it,' he said, referring to the cost of the lost ball.

A footy was produced, Mr Sharrock saying, 'Suppose you'd like to see John have a kick, Mr Davis ...'

'Call me Bob ... yes ... that would be very nice, thank you.'

So impressive was the 18-year-old bush champion with his overhead marking and magnificent field kicking that Davis stopped them after five minutes. 'Mr Sharrock,' he said. 'If there was a game on at the [Melbourne] cricket ground next Saturday, John would be playing at centre half-forward.'

The boom teenager was to receive 400 pounds to sign – a small fortune back then – and he and Denis Marshall joined the club's trip away to New Zealand – the first time Sharrock had ever travelled beyond Melbourne. True to Davis's word, Sharrock started in the seniors in the first game of 1963 and played every match, including the '63 Grand Final.

TEEN STAR: John Sharrock was one of the most important signings as Geelong coach Bobby Davis built a premiership team in 1963
John Sharrock Collection

Later a successful racehorse owner – Tooleybuc Kid is his latest multi-winner – Sharrock was asked about his biggest thrill in sport, winning a big race or playing in a VFL premiership team. 'Definitely the '63 flag,' he said. 'I just wish I could remember it a bit better. Gary Young hit me behind the ear in the first 10 minutes and I couldn't see for about two quarters. If it wasn't for the smelling salts and the sherry ... that helped, I can tell you.'

Sharrock's biggest turf thrill came in 1975 when his horse Caratime won at Caulfield.

'It was Easter time and we'd just bought a new house. I had to go to the bank manager and borrow another $10 000. Everything was set to be approved. I was going to Swan Hill for a tennis tournament and rang Pat Courtney who was Caratime's trainer and he said to me without any hint of hesitation, "This horse will win tomorrow." I had $100 on him each way at 16-1 and took him in the quaddie with a couple of favourites in the middle pins. I was so excited when he won I forgot all about the quaddie and asking later, was told that the two favourites had also got up. I ended up winning nine or so grand plus the original two grand which was enough to buy the house. The day after Easter I went back to the bank manager, thanked him and said we didn't need his extra cash after all! It was as good a win as I've had and came just at the right time.'

Sharrock was to run third one year in the Brownlow Medal before knee injuries forced him out of League football at the age of 24. He resisted the opportunity to return, despite starring in the strong Ovens and Murray League.

Another big-name player to miss his club's premiership team photo was the larger-than-life Sam Kekovich at North Melbourne the day after the 1975 triumph. 'I'd put in a big night, actually a very big night,' said Sam, 'and slept in.'

WHAT MIGHT HAVE BEEN

Melbourne's football legend Ron Barassi believes the Demons could have won 10 premierships in a row, had star rover Stuart Spencer remained with the club in the mid-'50s.

'We won five from six from the mid-'50s and all of us believed had Stuey not gone to Tasmania that we would have won in the wet in '58 and gone on from there,' Barassi said. 'Stuey was on another level to us. He was quick, had courage, a big engine and was a wonderful field kick.'

At the 2014 launch of *Stuey, My Life with Stuart Spencer*, written by Spencer's wife Fay, Barassi said his old teammate had skills he could only dream about. 'He left us at 24 before he was even at his absolute top,' he said. 'Even then he was best and fairest in two premierships seasons [1955 and 1956] and best afield in the '56 Grand Final. He could play all right. He was our biggest star of all.'

Melbourne played in eight Grand Finals in 11 years from 1954 to 1964, winning six flags. They appeared in the finals in the other three seasons, finishing third in 1961 and 1963 and fourth in 1962.

ANOTHER DAY, A DIFFERENT DECISION: Stuart Spencer turned his back on League football at 24 after being best afield in Melbourne's 1956 Grand Final triumph. 'Football wasn't as big then,' explained his Tasmanian-born wife Fay, who is pictured with Ron Barassi at the 2014 launch

*Fay Spencer/*Stuey, My Life with Stuart Spencer

KEEN: Ron Barassi from Melbourne's halcyon era in the late '50s
Tom Mahoney collection

Given the decision again, Fay Spencer said she and Stuart would have remained in Melbourne rather than moving to Hobart to work in the family's transport business. 'Football was not as big as it is now. We didn't have a crystal ball. We loved our time in Tasmania, but as Norm Smith was forever reminding me, things could have been different. All those flags ... it would have been wonderful,' she said.

The Denis Cordner-Barassi-Spencer following-division was one of the most noted in League history, Barassi saying in his early days that he often had a free run at the ball as his opponent would be looking to 'double-team' Spencer – so dominant was he.

'The first time we played together I said to Denis, "Where do you want me to stand?"

'"Just keep out of my bloody way, Ronny," said Cordner.'

3
Bush Royalty

'Graeme, how in the bloody hell
are we then going to get home?'
'We'll find a way ... we'll thumb a ride ...'

VERSATILE, EVEN AT 16

Tiny Waikerie in the South Australian Riverland had unearthed a teenage prospect apparently worth travelling miles to see. The legendary Neil Kerley had heard of the 16-year-old kid. His name was Mark Ricciuto and he'd been taking all before him in his first year of senior football as a running half-back.

Kerley duly arrived at a minor round game and was initially dismayed to learn that the teenage prodigy was going to play permanent forward pocket this day, as Waikerie was short of goal kickers.

Ricciuto kicked 10 and within weeks had been invited to train with the Adelaide Crows, beginning one of the great careers, which was to include a Brownlow Medal.

AS DECORATED AS THEY COME

Tony Hickey had only just progressed from three-cornered pants when he was first involved in Thursday-night selection at Robinvale FC. His farming father, Pat, was chairman of selectors and young Tony would sit on his knee and listen to all of the deliberations. 'Mum told Dad that if he wanted to be a selector, he'd have to take me to the footy club with him, so he did,' said Hickey.

Eleven Sunraysia premierships and 12 best and fairests later, young Tony hasn't regretted even one day of a lifetime in football. He is an icon at Imperials where he played 330 games and won 10 best and fairests.

Ten of his premierships were at 'A' grade level. The last one in 2010, was with the 'Impy' reserves. 'The seniors had been knocked out. Only the bare 18 had qualified to play in the rezzies. I wasn't going to keep a young bloke out. But they had no one else, so I played.'

Hickey says he's a better person for football and while he would have liked to have at least trialled at North Melbourne when he had the opportunity in 1987, the lessons learnt along the way impacted on every part of his life.

'In 1992, I was lucky enough to play under Pedro O'Neill who was coaching our Vic Country rep. team,' Hickey said. 'He was down from the Latrobe [Valley League] and he had a great way of encouraging everyone and making them feel welcome and part of a unit. Until then I was doing what most coaches were doing, the old fire-and-brimstone stuff without thinking too deeply about it all. Rather than driving and berating players, I started to go the other way, like Pedro did and was constantly encouraging and reassuring them and reminding them of exactly what they could achieve if they could implement what we were trying to do as a team. We had a very young side and they were very responsive. I'm proud that we won four flags on end from '92 to '95. They were very special young men and to have helped mentor them in those years was probably the highlight of it all, especially as I still see many of them all now.'

Originally from Robinvale and schooled at St Pat's College, Ballarat – one of footy's most noted recruiting nurseries – Hickey went to Melbourne to study and was playing midweek footy for one of the university teams when 'spotted' by North Melbourne's master recruiter Greg Miller, whose summer 'CV' of recruits included fellow country lads in icons-to-be Wayne Carey and John Longmire, both bought for a song from the Sydney Swans.

'I wasn't smart enough to get a degree and train the hours needed to make it,' Hickey said. 'I always wanted to have a big crack at it, but didn't think I could make a living out of it. Greg talked me into it and picked me in the reserves. I'd finally agreed that yes I'd do it and rang Greg and said I was in. In the very same week I got a job in Mildura and that was that. I decided to come back to the bush. I regret it now, but I don't regret the mates I made and the achievements of our club.'

Other than six months under Des Tuddenham at East Ballarat and a season at Karween-Karawinna where he won another best and fairest, Hickey played all his football in Mildura, gaining a reputation as one of the fittest and most skilled players outside the Big Smoke.

Hickey's extraordinary fitness reserves and inner drive were a secret of his success. He had a favourite five-minute course, where he would run up and back and try and beat his time every time, before doing a cool-down and stretching session. 'I basically trained *every* second night and was running all through summer and winter. To top that all off, my Dad would massage me. He had big strong farmer's hands and it all helped to keep me a step ahead of the opposition.'

Playing most of his football in the midfield, the 175-centimetre (five feet, nine inches) Hickey found he was being tagged, even playing off a half-back flank.

'The only way I thought I could compete was to be fitter than anyone else up here,' he said. 'So I built a fitness base. Then they started double-teaming me, rotating two off me, quarter by quarter. I had to accept that my possession rate would drop. Instead of getting up towards 40, I was getting high 20s and low 30s. I always took it as a compliment though. If there were two or three players worrying about me, that was limiting what they could do for their team and it left some of our boys free.

We'd turn that into a positive and get some of our young runners involved.'

Among the best players of his time were the much-travelled Phil Bradmore, who was Hickey's assistant for a time; Imperials centre half-forward Phillip Nash; and back in his Ballarat League days, Beaufort's tough-as-nails centreman Gary Lofts, who later went to St Kilda.

Hickey says each of the flags at Imperials were significant achievements, especially 1987 when the team was undefeated. Victoria's country championship victory at Port Lincoln is also an enduring memory.

Only one other Victorian country footballer has also won 12 senior best and fairests: Robbie Walker from Wangaratta Rovers. Bernie Beadle also won 12 in Tasmanian country ranks with Margate.

A UNIQUE BROTHERHOOD

The secret to coaching premierships, Laurie Burt says, revolves around work rates, unshakeable belief and trust. Burt's formidable record included four flags and a winning strike rate of 75 per cent, spread over his 230 games as coach of Wangaratta Rovers, one of the mightiest and most successful of all Victorian country footy clubs.

At a sell-out premiership reunion of the 1971–72 and 1991 teams at WJ Findlay Oval in 2011, premiership coaches Neville Hogan and Burt told of the good times, the play-offs and the unique Rovers' brotherhood.

'Not only did we have good players, we had good families and they are still all involved now,' said Burt. 'It's a key reason why we have been so successful for so long.'

A schoolteacher, Burt arrived for one year and is still in Wangaratta almost 30 years later. His stumpy legs and squat stature made him the most unlikely of footy heroes. But as the club's champion player Robbie Walker told me, 'Laurie was fabulous for our club and the whole town. He was always reinforcing the team aspects, the guys who were injured or others who had missed out, the supporters who'd backed us all year and the whole community which was behind us. We weren't playing just for us, but for them as well. The flags weren't just ours. They belonged to the whole town.'

Walker, a six-time Ovens and Murray competition best-and-fairest winner, rates the club's 1994 play-off as the sweetest moment of all as it meant back-to-back premierships for the Rovers and also for Burt, who'd started as a player as a 30-year-old in 1984 before becoming the club's senior coach in 1987.

'Laurie didn't want to leave anything to chance,' said Walker. 'He was just what we needed, the right bloke at the right time. We beat Wodonga in both those Grand Finals but they were real contests. They always were against Wodonga. When you have success when you're young, you tend to take success for granted. It's only later on that you realise how hard they are to win. These ones were flags all of us really savoured.'

Pre-finals that year, Walker had worried that the club may have been becoming complacent after its unprecedented run of 36 victories on end and was in danger of underachieving come September. In 1992, the Rovers had been premiership favourites only to go out in straight sets. But Burt told some home truths, reminded the playing group of how hard they'd worked since before Christmas and how everyone started equal again. 'It's whoever wants it most,' he said. 'Together we can do it. But one weak link, one weakness … it's all over.' The Rovers won the flag, its third in four years, by 10 goals. Back in 1988, Burt and Walker's first flag, the Rovers had shocked a more-experienced Lavington and in 1993, the Rovers cantered clear of Wodonga after an 'all-in' in the player's race at half-time.

Coming from cosmopolitan Coburg where most of the locals didn't even know where the local football club was, Burt says it was an extraordinary feeling to walk down the main streets of Wangaratta early on Saturday match days and be questioned about how the team was going and 'will we win today?'

'It was one of the secrets of our success outside a playing

list and an administration with so many rock-solid champion people involved,' he said. 'The whole community was behind us. You couldn't help but be lifted by their passion.'

A born coach and a master psychologist, Burt was the architect of the club's four premierships in his illustrious 11-year reign. His hunger for the game has never abated since his formative days as a junior at St Andrews FC through to the Victorian Football Association, where he played 150-plus games. With an inherent ability to read the play and a good driver in heavy traffic, he was twice placed in the top three in JJ Liston Trophy counts and a regular VFA representative. When he joined the Rovers he soon became a favourite with even the stern judges who congregate at the bar end at Findlay Oval. They liked the way he burrowed in for the hard ball. This was no hit-and-run import after an easy kick and some quick dollars. Burt was the quintessential clubman and he wanted to be involved in everything happening around the club. When club legend Merv 'Farmer' Holmes retired as coach, his successor was obvious: it had to be Burt. Few could 'read' his players and get into their heads like the little stocky bloke with the tree-trunk legs. And he's still involved now, as a mentor to the kids.

GOODE AS GOLD

As a child growing up in Gippsland, the Moe Rec. was Frank Goode's second home.

He and his best mate John Somerville, another League footballer in the making, would be down at the reserve 12 months of the year, kicking right and left-footers, honing the skills that were to lift them into the best teams in faraway Melbourne.

Somerville was to play in Essendon's 1962 premiership team. Goode was a groomsman at his wedding.

Having played in a premiership team at Heyfield under Gerald Marchesi as a 16-year-old, Goode took a more complicated path to League football, which included games with Melbourne High Old Boys, North Melbourne Under 19s and back in the bush with Moe and Kerang. His father Ray was keen for him to finish the year at Kerang where he was the leading goal kicker, but Goode said he was 'going to the city and that's that'.

A strongly built full-forward who could also play on the ball and in defence, Goode's burning desire to make it in Melbourne saw him trial one weekend at Hawthorn. He was in the early intra-club game at Glenferrie Oval and did so well that he and another of the rookies Alan Joyce played only the first half before being withdrawn to play in the feature practice game.

'A fella called Graham Cooper gave me an early whack, probably just to see what I would do,' said Goode. 'I got a few kicks and got my name in the *Sporting Globe* that night as being a kid with promise from Kerang.

'The *Globe* was the footballer's bible back then and Tony Trainor who was president at North Melbourne saw my name and realised I was tied to North as I'd played a game in the thirds a few years earlier. He arranged for me to get a transfer in the National Bank to Melbourne and when I came out on my first day for lunch, there was [coach] Wally Carter and [captain] John Brady there to sign me up. I played my first senior game soon afterwards [in 1961]. Who knows what would have happened at Hawthorn? They won their first flag that very year. All I knew at the time, though, was that I wanted to play League footy and Tony wanted me to play at North. That was good enough for me.'

The lessons learnt playing open-age football from his mid-teens in the bush were invaluable and allowed Goode to compete immediately at VFL level. 'We had some excellent footballers particularly at Heyfield when we won the flag,' he said. 'Mike Collins went to Melbourne at the same time as me. His brother Geoff was an interstate player and he was on a back flank with us. Howard Oakey's son Ron was an excellent footballer. So was Jimmy Beha who played in six or seven premiership teams and Bob Jacobs who was a real Coleman of the bush.'

Youngsters learnt how to use their bodies and protect themselves in the bush. 'The kids are great today,' said Goode, 'but some of them are fast-tracked so quickly they don't learn the basic fundamentals; they don't have that experience which we had at open-age levels.'

In one of Goode's first games, against powerful Melbourne, he was in at the pre-match listening to Carter who was telling his boys how one of the young Kangas was going to stand the great Ron Barassi and do this and do that. 'Then he told everyone it was me! I think I kept him to something like 18 kicks but I knew when it got to the business end when everything was on the line, there was nothing I could do to stop him. Ron was a fantastic player.'

Goode twice led North Melbourne's goal kicking and in one interstate game in Sydney, kicked nine goals for Victoria against New South Wales at Trumper Oval, including seven in the second half. 'Les Foote was one of the coaches and I'd kicked a couple in the first half and given a few away with handballs. Les told me at half-time that my job at full-forward was to kick goals and not to handball – and I finished with nine.'

His big-time career ended in 1968 when his troublesome knee collapsed in a pre-season practice game in Adelaide. 'They got me to room with a 16-year-old kid from Myrtleford. His name was Sam Kekovich. Sam was larger than life even then, took one look at me and said, "How old are you?"

'"28."

'"You're stuffed!" he said.

'And I was. I broke down in the first quarter and never played again!'

Goode went on to coach at both senior VFL and VFA level and also worked on the VFL tribunal. His younger brother Bob also played at North, via Yarrawonga.

MORNINGTON PENINSULA LEGENDS

Few sets of footballing brothers on Melbourne's Mornington Peninsula rival the feats of Frankston pair Greg and Joey Lane.

They were the standouts among five brothers to represent powerful Frankston YCW (Young Christian Workers). Greg also played League football with St Kilda before being an exceptional player with two clubs in Tasmania. He was a noted coach as well. Joey played in five Peninsula premierships and more than 400 games.

Greg's personal high came in 1988 when he returned to Frankston 'YC' ranks as playing coach and lifted the team into a Grand Final. He broke his hand on the eve of the finals and missed the decider, won by Rosebud. 'We had a team of terrific young fellows coming through, including Joey, Paul Theobald and Mark Berenger who were all in their first year of senior footy,' he said.

'When you combined them with people like Brendon Long – an absolute legend at the club – Brendan Delaney and others, it made us pretty hard to beat. It was a privilege to be involved.'

Greg's work commitments took him across Bass Strait to Tasmania and his successor Brendan Lacy won a flag in 1989 before the club won three flags in a row from 1991 to 1993 during a golden period in the '90s.

Greg had started on the Peninsula as a 10-year-old. He idolised the club's senior stars including Peter Hamilton, Paul 'Whistle' Willis and Ewan Cole. 'When I got old enough, I was able to play in the same team as them all,' he said. 'My best mates at school Jim Brouin and John Kenter had played with me all the way through the under-age grades including a couple of flags in the Under 17s. They were great days.'

The most outstanding players of his time at Jubilee Park included Jim Renouf, Paul Maher, 'Bomber' Brown and Chris Doherty.

An in-and-under midfielder, Lane had two and a half years at St Kilda playing a dozen or so games in 1983–84 before shifting to Frankston where he represented the Victorian Football Association's combined side.

'Maybe I could have played a few more [at St Kilda], but I'd just got married and was living in Frankston. Work commitments were building. Training two nights a week was better than doing five nights at Moorabbin.'

Greg represented Penguin FC for a year and also played in Hobart before returning to Frankston YCW as senior coach.

He is particularly proud of his younger brother Joey's achievements – 'five flags in seven Grand Finals is a mighty effort'. Joey was also a first XI sub-district cricketer at Frankston.

Even when working interstate, Greg would receive texts of the Mornington Peninsula Football League (MPFL) scores by 6 p.m. most Saturdays. 'You never forget your mates,' he said. 'It's one of the great aspects of sporting clubs and I get back to "YC" whenever I can.'

SPOOKY TALE

So hypnotised was one Mornington Peninsula club full-back by Luke McGuinness' goal-kicking brilliance one day that rather then watch the ball, he stood nose to nose with McGuinness, his back to play, watching only his eyes … à la Lee Adamson v Peter Hudson that memorable early '70s day at VFL Park.

'That was down at Dromana. I burst out laughing,' said McGuinness. 'It didn't do him much good. Think I kicked 10 that day.'

A two-time-premiership player at Mornington, McGuinness played into his 40s, and amassed more than 300 games and kicked almost 1000 goals in the Mornington Peninsula, the majority with Keysborough, his home for 12 years. Sixteen goals in a game and 120 in a season were McGuinness' best hauls, both at Keysborough.

The only competition goal kicker ahead of him is

LUKE McGUINNESS' MPFL RECORD

Year	Games	Goals	Average	Club
1994	4	10	2.50	Mornington
1995	17	9	0.52	Mornington
1996	20	46	2.30	Mornington
1997	16	34	2.12	Mornington
1998	16	25	1.56	Mornington
1999	18	34	1.88	Mornington
2000	20	104	5.20	Keysborough
2001	17	35	2.05	Keysborough
2002	18	67	3.72	Keysborough
2003	19	120	6.31	Keysborough
2004	17	72	4.23	Keysborough
2005	17	43	2.52	Keysborough
2006	20	107	5.35	Keysborough
2007	19	64	3.36	Keysborough
2008	20	77	3.85	Keysborough
2009	16	47	2.93	Keysborough
2010	14	22	1.57	Keysborough
2011	16	19	1.18	Keysborough
Totals	304	935	3.07	

Table: Doug Dyall

Mornington's Simon Goosey, a bush football legend, who amassed 1847.

Other than a few games as a 12-year-old, McGuinness preferred tennis right up until the age of 20. He created a sensation on his senior debut for Mornington by kicking eight goals against rough-and-tough Pines.

With Goosey entrenched in the goalsquare, he took over at centre half-forward and helped Mornington into four Grand Finals in a row for two wins and two losses.

Crossing to Keysborough, he promptly played in another play-off, his fifth on end, in 2000.

Known throughout League circles as 'Spook', the 191-centimetre (six feet, three inches) McGuinness says his longevity was all to do with starting late. 'Most of my mates my age finished early, but unlike me they played through all their teen years too and had had enough. I'm proud I was able to play longer than most.'

A ONE-MATCH WONDER

Among the rollcall of literally thousands to play League football are hundreds who played just once.

Riverina legend Brent Piltz says his signature day of big-time football lasted less than 10 minutes at the Docklands and was soon forgotten as Essendon came from behind to defeat his adopted team for a year, the Sydney Swans.

A decorated key position player in the bush, Piltz believes he entered the AFL system 'too late' to be more than a one-match player, but the benefits of training with the best were a wonderful rub-off on his return home.

He played in two premierships at North Albury and won a best and fairest at Myrtleford where he rejuvenated his career. As Henty's co-coach in 2014 he spearheaded Henty's first flag since 1996.

Piltz was born and bred in Henty, located in picturesque wheat and sheep country, halfway between Albury and Wagga Wagga. He played his first open-age season as a lanky 17-year-old in Henty's 1996 premiership side, before crossing to the more powerful and lucrative Ovens and Murray League and playing in North Albury's 1999 and 2002 premierships. In 2001, he represented Port Melbourne in the VFL and played a one-off game in the AFL, off the interchange bench, with Sydney.

As one of North Albury's most versatile, he initially played in key positions up forward before settling back into centre half-back and becoming known for his expert 'sweeping' roles.

In all, he played 217 games with North and 40-odd games in two seasons at Myrtleford.

Piltz contested seven Ovens and Murray Grand Finals including the 2005 epic when Myrtleford lost after the siren by a point. He was also a part of the Victorian Country team that contested the 2002 Australian Country Championships in Renmark, South Australia.

Among the most noted players of his time was Corowa's Craig Tafft who was also around the 190-centimetre (six feet, two inches) mark, had a good reach and was quicker. Best of his teammates at North Albury was Sydney Swan legend-to-be Brett Kirk.

Asked about his own ever-so-short big-time career, Piltz said he needed to make an immediate impact – and didn't. 'I was a mature-age recruit at 22. Had I come earlier and been in the system longer it could have made a huge difference. But that's football. You have to take your opportunities.'

BREAKING THE DROUGHT

For all of Briagolong-born Jimmy Pleydell's two decades at Carlton, Essendon, Cooee and back at home in Gippsland, one moment remains indelible: watching on as Maffra broke its premiership drought in 2002. It was the club's first flag in 54 years and Pleydell reckons he had never been more nervous before any game of footy.

'My son Chris played that day and won the Medal [for being best afield] and we got up [against Wonthaggi] by 14 or 15 points in a close one at Moe,' he said. 'It was a great moment, especially after all those years of battling.'

It was the first Grand Final Pleydell had ever been associated with.

He had four years at Carlton without playing a final, and two years in northern Tasmania with Cooee before heading back to Maffra where he followed in the footsteps of his big brother Bill by winning consecutive club best and fairests in 1968 and 1969. Even back in Gippsland his footy seasons would finish each August, without any September action.

A long-kicking left-footer, Pleydell played 37 senior games at Carlton in the mid-'60s around the time Ron Barassi swapped from Melbourne. Originally from Yarrawonga, he and John Lloyd (Matthew's dad) lived in the same inner-city house for the club's country recruits. Barassi was all about immediate success though and both were quickly moved on – John after playing 29 games. Had he played just a few more, Matty Lloyd would have been eligible to play at Carlton under the father-son rule of the time.

Pleydell also had a month at Essendon before transferring to Cooee where he played his best football in the strong Northern Tasmanian FL which included 'Mr Magic' Darrel Baldock, then with Latrobe.

'One year, we were the only team to beat them in the home and aways but we didn't even make the Grand Final,' he said. '"The Doc" [Baldock] was an amazing player. You could keep him quiet for all but five minutes of a game yet in those five minutes he'd kick three or four [goals] and beat you by himself.'

Pleydell was runner-up to another ex-League player, Footscray's John Jillard, for the competition best and fairest one year before heading back to Maffra where he played full-forward, centre and even in the first ruck despite being just 178 centimetres (5 feet, 10 inches).

'I was reasonably athletic back then and could jump a bit so I'd run in at the centre bounces and try and leap a bit at the taller, heavier blokes,' he said.

'We struggled to attract players back then and couldn't put good enough teams on the park. But it was still mighty fun, working in with the young fellas and watching them improve week by week.'

While Jimmy went on to League football, two other Pleydells gave even more service back home, big brother Bill aggregating 250 games and Jimmy's son, Chris, playing more than 100 in the seniors, including the epic 2002 Grand Final.

'It was amazing, after all those years of not going anywhere near a place in the Grand Final, we won it in 2002 and won another six in the next eight years. It's funny how footy goes sometimes,' Pleydell said.

For years his old Carlton teammate Ian Collins would send tickets to games at the Docklands for Pleydell and his family. 'That's the great thing about footy. You're never forgotten,' said Pleydell. 'I played my first game [with Carlton] the very same day [in 1964] as [Adrian] "Gags" Gallagher. Now he really could play ...'

ROBINVALE'S 'MR FOOTBALL'

Few in country circles are as rated, or as decorated, as diminutive Sunraysia farmer Don Falvo who played more than 400 'A' grade games.

A pepper-and-salt on-baller at his best when it counted most at springtime, Falvo is still known at John James Oval as Robinvale's 'Mr Football'.

A non-drinker and non-smoker, he played in his first premiership as a 15-year-old in 1991, after the club's senior coach Michael Woods had pleaded with his parents to allow him to play.

'I was in the Under 15s and only knee-high, but Michael invited me to training. There was a pre-season [open-age] carnival between the towns and that helped convince Mum and Dad that I'd be all right playing with the men. I always had pace and that kept me clear of any trouble.'

One of his teammates was Pat Healy, another of the Sunraysia's most revered. 'My first year was Pat's last and I was so lucky to get to play with him,' Falvo said. 'He's still the best player I have seen in these parts. He was so versatile, a great mark and could play forward or back. He kicked 100 goals in a season several times.'

Eight Grand Finals later, for two more flags in 1997 and 2010, Falvo became Robinvale's co-coach alongside another ex-premiership teammate, ruckman Darren Atkinson.

'We went through 2010 undefeated and played off again in

2011 only to go down by a kick or two. Nothing beats Grand Finals, but like in the Olympics, you have to do the work to deserve a place. Darren and I found it much easier to set an example when we were out there with them.'

In addition to his 400-plus senior games, a north-west record, Falvo also played more than 20 representative games for the Sunraysia League, before opting to play only at club level 'to give the younger fellas a go'. He won almost a dozen club best and fairests and four McLeod Medals for being the competition best and fairest.

Small and lightly built at 174 centimetres (5 feet, 8½ inches) and 78 kilograms (12 stone, 4 pounds), Falvo said he was fortunate to have maintained his pace. Locals still shake their heads in wonder at his three and four-bounce runs capped off by a long bomb goal from the 50-metre line à la his all-time football hero, Collingwood's Peter Daicos.

If it wasn't for a knee injury, Falvo would still be playing. He says his only regret was not actually winning more Grand Finals. One which particularly grates was the infamous 1999 play-off with Imperials when Robinvale's Matt Curran was abruptly red-carded midway through the first quarter by an emergency umpire, for allegedly spitting at an opponent. Forced to play the rest of the Grand Final with only 17, Robinvale lost by two points – and Curran was later cleared at the tribunal. It was officialdom gone crazy and cost 'the Vales' the flag.

MR DYNAMIC

In the swinging '70s, John Burns was as dynamic a centreman as there was in Australian football. He played in three VFL Grand Finals in a row and in 1975, kicked four first-half goals as North Melbourne broke a 50-year premiership drought.

But one humble accolade still stands almost as tall in the Burns 'CV': the bush season Geelong's silky-skilled Brownlow Medallist Alistair Lord stood aside for the super-slick teenager-on-the-rise, allowing Burns to play ahead of him in the pivot.

'That was my first year of Hampden League footy in 1968,' said Burns. 'It was my first year out of the Under 18s. Alistair had won a Brownlow in the centre at Geelong. He was like a God to us and here he was saying he'd ruck-rove so I could play in the centre. I've never forgotten that.'

South Warrnambool made the finals, Burns impressing enough to think that he would attract the attentions of Fitzroy's Hampden recruiting scouts. Disappointed when overlooked, he headed across Bass Strait to Tasmania, intent on increasing his profile by playing in a renowned recruiting nursery which had seen so many champions like Darrel Baldock, Ian Stewart, Royce Hart, Peter Hudson and Verdun Howell wooed by mainland clubs. He was both NTFA (Northern Tasmanian Football Association) and East Launceston's best and fairest.

'Footy was what I was good at,' Burns said. 'As a teenager growing up I had no parents. Mum died when I was five and Dad when I was 12. I was a larrikin but I was a loveable larrikin. I was supposed to get drafted. When it didn't happen, I made other arrangements. It made me fight even harder to get the break I wanted. Maybe it was good for me in the end.'

Ironically, the very year Burns shifted states and played in the 1969 Australian national football carnival, South Warrnambool won the Hampden premiership.

'Alistair still reminds me about that,' said Burns. 'I tell him if I'd been there, instead of winning by a point we would have won by 10 goals!'

Having played in Launceston and Perth, Burns was finally given his opportunity in Melbourne and began an exulted career at North Melbourne and Geelong, before being wooed west again as South Warrnambool's playing coach for three years.

'We made the finals only once, but I helped cultivate the younger ones which was to benefit Noel Mugavin when he came in as coach,' Burns said. 'We were a real working-class club and didn't have the money of some of the others. But it was still satisfying. And they still couldn't catch me – even then!'

Burns' blistering speed and ability to run sideways at pace like

OLD MATE: Barry Cable

a crab to evade his pursuers was his trademark. He was regularly invited to join the pro-running circuit. 'One of my mates from Fitzroy, Ian McRae, won all sorts of gifts including Maryborough and said I was mad not to also have a go. But I didn't want to hang around for two years just to get a certain mark. I have no regrets. You walk into a room where your old mates are, whether they be at South Warrnambool or at North and you can just take up the conversation where you left off. I ran into Barry Cable at AFL House one day a few years back. He was doing a tape for an AFL Legends night and they had me in talking about the '75 Grand Final. That was such a special time for us all. It's like the four-minute mile. Being the first to do something, in our case help to win North's first flag, is something no one can ever take away from any of us.'

Burns was carrying a shoulder injury entering the 1975 finals and on Grand Final day, knowing he would be targeted, he had his 'good' shoulder bandaged and started out of the centre to lessen the chance of being caught in the early crossfire. He kicked the first two goals including a 60-metre torpedo which bounced through and was one of the best afield in North's history-making win.

Injuries stopped him from playing in two more Grand Finals in 1977. One of his few games all year was in the reserves late in the season at Arden Street when coach Ron Barassi asked him to sit on the bench. 'I was in the dugout, still far from fit and stood up and walked around the boundary and about 6000 people in the stand and on the terraces stood cheering me,' Burns said. 'They knew I wasn't right but they appreciated the contribution I'd made. You don't forget moments like that.'

ANOTHER BIG NICK

A teenage Michael Hammond had been taking all before him in Maryborough football in 1963. Some thought he could emulate some of the Big Smoke doings of another local ruck hero in John Nicholls.

Richmond recruiter Graeme Richmond's bush contacts were second-to-none. One very cold July day he fielded a call from one of his mates. A rival club had seen big Mike play at the weekend and was keen to sign him.

'Okay,' said Richmond, 'we'll be right up.'

Ringing Pat Guinane, the Tiger's high-profile centre half-forward and telling him to meet him at his Barker's Road house at 5 p.m., Richmond went to work and by the time Guinane had arrived a new, swanky car was in his driveway at home.

'I'm going to give it to Michael Hammond if he'll sign,' said Richmond, anticipating Guinane's question.

'Graeme, how in the bloody hell are we then going to get home?'

'We'll find a way ... we'll thumb a ride.'

Much to Guinane's relief, Hammond *didn't* sign that night – but Richmond got his man the next time, Hammond playing 31 games in three years.

THE ICING ON THE CAKE

Grand Finals are rarely won when you're just four points up at three-quarter time opposed by a quality opponent, kicking into a howling gale.

As he gathered his team together in the three-quarter huddle at Friendly Society Park, Camperdown's captain-coach Stewart Lord insisted that his team had shocked all year and could do it again – *if* they listened to what he said.

In 1963, Lord had tasted the delights of a VFL flag at Geelong, just 12 months after his twin brother Alistair had won the Brownlow Medal.

But this was to be the sweetest 30 minutes of all.

Mortlake, coached by Peter Lyon (Garry's father), had lost the previous year's Hampden League Grand Final by a point and were primed to avenge the loss and steamroll home.

'No one thought we could win that year,' said Lord. 'We were a very young side and had come from fourth. But they were good listeners and all year had been trying to put into practice everything I said. The wind always blew from Port Fairy to Warrnambool, but this day it was coming from the east [the opposition direction].

'We were less than a goal up at the last change and kicking to the city end against this big breeze. I dropped our two ruckmen and myself across the half-back line to see if we could keep them out. The South Warrnambool ground had a slope of six or seven feet [1.8–2.1 metres] with a bike track going right around it. It was easy to box sides out if you knew what pockets to keep them in.'

Gathering his players in close at the last change, Lord spoke passionately, insisting that while their lead was marginal and the wind strong, the game was far from lost. 'We can win this, if you do as I tell you,' he told them. 'Play as I want you to play. Kick where I want you to kick.'

Just as the huddle was breaking up, he spoke with matchwinning forward Graeme Langsworth and said he'd won a flag for the club two years earlier with a moment of brilliance. If ever there was a time to shine again, it was now …

Within minutes, Mortlake had snatched the lead and continued to attack incessantly only to be turned back again and again by Lord and Co. Approaching time-on, Camperdown finally crossed the centre and Langsworth, quiet all day, bravely split a pack like he was Alan 'Bull' Richardson, Matty's father, and kicked a magnificent running goal to re-wrest the lead, triggering a joyous volley of car horns all around the park.

'The game was on the line. We were behind. Stewart had moved himself back into defence. Someone had to do something,' said Langsworth, a Collingwood six-footer who had played with Essendon reserves. 'The ball was there. I saw it and just went for it. It's one of those favourite moments you live and re-live.'

Lord regarded Camperdown as a true 'family club' in the mould of Hawthorn. 'The whole town was behind us,' he said. 'When I first got there we sat down with a group of local businessmen. I told them that we could win a premiership if they were prepared to put something into the club. I told them that I'd get the players and I did. Everyone was so closely knit. They became friends for life.'

Camperdown's standout players of Lord's era included key defender Graeme Bourke, rovers Peter Stephens and David Lane, key forward Ian McGregor and man-mountain ruckmen Trevor Potter and Bert Peperkamp.

'Trevor and Bert were both six-foot-five [196-centimetre] fellas and good strong country players. Peter Stephens could have played in any League side as rover. He should have gone down [to Melbourne]. It was our good fortune that he chose to stop at Camperdown.'

Stewart and his equally handsome younger twin brother Alistair were the darlings of football in the Western District in the '60s and early '70s. They'd played with Cobden as teenagers and locals loved it when they both returned from Geelong into the Hampden League, Stewart at Camperdown and Colac and Alistair at South Warrnambool and Cobden.

Still inseparable, the twins live in adjacent streets in the same inner-Geelong suburb, a couple of Alistair's magnificent drop-kicks from Kardinia Park. Football has been their life and the premierships, in the city and the bush, a magnificent bonus.

FAST-TRACKED AHEAD OF HIS TIME

Briar Hill boy Ray Willett had only just turned 19 when he played in his first Grand Final in 1960. It was his fifth senior game and he can't remember touching the ball even once. Embarrassingly this day there just happened to be 97 500 present! The venue was the Melbourne Cricket Ground and Willett was Collingwood's full-forward …

'I had plenty of mates that day,' he said. 'We kicked a record low score of two goals two for the entire match and we were slaughtered [by eight goals]. Melbourne had a tall defender by the name of John Lord and he was impassable at centre half-back. I ran around like a chook with its head cut off and didn't get near the ball.'

Over 20 senior games spread over two and a half seasons Willett wore the No. 6 and No. 8 guernseys soon to be made famous by Peter McKenna and Des Tuddenham.

Other than being best afield against Essendon in his first semifinal in 1960 (with 20 kicks and 12 marks) and one goal performance against Fitzroy from a forward flank in 1964, he admits to having underachieved.

Back in the '50s and '60s, most played for the honour rather than the cash. Eventually they realised they had to financially capitalise on their skills and experience and went out coaching. Nowadays they tend to play until they drop as no secondary club can afford them and an extra year's salary is probably worth two to three times the wage they could get outside the AFL system.

Willett was a schoolteacher and was relieved to be posted to a one-room school at Strathallan, midway between Echuca and Rochester, where he immediately began one of the great bush careers, playing in back-to-back flags at Rochester and winning three competition best and fairests at Mooroopna. In his first year at 'Rochie' he won the competition best and fairest and the League's goal-kicking award – an unprecedented solo.

'Rochie played in eight Bendigo League Grand Finals in a row,' he said. 'It was a privilege to be part of two of them. In 1962, my first year, we were undefeated including the second semi and the Grannie. That September was incredibly wet in Bendigo and the authorities put back our first final by a week. It meant that we hadn't played for three weeks and we were off the boil and only just limped to the line. Then we had another two weeks to wait for the Grand Final [against Golden Square].'

APPRENTICE: Ray Willett had played only a handful of games when named in Collingwood's 1960 Grand Final team. The Magpies had a shocker, kicking just two goals all day
Ray Willett Collection

The impact of ex-Demon Noel McMahen, captain-coach in the first four of Rochester's run of eight Grand Finals was profound. 'Noel introduced the Melbourne way of playing and it was highly effective. We also had a dynamic secretary in Jack Green who made everything hum along nicely. He was as good as any of the big boys in Melbourne and I think he had some time at Essendon. He was a superb operator.'

In 2012, Willett was proud to attend the club's 50-year premiership reunion. 'It didn't matter that we hadn't seen each other for years,' he said. 'We were all like brothers, the greatest of mates.'

Despite back and knee problems, so successful was Willett at his next club Mooroopna that he was asked to coach. 'I wasn't sure how I'd go. As it proved, it wasn't for me,' he said. 'I was always nervous giving them the pre-game rev-up and one day instead of saying: "I want 18 men for 100 minutes" it came out the wrong way around: "I want 100 men for 18 minutes!" We won the game and our vice-captain Stewie Florence told me later that those 80 extras across the half-back line made all the difference!'

Willett's back regularly went into spasm and he'd hang from the rafters of his garage with one of his kids swinging on his legs to stretch the joints and get him mobile again.

With five years of Ovens and Murray football at Corowa and five more at neighbouring Wahgunyah, Willett played with and against some of the most notable country players of the '60s and '70s. The toughest was Rochester's Con O'Toole who played at centre half-forward and was captain in Willett's only two bush flags in 1962 and 1963. Mooroopna's Jimmy Read, a St Kilda premiership winger, was the best tackler he saw and the much-travelled Ovens and Murray legend Johnny Clancy the best rover. There was no superior ruckman than Mick Nolan from Wangaratta Rovers. 'He made brilliant use of his big frame in the ruck duels and was a beautiful tap of the ball. His rovers always enjoyed an armchair ride. He was also a great character and the first to offer you a beer or a softie after a game.'

Way ahead of all his football feats and decorations over a 300-game career were the mates he made. 'The unsung, unpaid people at all the clubs I was at are the real heroes,' Willett said. 'The trainers, the gatekeepers, the timekeepers, the girls in the canteen – they were all fantastic and make country footy what it is today.'

BUSH ROYALTY

When Carlton full-forward Allan White snapped a matchwinning goal virtually on the siren at Princes Park late one year in 1959, teammate Serge Silvagni was so excited that he planted a huge Italian kiss right on White's cheek. 'It was the 17th round [of 18] and we were going for the double chance and it got us over the line by just two points,' said White. 'Gary Young [of Hawthorn] kicked eight goals that day and I got five. We were going goal for goal in that final quarter.'

STAR SPORTSMAN: Allan White (left) with Maryborough's John Nicholls in 1957. He beat 'Big Nick' for the club's best first year player award
Ken Piesse Collection

White had three years in the big time and famously, in 1957, was named Carlton's best first-year player ahead of legend-in-the-making John Nicholls from Maryborough. But after just two more years at 12 pounds a game, the lure of double the money up at Mildura and a more laidback lifestyle back in the bush was compelling.

'I'd been born in Carlton and went to Lee Street [Carlton North] Primary before the family moved out to Fawkner and

I worked in the bush with Dad cutting wood and carting it to Melbourne,' he said. 'All we had back then were axes, so it helped develop a good pair of shoulders which stood me in good stead with all my sport.'

White played finals in two of his three League years, including the famous 1957 'hail storm' semifinal against Hawthorn. Only once afterwards, at Alexandra, at bush footy level did he ever experience more atrocious conditions.

Blues legend Ken Hands rated White as the best field kick he ever saw. Once in the reserves, White kicked 9.1. His best at country level was 13 in three quarters for Avenel.

He has few regrets about leaving League ranks in his mid-20s, as Mildura Imperials had promised him 25 pounds a game. 'We didn't find out until we got there that the rent on the home they'd arranged for us was 20 quid a week! The other five went into a barrel [of beer] I'd buy each year for the players. So basically I played for nothing,' he said. 'I just worked out in the bush chopping wood. Had I been a bit sharper I would gone to the Association [the old VFA] where you could have really made some money.'

A sports fanatic, who has always been a player rather than a watcher, White won nine Avenel Golf Club championships, three Victorian Veteran Sandgreen championships, 19 Avenel Bowling Club championships and three Goulburn Valley champion of champions titles. He reduced his handicap to four at Avenel and played at No. 1 in the pennant team when it won nine titles in a decade. At Euroa one year, three tied for the club championship and had to go out and play three extra holes to decide the winner. White went birdie-birdie-birdie to win by three shots. When the local television station came to Avenel to interview local sports legend two-time Essendon premiership defender Ian 'Bluey' Shelton, Shelton told them they had the wrong man. 'You should go and talk to Alan White,' he said.

HIS HIGHNESS

F ew had the same Western Districts football pedigree as Reg Burgess, who quit League football at 26 to work back on the family farm. Originally from Edenhope Secondary College, Burgess was one of many VFL champions lured back to the bush in an era of staggering payments that saw a stream of big names exit League football prematurely.

'Everyone bar the captain got only the basic wage [in Melbourne],' Burgess said. 'I was on six pounds a game and then eight quid in my last few years. If you played some finals you might get 200 pounds for the entire year. In my first year coaching at Casterton I got 1500 quid, which was more than I'd made in all my [seven] years at Essendon. It was pretty handy money. My oldest mates still refer to me as "Your Royal Highness". Mind you it was a 100-kilometre trip up and back three times a week, but it worked out well with me being able to help my brother with the farm work [at Apsley].'

A two-time Essendon best and fairest, versatile ahead of his years, Burgess was ranked 13th in *Champions of Essendon*, a book on the greatest Bombers of all time, released in 2002.

Known as the perfect midfielder with superb ball-handling skills, Burgess loved his time in the Big Smoke, especially the opportunity to play under his idols Dick Reynolds and Billy Hutchison. 'And then there was a bloke called Coleman who was simply out of this world,' said Burgess. 'I got to play eight games with John and they were all unforgettable.

'He'd just say to us to "put it out there in some space" and invariably he'd get it. Everybody thought the world of him. On some training nights when the school holidays were on, there'd be 4000 and 5000 people all milling around the [players] race just see him run onto the ground! I was so lucky to play with him.'

Burgess believed himself so privileged to be playing football at Essendon that each Friday he'd clean his boots, wash his laces and polish his stops. His midfield teammates included some of the who's who of the most elite Bombers including Hutchison, Jack Clarke, Hughie Mitchell and John Birt.

The highlights of Burgess's 124 games with Essendon were his Grand Finals, in 1957 and 1959, where he opposed Melbourne champions Laurie Mithen and Brian Dixon. 'We ran second on both occasions, but it was still a thrill playing in front of 100 000 people,' he said. His duels with two other leading country boys of the '50s, Brendan Edwards (Hawthorn) and Thorold Merrett (Collingwood) were always memorable. 'Everyone stayed in their positions back then so you would have a series of one-on-one contests against your direct opponent,' he said.

Burgess was a tall wingman for the time at 175 centimetres (five feet, nine inches). He could sprint with the speedsters, fly with the ruckmen, handle the ball with poise and polish and was a long and penetrating kick. He represented Victoria nine times and was an All-Australian in 1958. He admits he 'could have given a bit more' at Essendon but he loved being back in grassroots football and being closer to his family.

His coach Reynolds regarded him more as a 'dry-tracker' but that was underrating his sheer skill and tenacity. During his final season, Footscray's Western Oval was awash and Burgess played a blinder, taking one of the marks of his life when he threw himself headlong into a giant puddle and grabbed a sliding mark. 'I clutched that ball like it was the Crown Jewels,' he said. Later Reynolds quipped Burgess had in one memorable moment swum 25 yards to earn his *Herald* Learn to Swim Certificate!

Burgess won premierships in each of his three years with Casterton from 1961 to 1963, the town's teams of the late '50s and early '60s including John and Barry Gill, Alan 'Bull' Richardson and David Robbie who all played League football.

In the 1962 play-off against hot favourites Portland, coached by Collingwood's Mick Twomey, Casterton trailed by 26 points at three-quarter time before kicking four goals to nil in the final term to snatch the flag. 'And we kicked only eight goals all day,' he said. 'Portland had a young Peter Hogan in its team that day. He went to Richmond. Every [Western Border] team had a big name or two. But not everyone could settle in Melbourne. Our own Peter Kellett preferred to play his footy locally. He was only little but he could really play. And Portland's Denis Bell came back home again after a run at Collingwood [in 1961]. The big city suits some and not others.'

REG. BURGESS
ESSENDON

Burgess started and finished his career at Apsley on the South Australian–Victoria border. As a 17-year-old he was the Kowree-Naracoorte competition's best and fairest and played in Apsley's XVIII team which made a Grand Final in 1951. In 1952 they won the flag with Burgess again starring.

Burgess has an extra strong link to Essendon. His son-in-law Roger Merrett was a powerhouse at the club in the '80s and early '90s.

A TOUGH NUT

Billy Lieschke's League career was restricted to just one game, as a teenage reserve, late in the 1962 season at Footscray. He suffered a near-critical head knock and had three holes drilled through his skull to relieve the pressure on his brain. He was lucky to live and doctors advised him against playing *any* form of sport again.

But he was a tough nut and returning to Albury where he'd first played senior Ovens and Murray football as a 15-year-old, he won his club's best and fairest in 1963 and was one of the best afield in their 1966 Grand Final win under Collingwood legend Murray Weideman. He also represented the Ovens and Murray League and made Albury's Team of the Century, in a back pocket. Later he joined Acton in the Canberra League and had a season with Natimuk before continuing his football love affair as an umpire in the Wimmera League.

A ROSE AMONG THE THORNS

Evelyn Rogers always regarded herself as 'a bit of a tomboy'. Even into her mid-70s, the Daylesford great grandmother was known to have an occasional kick of the footy with the kids.

Originally from Erica, near Walhalla, Evelyn was the talk of the town in 1955 when she replaced her husband Bernie in Erica's team one Saturday and kicked half her team's score against Yinnar. It was the first recorded instance of a girl playing men's open-age football and warranted an entry in my *Football Legends of the Bush* (2011) and in 2012, a front-page photograph in the farmer's 'bible', the *Weekly Times*.

Remembering the great moment, Evelyn said, 'We were down to 12 or 13 and would have had to forfeit. The night before, Bernie was injured in a car accident, not badly thankfully. I'd been running the boundary most of the year and the opposition had no problems with me playing, so I did.'

Erica kicked only two goals all day, one coming courtesy of a free kick to Evelyn who calmly punted the ball through from 'pretty close in … but it was on a bit of an angle'.

'One of their players pushed me in the back and then remonstrated with the umpire and I got a 15-yard [13.7-metre] penalty. I'd always been able to kick, with both feet. I taught a few of my younger brothers.'

The eldest of five, Evelyn has lived in Daylesford for almost 30 years. She has 10 children, almost 30 grandchildren and 'a dozen or so' great grandkids. 'It's hard to keep up with them all,' she says.

One of her daughters Shirley Elderfield says her mother has always preferred 'to have a bat or ball in her hand than to just sit inside and sew'.

'She won a long-kick competition one day and still has the trophy to prove it,' she said. 'We're very proud of her.'

4

Goals & Goalmen

*'McKenna could unleash 60-yard
drop-punts and land them directly on
top of the goal umpire's hat ...'*

SHEER NECTAR

It seems I've been tripping off to the football all my life. From the early '60s my father and I would drive to Hawthorn home games, walk under the railway underpass at Glenferrie Oval and scramble for a vantage spot on the outer terraces. Having armed me with a Herbert Adams pie – always in foil – Dad would push me through to the front, making sure I had a pen to note the goals and the quarter-by-quarter scores in my *Football Record*.

We'd go most weeks, revelling in the goal-kicking deeds of John Peck, the artistry under fire of Graham Arthur, the sticky-fingered high marking of undersized full-back Phil Hay and the raw courage of ball magnet Ian 'Liberty' Law. 'Pecky' could torpedo his goals around corners and topped the League goal kicking three years in a row. I was one of hundreds to wear his No. 23 on the back of my Hawthorn jumper.

Later we witnessed the emergence of a young Leigh Matthews, who even at 18 had a tank-like physique and an implacable attitude. The leaping of Peter Knights was wondrous and the athleticism and drive of Don Scott admirable. Knights was a jumping jack who we reckoned took Mark of the Year every week. Once Scotty outpaced North Melbourne's headlining

DRIVEN: Few were as athletic, determined or as loyal as Hawthorn's powerhouse ruckman Don Scott
Don Scott Collection

ruck-rover Sam Kekovich in a 50-metre sprint across the centre wicket area at Glenferrie. Years later he told me how that one contest was the makings of him, giving him renewed self-belief that he could compete against anyone.

The crowd was always so close to the action at Glenferrie, the narrowest of all League grounds. John Kennedy had a long-time runner in Normie Lord, but often didn't need him. Frequently, especially late in a quarter when he demanded 'shut-down' football, 'Kanga' would stand on top of the Linda Crescent coach's box and in that booming voice of his, call his players back behind the ball. When he piloted his third and final premiership in 1976, he clambered on top of the lockers in the Richmond rooms for a better look at the celebrations and stayed there like a proud father watching over his flock.

The arrival of Peter Hudson as the team's highest-paid and most glamorous player changed perceptions about Hawthorn. Suddenly it was no longer an unskilled easybeat. Rather, from 1971, it was *the* team to be feared. So good was Hudson in the one-on-ones that Kennedy cleared out the rest of the forward line, often leaving Hudson and his opponent one-out 60–70 yards (55–64 metres) from everyone else. 'Huddo' won the goal kicking five years in a row, with four centuries. He regularly kicked the majority of Hawthorn's score. Maybe there was too much reliance on one man, but boy, was it exciting!

Hudson's two major goal-kicking rivals of the time Peter McKenna and Doug Wade invariably had better 'service' from players further afield. Barry Price's bullet-like stab passes to a leading McKenna were a joy to behold, even for non-Collingwood supporters. McKenna could unleash 60-yard (55-metre) drop-punts and land them directly on top of the goal umpire's hat. He'd learnt to kick on the soccer fields of Heidelberg when 'goals' would only be allowed – even from a long distance – if the ball landed in the actual soccer net. 'I had to learn to kick long and low,' said McKenna. 'I was able to kick my drop-punts 10 metres longer than almost everyone else.'

Wade, bulkier and tougher, would roost monstrous torpedoes that went on and on. His over-the-head snaps in heavy traffic were remarkable and sunk many a team late in a game. Wade had enormous pride and bristled at first in the lead-up to the 1975 Grand Final when coach Ron Barassi told him he was playing, but on the proviso that he *didn't* fly for even one mark. Wade, one of North Melbourne's mature-age imports, had visited Barassi on the Thursday night before the game, demanding, 'Am I in, or am I out?'

'Do you want to have a game of chess?'

'No, I don't want a game of bloody chess. Am I in or am I out?'

'You're in ...'

In a low-scoring final, Wade kicked four goals, including three on the run, from crumbed balls that he'd expertly roved. Not once do I remember him contesting a pack mark. And North won its first flag. It remained Wade's finest September moment, one where he had to play like a defender.

Hudson possessed neither the blinding leading speed of McKenna, nor the intimidating bulk of Wade, but it was uncanny the way he could position himself in the front position just as the ball was at its highest point and about to drop. The supply was weird and wonderful from Bob Keddie's veering-around-the-corner drop-punts, Alan Martello's torps – which would fly either 35 yards or 60 – and Des Meagher's scrubby, bouncing left-footers, yet 'Huddo' would invariably be in the right place at the right time, having tilted his opponent out with his hips. When taking a set shot, he was one of the first to go through a set routine before unleashing his own favourite flat-punts. They looked inelegant and inadequate when compared with McKenna's majestic low-flying drop-punts and Wade's booming torpedoes – yet he was more accurate than both. His goals-per-game average was also superior at 5.64.

Only once, on debut in 1967 against Carlton when he ran around opponent Wes Lofts at Princes Park and twice stab-kicked the ball through, did I ever see him kick anything but flat-punts, some of which on the good days would 'torpedo' deliciously. 'I never dared to kick any stabs again after that first game,' he said. 'John [Kennedy] didn't like them ...'

The most memorable goal I witnessed from Huddo wasn't from a spectacular mark or an impossible angle. Rather, it was in 1969, when he was chasing his opponent, Footscray's Peter Welsh around the outer wing at the Western Oval. Welsh had

PINCHED: Champion goal kicker, high-flying Doug Wade initially signed at Melbourne as a 17-year-old before sweet-talking Bob Davis and Geelong changed his career path
Drew Payne/Ken Piesse Collection

a break on him and was bouncing the ball around the boundary line, with Hudson in close pursuit. Football folklore has it that Welsh took six or seven bounces; in reality it was probably three or four. Just as Huddo seemed exhausted and ready to stop,

FIVE OTHER FAMOUS GOALS

2012: Tom Hawkins (Geelong) – his goal after the siren maintained the Cats' miraculous record of wins in a row against Hawthorn.

2010: Lance Franklin (Hawthorn) – the most astonishing goal I have seen; running like a Stawell Gift finalist, hugging the MCC member's boundary, the 'Budster' ran away from a despairing Bomber Cale Hooker and after three bounces drilled it through from an impossible angle from 40 metres to tie the scores midway through the final quarter. Three minutes later he followed with one almost as good… footy perfection.

1987: Gary Buckenara (Hawthorn) – a curving drop-punt after the siren pole-vaulted the Hawks into another Grand Final, denying Melbourne icon Robbie Flower of the chance to play off for the first time for the flag.

1970: Alex Jesaulenko (Carlton) – a left-foot snap in time-on, which bounced through to sink Collingwood in the most extraordinary comeback in Grand Final history.

1960: John Peck (Hawthorn) – his goal after the siren gave Hawthorn its first-ever victory after 35 years against Collingwood at Victoria Park.

Welsh bounced the ball on a harder part of the ground and it rebounded straight over his shoulder, straight into Hudson's hands! He took off, this time with Welsh in pursuit and after three or four bounces put it through the high-diddle-diddle. It was nectar, sheer nectar.

Had Demon Barry Bourke not accidentally fallen across my hero's knee in the opening round of the 1972 season, Hudson was on schedule that day to break Fred Fanning's record of 18 goals in a game. He'd kicked eight or nine in the first 50 minutes and was playing with imperious confidence. Just as many can remember where they were for a particularly significant moment in history, like JFK's assassination in Dallas in 1963 or Warnie's flipper which castled Richie Richardson at the 'G in 1992, I can recall exactly where I was at the time of the Hudson tragedy – up a ladder helping to paint the back verandah of our family home in Beaumaris!

HASSA'S SIGNATURE MOMENT

Fifty years after Hassa Mann's miracle goal that sent Hawthorn spinning from first to fifth in the penultimate round of 1964, I can still remember that hurried, inspired snap from the Linda Crescent boundary at the 'Sardine Tin', as we called Glenferrie in those days.

Hassa was one of the guests at the 2014 launch of the biography of Stuart Spencer, which I published, and knowing my liking for the Hawks, took particular delight at retelling every detail.

It was a desperate finish and there must have been only a minute or two to go. John Kennedy had packed the back line but somehow after a stoppage Mann found enough room and with not even a half-look at the swimming-pool-end goals, roosted the ball high. 'Originally I was thinking I'd get it to the top of the goalsquare, but there was a little breeze and it picked it up perfectly and took it straight through,' said Mann. 'I was as surprised as everybody else!'

In a lifetime of watching football all around the country, it remains the goal I most remember – along with Alex Jesaulenko's hurried left-foot snap which bounced and bounced straight through the city-end goals to sink the Magpies in the 1970 Grand Final. The roar of acclamation that accompanied the match-sealing goal was as loud as any I've ever heard at the MCG, but there were 121 000 present – the biggest football crowd in history.

Malcolm Blight's 75-metre goal after the siren at Princes Park is a favourite among North Melbourne supporters. But more recently, Ash McGrath's sealing goal after the siren against Geelong at the Gabba in 2013 was just as impressive given it was from 60 metres out and saw the Brisbane Lions overturn a 52-point deficit late in the third quarter to win by five. 'This is better than a fairytale,' said Fox Sports commentator Anthony Hudson. 'You can't dream these scenarios.'

NEW STATUS

As gifted as Tony Lockett was in his formative years at St Kilda, his massive frame and fitness was always a conversation piece. Cynics dubbed him the Refrigerator and claimed the team could adequately warm-up by running a couple of laps around him. When he was late onto the ground one day, one said he'd got caught in the race or was busy downing a few pre-match hot dogs out the back.

But Lockett re-addressed his love of fast food and fizzy drinks, lost 11 kilograms in just five weeks at the start of the 1986 season and turned around his career, winning a Brownlow Medal and becoming the greatest goal kicker in history.

Now he's back enjoying the anonymity of bush life, in the picturesque southern highlands of NSW.

ONE IN A MILLION

Gary Ablett snr was feeling peckish and asked one of the trainers to go and get him a roast dinner from the Geelong Social Club. 'Are you serious? It's already half past one, Gary. The game starts in just over half an hour ...'

PECKISH: The Cats were warming up but Gary Ablett snr still wanted his lunch ...
Ken Piesse Collection

'Yeah, I know. I'm hungry.'

The dinner was duly fetched and devoured while his incredulous teammates warmed up without him.

Ablett hardly had time to even do some stretches but still played a blinder.

DRILLING A TORP

It remains the most memorable of all of Ross 'Twiggy' Dunne's 238 career goals – his torpedo at the 33-minute mark of the final quarter to tie the scores and force a Grand Final re-match in 1977.

Having taken a fine pack mark ahead of North Melbourne defenders Frank Gumbleton and Brent Crosswell, Dunne slowly settled himself and ignoring the advice of the Richardson brothers, Wayne and Max, to kick a drop-punt, drilled his favourite torpedo through post-high from close range. 'I've heard I got a bit of advice but I honestly didn't hear a word from anyone,' Dunne said. 'The concentration kicked in and subconsciously everything else was blocked out. I suppose it was my most famous goal. I can't tell you what the second one was.'

Less than 72 hours after kicking the crucial final goal – in the first ever VFL Grand Final to be televised 'live' – Dunne was back at work at Victoria Park, selling tickets for the replay. '[As assistant-secretary] I was at the ground at 7 a.m. on the Tuesday. There was no let-up until late in the afternoon when it was time to go to training!'

Extra time is played only during the first three weeks of a finals series, not on Grand Final day. Should the scores be tied in a Grand Final, a replay is played the following week.

PICKING THE WRONG MAN

Williamstown's full-back Ronny Fenton had been keenly anticipating his clash for weeks with the VFA's glamour full-forward, Dandenong's Jim 'Frosty' Miller. At the pre-match, he told his mate, Willi's centre half-back Greg Boxall how he intended to 'fix Miller up today'.

Before the bounce he was 'into' the rough-and-tough goal-kicking icon, banging his elbow into his ribs and generally making a nuisance of himself. Next time Boxall looked around, Fenton was on his back having taken a screaming left hand from Miller right in the gob.

By quarter-time a fired-up Miller had kicked four and the game was fast getting away.

Boxall was first to his mate. 'Geez, you fixed Miller up all right Ronny ...'

'Great &c$#@ing mate you are,' came the reply. 'What bloody well happened? Why didn't you come to assist?'

'I was too busy laughing,' said Boxall.

Miller kicked nine and the men from Dandy won easily.

ALL-ROUNDER

In Victorian amateur football ranks, no one had a higher profile in the '30s than sporting all-rounder Bill 'Soapy' Pearson who in seven years with Old Scotch amassed 1023 goals at an average of 7.3 goals a game and almost 150 a year. The Collegians won four flags in a row, Pearson's personal high of 220 in 1934 including 30 against Brunswick. The great Norm Smith said Pearson was the finest exponent of the torpedo punt he ever saw. So straight and long was Pearson's goal kicking that on set shots teammates would automatically return to the centre for the next bounce – so sure were they of Pearson's accuracy. He was the amateur's Player of the Year in 1937 and also captained St Kilda CC and represented Victoria in the Sheffield Shield.

5
Interviews

Unimpressed by my 'pec' muscles,
Barass said, 'Where's your six-pack?'
'Back at the motel cooling down Ron ...'

A LIFETIME IN THE GAME – AND LOVING IT

I maintain three golden rules when interviewing cricketers and footballers: keep the questions short, listen to what they say and bounce off their answers. The more engaging and vibrant the conversation, the better the listening. Even when promoting his own books – and there were many – cricket legend Dennis Lillee wasn't always as affable as some, but after one six-minute one-on-one radio interview with me, he smiled and said, 'I enjoyed that.' Another former Australian cricketer George Thoms stopped in mid-sentence once and said, 'You're a very good listener, Ken.'

With the leading players – especially the older ones – I'll often ask for their autograph to go into one of my books or onto a keepsake photo. It's a permanent reminder of our meeting. One I didn't ask to sign was 79-year-old master batsman Bill Ponsford and I've regretted it ever since.

There was no time to ask Carl Ditterich for an autograph before Melbourne summer training at Dendy Park one night. He'd arrived late and said if I still wanted to ask him some questions for *The Age* I'd have to go jogging beside him, which I

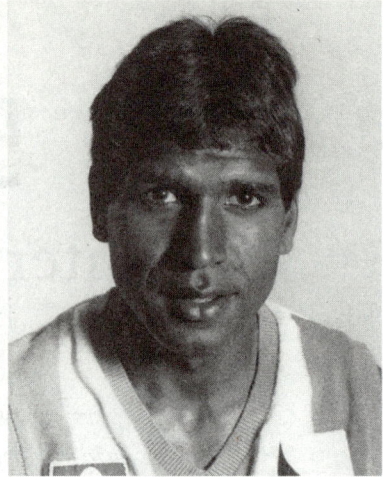

Left: SEALED WITH A KISS: Gerard and Lisa Healy celebrate Gerard's 1988 Brownlow
Greg Hobbs Collection

Right: HELPFUL: John Dugdale sat in on my interview with Jimmy Krakouer, the first he'd given at Arden Street

did, despite being in a suit with dress shoes. Halfway through the first lap he relented and gave me three or four minutes.

At Arden Street one day, North Melbourne's secretary John Dugdale – a midweek cricket mate of mine – sat in for my interview with Jimmy Krakouer, just to help Jim with his answers. It was his first interview with any of the Melbourne mainstream papers.

One Friday night, Sydney had just flown in for a game the following day and Greg Williams told me to come up to where the team was staying at 11 o'clock that night. 'Are you sure?' I asked. 'Match eve?'

'Yep, that's fine,' and it was, Greg chatting amiably about his career, his setbacks in twice being rejected by Carlton, how he had to wear calipers as a kid and how on any match day he would look to run for 90 per cent of the match to burn off his taggers. He also told of the complications of juggling football with the running of his and wife Mary's family's Sydney restaurant. 'The food's good and the turnover is fine,' he said.

INITIATION: Asking me to piggyback Mick Nolan was Ron Barassi's idea of fun. With 35 others watching on, there was no other choice ...
*Ray Jamieson/*Sporting Globe

'It's just the runners [those who don't pay]. Mary says it's my job to catch 'em and I never can. I'm not fast enough!'

His sidekick Gerard Healy and I were good mates. The year Gerard won the Brownlow Medal, he was increasingly worried by a groin injury and at the urging of his girlfriend Lisa, he went into a major Sydney department store to buy a corset to give him some extra support. 'And sir,' said the saleslady behind the counter, 'will you be wanting a matching bra with that?'

Gerard's physiotherapy clinic was for a time in the same Frankston gymnasium I frequented. After work one night he suggested a run, up Kananook Creek and back along Seaford Beach to the gym. I stayed with him for the first 200 metres but then he took off and beat me home by about five minutes. 'What kept you?' he asked.

In Adelaide for a Test match one year, I trained on Sunday morning with Ron Barassi and North Melbourne. 'Barass' had a wicked sense of humour, saw me and immediately told his players to do some warm-up laps of the oval ... by piggyback! My partner? 'The Galloping Gasometer' Mick Nolan, then weighing in at around 108 kilograms (17 stone).

Unimpressed by my 'pec' muscles, Barass said, 'Where's your six-pack?'

'Back at the motel cooling down, Ron,' I replied.

Having covered VFL and AFL football for 35 years, I've been privileged to have had a cuppa or a glass of ale with many famous names from old champions like Wells Eicke, Bob Pratt, Jack Mueller, Dickie Harris, Harry Collier, Laurie 'LJ' Nash and Jack Dyer through to Jim Stynes, Robert Harvey, Johnny Longmire and Darren Millane. Collingwood had just won their drought-breaking '90 premiership and Darren came home several hours late for our Monday morning appointment wearing footy shorts, a bandana, a Collingwood premiership boater and mismatched shoes. 'It was one helluva party,' he quipped. A year later he was dead, after zipping at high speed from one lane to another and burying his car under a truck. A good-time boy lost far too soon.

For years I 'ghosted' Denis Pagan's column for *North News*. We'd played midweek cricket with and against each other – Denis noted for his super-long sprint to the wicket before bowling at a modest military medium. One morning we were chatting in the portables at the Arden Street Oval when a girl came in off Fogarty Street. Her car had stalled and would we mind giving her a push start? Denis and I pushed this old bomb about 60 metres before it finally ignited and off she went. It was a cold winter's day but I was sweating from the exertion. 'Thought you said you were fit, son?' said Denis.

Denis loved football and North Melbourne so much that he could never go on holiday for more than four or five days. Once he left his wife Cheryl at faraway Cable Beach 72 hours into a carefully planned off-season trip, saying it was too steamy. The truth was he just wanted to be back at the club. He loved North and the club loved him. So did the media. Win or lose, he had a lingo all of his own at the press conferences and would trot out his favourite one-liners like 'dancing with your sister' and referring to the game as 'war without weapons'. Quizzed why North had lapsed in a particular quarter, he said, 'Well, the other side does turn up you know.'

One Friday night North lost and Denis was ropable. At the after-match 'presser' the assembled journalists were silent, no one wanting to ask the first question. Up stepped a bright-eyed and bushy-tailed young man working for the first time for the *Sunday Observer* who asked a question Pagan thought insensitive and inane.

Not even bothering to answer, he said, 'And where are you from, son?'

'Keilor.'

Every coach – and footballer – has a story to tell – and I was always an avid listener. Until the '70s and colour TV there was hardly any money in the game, except for the very biggest names. While they were paid peanuts, they were fabulous characters.

Ted Whitten was Footscray's Most Consistent player one year. His prize? A Strasbourg sausage!

LJ Nash was the king of the storytellers and would invariably be found holding court from his favourite stool at the Emerald Hotel just a few of his famed torpedoes from the old Lakeside Oval which he'd made his own in the '30s. The only time he'd ever pause was when Keith Miller entered. Even Laurie was in awe of charismatic Keith, the darling of just about every sports-mad kid, boy or girl, growing up in the '50s. Seeing our group, Nugget would say, 'Is it my buy, boys?' before launching into all sorts of entertaining chit-chat.

My old boss at the *Sporting Globe*, Greg Hobbs, had introduced Nash to me a few years previously. I shook the legend's hand, asked a question and two hours later he was still talking … mostly about himself! He'd once kicked 18.2 for Victoria in a state game and said it would have easily been more, but the rovers 'Beames and Bunton were selfish' and hadn't kicked the ball to him. And by the way, son, did I know that he'd started the game at full-back?!

I asked LJ just how high the acrobatic Pratt would leap for his marks. 'Dunno,' he said, 'all I ever saw were the studs in his boots,' before bursting into gales of laughter.

'Laurie,' I asked him another time, 'just who is the best footballer you've ever seen?'

'Son,' he said, pausing deliberately and looking me straight in the eye, 'I see him every morning in the mirror when I shave!'

Wells Eicke was in his mid-80s when I went down to his tiny flat in St Kilda. He'd debuted in 1909, first represented Victoria as an 18-year-old and remained closely associated to his old club as a committeeman right up until 1964 when he resigned in disgust at their move away from their home, the Junction Oval.

Premiership specialist Mueller spoke of the time he came home at 2 a.m. having worked the night shift at the local flour mill in Echuca to be met by Percy Page, Melbourne's 'Prince of Recruiters'. Page had taken the country train from Spencer Street and wasn't moving until young Jack signed. Mueller's father, Frank, a solicitor and former star sprinter, was unimpressed at the prospect of losing his son to the Big Smoke on a sporting whim. He far preferred his boy to have a steady nine-to-five job – like everyone else in the town. The conversation was meandering until Mrs Mueller stepped in. 'Dad,' she said, 'it might be his [Jack's] chance in life. We'd better let him go.' Mueller signed a Form Four and the very next morning at eight o'clock, two Hawthorn officials knocked, only to be told they were six hours too late! The young giant kicked four goals in his first match and seven in his second, launching a fabulous career which included almost a dozen Grand Finals.

Mr Page, then 81, was my link with so many past greats. On meeting he said to me, 'Do you take shorthand young man?' Having been to Mrs Travers' school of shorthand as a teenager at *The Age*, I could confidently say 'yes', but it was still comforting to have a mini-cassette-recording machine next to me. I always found being able to be part of the conversation, rather than furiously scribbling notes, led to unexplored and satisfying 'angles' and I was fortunate enough to interview a whole raft of oldies but goodies who invariably were only too happy to talk.

Some weren't as chatty, however ... like Des Fothergill who'd won a Brownlow Medal during the war and was equally accomplished at cricket. A teenage prodigy with sublime skill, Fothergill had first played at Collingwood under Jock McHale as a 16-year-old and won the Copeland Trophy in a team that made the Grand Final in his very first year. It was the first of his three club best and fairests – all before he'd turned 21. He was small but could find the ball and was a thumping kick. Despite his on-field genius, he didn't always please those in authority at Victoria Park, especially when he walked

RELUCTANT: Des Fothergill wasn't initially keen on being interviewed, but was delightful company, especially when we chatted about the century he made against Don Bradman
Ken Piesse/The Complete Guide to Australian Football

out without a clearance just months after finishing equal first in the Brownlow alongside South Melbourne's Herbie Matthews snr.

I rang him twice a week until finally he answered. 'Sorry … Ken is it? I don't do interviews,' he said, and then promptly hung up! A few weeks later I was north of the Yarra and close to where Des lived. On the off-chance, I went around, unannounced. There was a car in his driveway and I knocked on the door. There was no answer and no sound from inside. Finally, just as I was about to leave, I knocked once more and a voice answered, 'I'm in the bath. I can't come to the door.'

'Mr Fothergill,' I called. 'It's Ken Piesse the sportswriter. We've spoken on the phone. I'd love to talk some cricket and footy to you …'

'Go away. I'm in the bath.'

'But … I've come a long way to see you. I don't mind waiting.'

Five minutes later he shuffled out in his street clothes and dressing gown. 'The old bones get so cold nowadays,' he said. 'The bath is about the only place I can get warm … come in.' He was in his early 70s and still had a firm handshake.

I'd brought a football encyclopaedia I'd just had published. It included a short essay on his own sporting career, which contained so many soaring highs, and I showed it to him. He particularly liked the paragraph mentioning the century he'd scored against Don Bradman. 'They probably wouldn't let you play both footy and cricket these days, Mr Fothergill,' I suggested.

I told him how Freddie Freer was a neighbour of mine close to where I lived in Mt Eliza. He and Fred had both played for Victoria and in the Lancashire League after the war, Fothergill as a No. 3 batsman and leg-spinner with Enfield CC. He gradually warmed to the conversation and smiled when I asked him where his Brownlow Medal was. 'It's in my sock draw,' he said, bringing it out to show me, along with a Recorder Cup Medal (for Williamstown) when he'd polled an extraordinary 62 votes. Not surprisingly he'd won by a record margin. Other than a small exercise book of cuttings he kept in his kitchen, there was little memorabilia on show highlighting just how prominent a sportsman he'd been 50 years earlier.

It had been a privilege, he said, to have played 100 or so games 'for such a great club like Collingwood'. He'd upset a few when he'd left in mid-career but he needed the money and he had returned, before playing cricket professionally in the north of England where he was offered a lucrative retainer and attractive bonus monies.

He was just 15 when he first represented Northcote's first XI. In all, he represented Victoria 27 times, including one memorable day when he scored a career-best 102 against a South Australian team that included the Don. He'd also been a Big V footballer of distinction, joining an elite band to play two sports at the highest possible level. Before I left, with a steady hand and a flourish, he autographed my pride-and-joy football book, joining other greats who had signed like Jack Dyer, Bob Pratt, Jack Mueller, Darrel 'Doc' Baldock, Stuart Spencer, Lou Richards, Bob Davis and Ron Barassi. I'm proud to have met and been mates with them all.

'I'M NOT HOME, MUM'

So shy was Corey McKernan that when North Melbourne's Denis Pagan, then coaching the Under 19s, came knocking on his door, inviting him down to Arden Street, McKernan hid in his bedroom and told his mother to say he wasn't home.

He was an incredible teenage talent, tall, athletic and a magnificent mark. Pagan wanted to be convinced in his own mind that he was worth the trouble so joined chief recruiter Greg Miller at one of McKernan's school games at Gladstone Park.

'Greg was right. He could play all right and we went into the rooms and I asked him to come down to training the next night, a Thursday. We played him on the Saturday against St Kilda at Arden Street and he kicked 13!

'Fast forward to the '96 Grand Final and while "Arch" [Glenn Archer] won the Norm Smith, Corey could easily have dead-heated him. He had 29 possessions as a ruck-rover. He was seriously good.'

AHEAD OF HIS TIME

Among the youngest to win a Brownlow Medal (at 20), Brian Wilson had uncanny reflexes. 'I taught myself to watch the bounce of the ball so closely that I could judge and anticipate its bounce – how high and in which direction,' Wilson said. 'It allowed me to hit it flat out when others may have been waiting and wondering.'

Wilson's other trick-of-the-trade after a win was always to sit next to the best player on the field as he knew the Sunday paper photographers would make a beeline to them for an immediate after-match shot. 'It was all about profile and making sure you were in as many papers as possible,' he said. Unsurprisingly, he became a very successful businessman.

SPRUNG

Alex Jesaulenko could be both hard and laidback, depending on the day and the circumstance. We, the media, would be ushered into Carlton's boardroom after home matches where 'Jezza', having showered and dressed would talk openly about the game over a few longnecks. He was a believer in the old-time pleasant Sunday mornings and would be right in the mix, drinking with his team.

Come pre-season and training nights, however, he could be ruthless and absolutely unbending – even when it came to his best mates.

This hot pre-season night, Jezza told his players that everyone had to run the prescribed distance around Sydney Road and back to the club within a certain time – or go back and do it again. 'And there are no exceptions … none at all.'

Lumbering ruckman Peter 'Percy' Jones was in immediate trouble and was attempting the course for a third time with no appreciable extra spring in his step. A tram pulled up alongside him and the conductor, recognising him, said, 'Perc, you look tired. Do you want to hop on?'

Perc didn't need a second invitation. He was sitting back on that tram blessing himself when he spied the club's fitness instructor Peter Powell running back down the course obviously looking for him. 'I tried to hide, but too late, he'd spotted me,' said Perc. 'There was hell to pay of course. Alex wasn't impressed at all ...'

OLD-TIME LOGIC

Long-time League chief Jack Hamilton mixed a wry sense of humour with good old-fashioned football nous. Welcoming the newly appointed club promotions officers at the League's Jolimont headquarters in 1976, Jack said, 'Welcome guys. You will be like me every morning. You won't necessarily like what you see on the other side of the mirror when you get up. But you also won't know what is in front of you that day. It'll be ever changing. If you're on the back pages of the paper, that's good news, if you're on the front page, that's bad.'

CRIMMO

John Kennedy wasn't one to openly admit to having made a mistake, but if he had one selection regret, it stemmed around Hawthorn's inspirational captain Peter Crimmins and his non-selection in the 1975 Grand Final. 'The little bloke might have made a difference, you know,' admitted Kennedy years later. 'He was so loved, so admired ... the fellas may have lifted for him ... we'll never know ...'

Crimmins was on the comeback trail having had treatment for testicular cancer. He hadn't played a senior game for four months, but had had five reserves games including the first semifinal against Essendon just a fortnight earlier. He wanted to play, even as 20th man.

Kennedy agonised over the decision. Had he insisted, the other four selectors including acting captain Don Scott would in all likelihood have backed him. Instead, the vote was 50/50. Eventually Kennedy refused to take the risk, saying he wouldn't want to do anything to harm Crimmins' health.

A heartbroken Crimmins watched from the stands as his beloved Hawks were steamrolled by North Melbourne, heading for its first flag. He died just over a year later but not before members of the '76 Grand Final team had brought the Cup to his bedside.

FIXED UP BY TUDDY

Bill Serong knew he was on the way out at Collingwood when a pugnacious redhead just down from Ballarat stitched him up big-time in a trial game in 1962. 'I was told before the game that this untried kid Des Tuddenham was good and I needed to do well to stay on the list,' Serong said. 'I hardly touched it and they immediately cleared me to North Melbourne. Des, of course, went on to captain the club.'

Serong chose North as his new home as he'd been promised nine senior games and at eight pounds a week that helped him to keep his family afloat – his parents having died within months of each other shortly before.

'I was driving trucks around the docks during the day, training Tuesdays and Thursdays and studying at night [for his law degree] to help support my brother, sister and grandmother,' he said. 'I was having a decent sleep only three nights a week and reckoned I lost a stone and a half in the process.'

He still won the club's best and fairest ahead of champion quartet Noel Teasdale, Allen Aylett, John Dugdale and Laurie Dwyer before going bush at a then-record sum of 1500 pounds as Echuca's captain-coach. He finished his career in the VFA at Camberwell.

Serong was another League football star from St Thomas Christian Brothers College in Clifton Hill. Others included the three Twomey brothers – Bill, Mick and Pat – and Bernie Shannon (all Collingwood), Brian Beers (Collingwood and Fitzroy), Kevin Coghlan (Collingwood and Hawthorn), Eddie Hart, Eddie Goodger, Kevin Murray and Kevin Wright (Fitzroy), John Benetti, Sergio Silvagni and Kevin Hart (Carlton), and John Hudson and Maurie Lyons (South Melbourne).

'IT'S JOHN, CAM . . .'

It was a biting cold July morning in 1961. Hawthorn's Cam McPherson was buried under a mountain of blankets when there was a sharp rat-tat-tat at his front door. 'Who the hell could that be at this hour?' said McPherson, checking the time. It was 6 a.m. and it was still pitch-black.

He stumbled to the door to be met by his coach and fitness fanatic John Kennedy. 'Right,' said Kennedy. 'Get your runners on Cam. You and I have some road work to do!'

Minutes later the pair were pounding the frosty streets of Camberwell with Kennedy setting the pace.

WAKE-UP CALL: 1961 premiership Hawk Cam McPherson

Peter Haby/Hawthorn Football Club

'We did something like six miles [9.6 kilometres] that morning,' said McPherson. 'But we couldn't complain. We were to be part of the club's first premiership that year and that hard work went an awfully long way to us winning it.'

Premiership centreman Brendan Edwards said Kennedy was always dropping in unexpectedly on his players – most of whom lived in close proximity to the club's headquarters at Glenferrie Oval. 'John was very cagey about it all,' he said. 'He never told us

KENNEDY'S COMMANDOES: The Hawks training at Bondi Beach, 1969, from left to right: Ron Stubbs, Vin Crowe, Cam McPherson, Don Scott, Rod Olsson, Paul Tolson, Ted Johnson (partly obscured), John Fisher, Lance Morton (partly obscured), Bob Keddie, Jim Smith, Ian Bremner and Mick Blood (partly obscured)

who he would be dropping in on next for those morning runs of his. He was such a stickler for fitness and would do everything you could do.'

Another of Kennedy's pet training tricks was to send his players running up and down the muddy slopes near the Kooyong tennis courts. In time he made the players lug sandbags up and down the slopes. Kennedy's Commandoes were born.

'I wanted us to play on at all costs that year and to play that sort of running game meant you had to be fitter than everyone else,' Kennedy said. 'What we lacked in ability we made up in determination and extra fitness.'

On Grand Final day, Footscray led by 10 points at quarter time and eight points at half-time only to be blown away afterwards. 'Looking at the Footscray boys coming up the race at half-time I could see the effort had just about knocked the stuffing out of them,' said Kennedy. 'Most of them could hardly lift their feet, but my blokes looked fine. They'd hardly worked up a sweat.'

6

Larrikins

*Seeing the mad look in his eye, Graham
started running the big man up and
down the ground. Finally an out-of-breath
Lockett blustered, 'Okay, that'll do. We're cool!'*

THE BIG HAIRY CAT

'One of the best things that could have happened to the
Geelong FC was his missus getting pregnant,' said Tom
Harley of the club's power forward Cameron Mooney in 2007.

The fun-loving, undisciplined, out-of-control 'big hairy Cat'
transformed himself into a reliable ultra-team player, becoming
the star forward in the best team in the land.

His partner Seona gave birth to their first child Jagger, and
Mooney's football prospered.

At North Melbourne Mooney had found himself in a
winning Grand Final team while still on his 'P' plates. Having
been dragged early in the game by coach Denis Pagan, he failed
to register even one 'stat'. He was the last player up to the dais
to receive his premiership medallion and on the way down,
coach Denis Pagan had more words with him. He reckoned he
was the only player Pagan *didn't* hug after the game. Within a
week he was traded. And in time, given a fresh start by the Cats,
he was to become a three-time premiership player and an All-
Australian forward, one of the very best and most formidable
footballers in the game.

FEVALENKO

Sunday, 25 July 1999, was meant to be a red-letter day in the life of wide-eyed teenager Brendan Fevola. Honoured with the bestowing of Alex Jesaulenko's famous No. 25 Carlton guernsey at the start of the season, he'd been named for his senior debut – and against old enemy Collingwood.

Fevola set off from his home in Narre Warren nice and early for the compulsory team meeting, but his Nissan Bluebird developed a wobble about Waverley Park and slowly but surely came to a complete halt.

'No matter what I did, the car wouldn't restart,' said Fevola, 'and no one was stopping [to assist]. Just as I was despairing about making any of the meeting, my Mum came racing up the freeway on her way to the game, realised it was me and backed back 100 metres. I jumped in and she raced me up to the 'G. I was still late for the meeting mind you, but thankfully "Parko" [coach David Parkin] didn't get too upset and told me I was starting [on the ground]. I had all these expectations, all these hopes of taking a speckie first up and kicking a long bomb goal with my first kick. But nothing like that occurred. I was taken from the ground early and didn't reappear until the final quarter. My stats for the day? One handball! It wasn't the most auspicious of starts … but I did get better.'

Hyperactive and impulsive, a drinker and a gambler, Fevola was proclaimed an overnight champ from the time he kicked 12 goals in the only New Year's Eve football match ever played – the Millennium match of 1999. A three-time All-Australian and two-time Coleman Medallist, he played more than 200 games and kicked 600-plus goals but is just as well remembered

MILLENNIUM MATCH: Brendan Fevola kicked 12 goals in the only New Year's Eve match ever played
Tom Mahoney

for his bouts of depression and drunken ways which cost him his career at Carlton.

TREADING A FINE LINE

Hawthorn's Mark Graham was opposing Gary Ablett snr at VFL Park in the early '90s and took a mark from a misdirected ball while running back towards goal. Ablett had been caught out of position and his late lunge resulted in a 50-metre penalty.

'The penalty took me almost up to the centre line,' said Graham. 'Gary was running backwards and I was pushing him along, trying to run faster than he could go backwards. He wasn't too happy. I eventually passed the ball and was jogging back alongside him towards goal when he said, "It's coming ..."'

'For the next two and a half quarters I just wondered where and when I'd get my jaw broken. Given Gary's history, particularly the '89 Grand Final when he barrelled into Dipper, I was very wary of where Gary was, put it that way. He could make mincemeat of you.'

Another time at Waverley, Graham was full-back against man-mountain Tony Lockett, then with Sydney. Next to him was Luke McCabe, playing in a back pocket on 'Captain Courageous' Paul Kelly, one of the AFL's very finest. McCabe was niggling Kelly at every opportunity. Several times Lockett came over, warning McCabe of the consequences if he continued the harassment.

At the quarter-time break, Graham raced across to McCabe and said, 'For Christ's sake, will you leave Kelly alone?! I'm going to end up getting &$#@ing bashed here.' Thankfully he did stop, but it was a close thing. Big Tony was getting hot under the collar.

Another time Graham had been in the right place at the right time and flattened another of Lockett's teammates, Troy Luff. Lockett wanted instant revenge and seeing the mad look in his eye, Graham started running the big man up and down

the ground. Finally an out-of-breath Lockett blustered, 'Okay, that'll do. We're cool!'

FULL-FRONTAL WOK

There has never a footy autobiography quite like it. Cocky, confident, bizarre Warwick Capper's *Fool Forward* could almost have had a brown paper wrapper around it and sold purely in the 'Adults Only' section.

WOK: This particular Saturday night at Waverley Park, Warwick Capper spoke so fast I couldn't understand even one word
*Tony Greenberg/*Inside Football

Included were nude full-page colour photos of 'Wok' and his wife Joanne simulating sex for one of the adult magazines, plus a range of Capper boasts and observations. From the benefits of wearing shorty-shorts to up-close-and-personal observations about the luscious Leanne Edelsten, he held nothing back. His opinion of several of his opponents was typical 'Wok':

- Rick Kennedy – 'A prick … an absolute lunatic on the field. He'd always pull my hair and pull my shorts up my backside – the funny thing was that I liked it …'
- Michael Christian – 'I often sat on his head talking mark of the year. I'd yell, "Cap-ppar … Cop thaattt."'
- Mick Gayfer – 'A cheat. He'd hold your jumper all the time.'

Life after football saw Capper work as a roadworks signaller, a stripper and a sportie night 'celebrity'. He even made a porn movie. He remains the only footballer I have ever interviewed (Waverley Park, 1986) where I was unable to understand even a single word he said.

'WHO'S PAYING FOR THIS CALL?'

Carlton was on its end-of-season trip to the USA at the end of the 1993 season. Steve Silvagni wanted some news from home and rang the club, reverse charges, only to be rebuffed by the club's secretary Sharon McColl who said he had to pay for his calls.

The boys soon worked out that there was one set of rules for them and a different set for captain-elect Stephen 'the King' Kernahan, so putting on their deepest voices, the lads tried again. 'Hi Shazz, Sticks here, can I talk to "Goughie" [the club's general manager Stephen Gough]?'

'Sure, Stephen.'

Elated at their success, they got through to Goughie, one pretending he was an Indian businessman from Bombay who was wanting to join 'the great Carlton Football Club'.

Everything was going well until his 'Indian' lapsed into 'African' and onto a version of 'Chinese' ... all in the same call.

Amidst the hysterical giggling in the background, Gough roared, 'Who's paying for this call? Right boys ... you've got 30 seconds – and I know who you are!'

The lads quickly rang off, but it was still terrific fun ...

A LIFESAVER

David Cloke (Travis's Dad) was on his way to back-to-back premierships with Ainslie in the early '90s. One night, very late, he fielded a phone call. One of his players was on top of a six-storey building threatening to jump. He had serious drug and alcohol issues and believed his parents simply didn't care. Cloke spoke to him for two hours before the lad finally agreed to come down, via the stairwell.

Football was a salvation for him, but his off-field problems were clouding everything. Cloke made him promise to ring him if he ever again felt suicidal. 'I am one phone call away,' he said, 'day or night.'

A fortnight later, the lad phoned again. He was at the top of Ayers Rock and had run out of money. Cloke immediately wired $200 to get him back to Canberra and went and had another heart-to-heart with the boy's parents.

Cloke told them the lad felt nothing he did could meet their expectations. Both were high-up public servants and busy six days a week. Nothing could make their boy happier, Cloke said, than for them to come and watch him play a game or two. They did; the lad ended up being part of a premiership team. Afterwards as the celebrations flowed, the lad approached Cloke with his premiership medallion. He'd been among the best six afield and wanted to present it to Clarke as a thank you.

'You've probably got nearly everything in life with what you've been able to achieve in footy,' the lad said. 'I've got nothing except this medallion. I want you to have it.' Cloke was touched, thanked him and politely refused. But he was glad to have assisted in the rehabilitation of a young man who had lost his way.

LONG MEMORIES

When Mil Hanna's cheque for trip-away raffle monies was dishonoured and returned to the Carlton FC one year, the players stuck both the cheque and the offending letter on the club noticeboard for all to see. Years later many continue to call him 'Miser Mil ...'

WHAT A STENCH

Essendon's annual beer and prawn fundraiser was winding up. Billy Duckworth was cleaning up some of the prawn shells. Instead of binning them, he put them in a plastic bag and placed them neatly in the bottom of coach Kevin Sheedy's commodious footy bag. Sheedy slung his bag into his boot where the said prawns remained fermenting for two days. Kevin was livid. Back at training, the first words he spoke were 'Where's Duckworth?' Boy those shells stank!

JUST GOING FOR A JOG, LADS ...

Few loved training and running like Terry Daniher. At the end of one season he reckoned he needed a bit of a 'hit-out' so having had a beer at the local Ungarie pub, he ran back to the family farm, 16 kilometres away!

FITNESS FANATIC: Terry Daniher jogged just about every back road of Ungarie as part of his annual summer training before returning to the Big Smoke

ANYONE SEEN MY CAR, LADS?

Essendon's long-time club doctor Bruce Reid was walking out to the middle of Windy Hill for training as usual when he noticed a car parked slap bang in the centre wicket area, almost entirely encased in toilet paper. On closer inspection, he realised it was his. Boys being boys, a few of the Bomber lads had borrowed his car keys and shifted his pride and joy from its normal park before giftwrapping it with every roll of Sorbent they could find. The Doc saw the funny side of it … eventually.

I WARNED YOU, MICK …

Speedy Cat Mick Turner was having a birthday on Micky Egan and had kicked three or four and was feeling so good about himself that he started to mouth off a little. Rick Kennedy, Footscray's protector, overheard some of the barbs and told Turner to shut up or there would be retribution.

'Yeah?' said Turner. 'You're as weak as piss.'

Soon afterwards Turner had his jaw broken, for which Kennedy received a month's holiday …

GET YER OWN

Ron Barassi called a team meeting immediately after Melbourne training one night. It was a cold July night and dressing gowns were called for. Brent Crosswell was closest to the property room window and Greg Wells called across to throw him a gown.

With a look of utter disdain, Crosswell stood as tall as he could and said haughtily, 'Me? Me? … With 258 League games, 12 finals, six Grand Finals, "x" number of best and fairests … you want me to get a dressing gown for you! Go and get nicked.' And with that, he marched off imperiously into the coach's room leaving Wells to go and get his own.

FRIDAY NIGHT LIVE

Drew Morphett was co-hosting the original *Footy Show* on Friday nights on ABC TV in 1985. Normally it was pre-taped – it was 'safer' that way, the team of Drew, Ron Barassi, Doug Heywood and Ian 'Clelo' Cleland meeting at lunchtime for a pizza and a few reds and then going on to the studios at Ripponlea.

This particular Friday, the very first night game was being played at the MCG and it was decided that the whole show would be recorded 'live' to enable a cross or two updating the score and any news. Special studio guest Ted Whitten had agreed to meet Drew and Co. at the restaurant in Glenhuntly Road by a certain time – but was late … very late.

Finally he arrived, bowling over every second chair as he made his apologies.

Clearly he'd had a skinful.

'He's too pissed. He can't go on,' said Drew's right-hand man, the show's executive producer Robbie Weekes.

'You tell him he's too pissed,' said Drew, immediately ordering multiple cups of black coffee for Ted.

They finally got into the studio and began the show, 'Barass' on one side of Drew and Teddy on the other.

It was just after the first live cross when the bickering started, back-and-forth.

'I'm Mr Football!'

'No you're not. You're *Mrs* Football.'

Teddy was becoming belligerent and started to wave his arms around. Poor little Drew reckons he all but got a depressed fracture of the cheekbone ducking Teddy's elbow.

'I never did watch a tape back of that show, but it's the one I remember the most,' said Drew, one of Australian sport's broadcasting doyens.

A GRAND FINAL SHARK

The race to gain a seat on Grand Final day is always intense and some of the stories told to gain admittance have to be admired. Footy folklore has it that there is one blue-collared gent who hasn't missed a 'Grannie' for years. He comes dressed in blue overalls with his toolbox, and uses a 'temprite emergency' as his entry ticket …

In 1982 on the eve of the Carlton-Richmond showdown, a man rang League headquarters in Jolimont claiming he'd been the victim of a shark attack the previous weekend and was lucky to be alive. Grounds administrator Jill Lindsay listened sympathetically and said she could probably swap his standing-room ticket for a restricted-viewing seat if he came in the following day. Unfortunately for the man, Jill happened to be looking out the window just as the shark attack man was athletically dodging traffic and running across Brunton Avenue before inexplicably slowing down and limping up the 12 stairs into the building with the help of a walking stick! Jill admired his front, before showing him the door. 'Oh well,' said the man, having been 'sprung'. 'It was worth a try!'

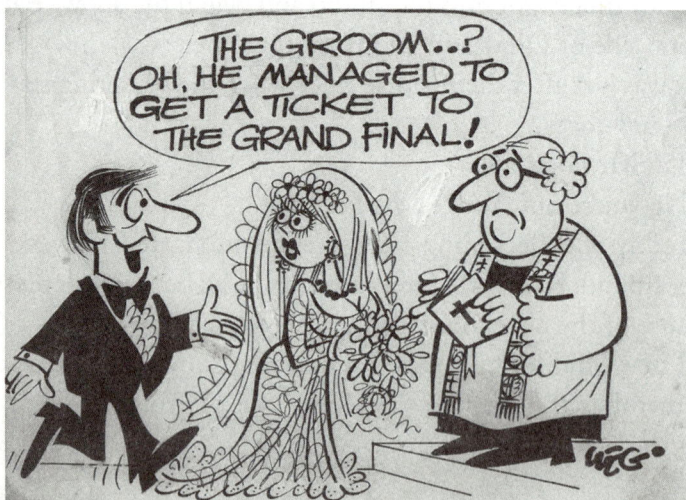

CLASSIC WEG: Bill Green's whimsy was always evident in his cartoons with *The Herald* and onwards as a long-time freelancer. I was fortunate to be one of his mates

WALKING TALLER

No ruckman of the '60s and '70s was as feared as Carl Ditterich. Athletic and imposing, he was the consummate team player and protector. My mate Trevor Barker always spoke in reverent terms about 'the Shadow'. 'No one dared misbehave when he was around,' he'd say. 'You just had to say how so-and-so was bothering you and he'd fix it.'

When Ditterich switched to Melbourne, Demon players walked taller, just as their St Kilda counterparts had for years.

Stan Alves, one of the club's premier players, was being closely tagged as usual and at a stoppage, seeing the stopper continue to harass and annoy his star player, Ditterich approached. 'Stan,' he said, 'I want you to charge straight at me, but make sure when you're one step away from me, zag and make sure you zag to my right – which is your left. Got it?

'Got it.'

The ball was bounced and Alves, on cue, sprinted straight at Ditterich and zagged at the last possible moment.

'All off a sudden behind me I heard this "Orrrrr" – this unbelievable sound of someone having the wind knocked out of them,' said Alves. 'I look back and there was my tagger lying flat on his back with big Carl jogging away. Mission accomplished.'

THE SHADOW: Carl Ditterich's attack on the ball and the opposition was always ferocious. Woe betide anyone misbehaving in his vicinity . . .

FOGGED IN

Peter Keenan wasn't called 'Crackers' by accident. He was Ian Ridley's No. 1 ruckman at Melbourne but was incredibly temperamental. For weeks this particular year he'd been struggling to get near it and declared he was 'fed up with everything', including coach Ridley, and was heading home to Tungamah. 'Seeya boys,' he said. The next morning, very early, there was a phone call. It was Keenan. He'd got as far as Seymour, but the fog was so bad he couldn't continue and was coming back!

ONE IN, ALL IN

All hell broke loose early in the 1976 VFA Grand Final after Port Melbourne's Fred Cook was flattened by Dandenong's Alan Harper at the Junction Oval. A huge melee formed with players running from all corners of the ground to be involved. The only two who stayed in their positions were Port's half-back George Allen and his opponent Pat Flaherty.

'No need for us to get involved in that, George,' said Flaherty.

'Bullshit,' said Allen and downed him on the spot.

COMING BACK FOR MORE

St Kilda's matches with Hawthorn in the '70s were rough and tough, the 1971 Grand Final as spiteful and physical as any play-off since the infamous 1945 'Bloodbath'.

Stuart Trott was one of many to be flattened in '71, by the emerging Hawk Leigh Matthews. He'd been best afield for the first three quarters.

Come the Grand Final replay at Moorabbin in 1972 – which St Kilda won easily – Matthews was close to the ball as it went over the boundary line before being clobbered by Trott. It was the classic square-up. 'He broke my nose,' said Matthews, 'and I thought, "You bastard."

'I waited for the boundary umpire to turn his back and throw the ball in and I simply whacked him back. The battles back then between Hawthorn and St Kilda were very tough games as both sides were coached by hard, unrelenting coaches [John Kennedy and Allan Jeans] and were stacked with their share of big, heavy fellows. More often than not it could be wet down at Moorabbin or at Glenferrie Oval so it was usually a hard slogging match. With players like Carl Ditterich, Neil Ferguson and Mick Porter, the games were always tough. But you didn't take the grudges off the field.

'As it turned out Trotty ended up with us at Hawthorn [in the pre-season of 1975]. I didn't know it at the time and there was a circle of us with John saying something and I spied him over the other side of the circle. My immediate thought was that he'd come back for more ...'

KEKOVICH AXED!

Before the arrival of Ron Barassi at Arden Street, North Melbourne was an also-ran, winning rarely. And even a few of its best players trained only when it suited.

Champion ruck-rover and man about town Sam Kekovich had gone bush to the Wagga Wagga Gold Cup race meeting with his mate Brian Mulvihill when they received word via coach Brian Dixon that anyone not training that Thursday night would not be selected for the following weekend's match.

Kekovich had been best afield the previous match, so thought he'd be fine – but he told Mulvihill he better head back as his form had been patchy.

'Keka' had a terrible day on the punt and woke up in Wagga the following morning to screaming front-page news in the morning *Sun*: KEKOVICH AXED!

Arriving back at Essendon airport, he was immediately surrounded by journalists and photographers. 'It was if I'd committed murder,' he said.

He duly took his demotion, playing off the bench in the reserves and told the kid next to him, 'I don't know how bad

HAPPIER DAYS: 'Slammin' Sam Kekovich takes a speckie ahead of his captain Barry Davis at the MCG in 1974. At his best he was unstoppable ...
*Geoff Poulter/*Inside Football

your week has been son, but I've lost all my money, been splashed on the front page of every paper in Melbourne and I'm sitting here with you at 11 a.m. when I should be back home asleep!'

FUN WITH TOMMY

Reacting one summer to the call from Essendon's coach Jack Clarke for more fun in football, Richmond's Kevin Bartlett had a T-shirt made up with the following slogan: 'BARTLETT FOR COACH ... FUN, FUN, FUN'.

Tommy Hafey was addressing his players when he noticed Bartlett's T-shirt. 'Get that off!' he roared before bursting into laughter.

Visiting Hafey's holiday home at Sorrento one year, Brian 'the Whale' Roberts left 12 empty beer cans on his bed with a note: 'Guess who!'

Another time the Whale took the bell out of Tommy's whistle ... he didn't get away with that one either!

DON'T FORGET THE FUN:
Essendon's Jack Clarke

THE KISS OF DEATH

Lou Richards' regular tips in the Melbourne *Sun* were so consistently wayward that he was dubbed 'the Kiss of Death', his selections being used in many office sweeps as a penalty for those who failed to lodge their tips on time.

Lou's headlining antics guaranteed a rare profile for someone whose career had finished years earlier in the mid-'50s.

His outlandish, tongue-in-cheek dares saw him consistently in hot water and resulted in him having to do the following:
- piggyback a 17-stone (108-kilogram) Mick Nolan down Errol Street, North Melbourne;

- clean Swanston Street with a feather duster;
- eat a bucket of spaghetti with Carlton's Mario Bortolotto;
- and cut Teddy Whitten's lawn with nail clippers.

Lou and his long-time sidekick Tom Prior were also responsible for a range of nicknames that have stood the test of time:
- 'The Flying Doormat' – Bruce Doull
- 'The Galloping Gasometer' – Mick Nolan
- 'Lethal' Leigh Matthews
- 'The Junkyard Dog' – Dean Laidley
- 'The Bionic Man' – Greg Smith
- 'The Kookaburra' – Alec Epis

Epis could talk underwater with a mouthful of marbles and Lou said when he interviewed him, even he couldn't get a word in.

Writing about Richmond's boom youngster Mark Lee one year, Lou said, 'Mark Lee, Richmond's new ruck sensation, reminds me of my old mate Jack Dyer … except for a few things:
- At 199 centimetres (6 feet, 6½ inches), Lee is about a metre taller than 'Captain Blood'.
- At 102 kilograms (16 stone) he is about 42 kilograms heavier and it's all muscle.
- He is pleasant and modest.
- And … he's got brains!

A star of TV, newspapers and radio, Lou called himself football's first 'multimedia megastar'. He'd been retired with a fortnight to go in the 1955 season and Harry Gordon, sports editor at the Melbourne *Sun*, asked Lou to come and do a column for his paper in 1956, replacing Jack Dyer who was overseas for the season.

'I was so good, Jack couldn't get a look-in when he came back … the big lug,' said Lou.

Surprisingly for one with so much confidence, off-camera Lou was always asking how a segment had gone – even me, a first-year rookie presenting the cricket.

Lou loved working with Bill Collins and soon learnt that Bill the practical joker loved to set up Lou. 'I'd have to give away a prize and I'd ask Bill, "Who's this?"

'"Harry," he'd say, and of course it wasn't, much to Bill's merriment.'

PECK v SAWLEY 1964

It was the sort of punch Johnny Famechon would have dreamed of throwing: a ferocious right cross that landed flush on Brian Sawley's jaw. The South Australian was unconscious before he hit the deck.

Victoria's John Peck stood over him, his fists still clenched ready to strike him again but Sankey was out to it.

As he left the Adelaide Oval that day, Peck and his fellow big V players had rocks and mud thrown at them. Three blokes jumped the fence and made a beeline for Peck before ruckman Ken Timms blocked their way, and the police restored order.

Peck claimed he'd been deliberately kicked by Sawley and said if a similar incident happened, he'd do it all over again. 'In the first quarter the ball was shot over our half-forward line and I took off after it,' said Peck. 'As I stopped to pick it up, I lost

FAMOUS PUNCH: The incident was detailed years later in the Hobart *Mercury* my footing in the mud. Just as I was falling I felt a boot whizz past my ear. The stops actually ruffled my hair. The bloke that owned that boot looked awfully like Sawley.'

In the third term Peck had dropped a mark and fell flat on his face, headfirst into more mud. 'I was just about to get to my knees when I was kicked – about two or three times – right in the small of my back ... and those kicks really hurt. I rolled over onto my side and there was Sawley grinning. I was so wild I didn't stop to think. I just jumped to my feet and clobbered him.'

Reported by three umpires, including a boundary umpire who ran 150 yards (137 metres) to get involved, Peck was suspended for two weeks.

In an interview years later with David Stockdale, Sawley claimed to 'have just nudged' Peck with his boot to make him get up. 'I didn't kick him,' he said. 'In some ways I don't blame Peck for what he did. I don't hold grudges.'

Peck didn't see or speak with Sawley again.

YES, I DID IT

Few were as honest as Ken Boyd who openly admitted to felling Carlton's John Nicholls behind play late at Princes Park in 1961.

'I'm not ashamed I hit John Nicholls last Saturday,' he said in the midweek *Sporting Globe*. 'I have a clear conscience ... early in the last quarter at a centre bounce, I was kicked in the stomach and the groin. I was in terrific pain and when I recovered I simply went back, turned Nicholls around and dropped him.

'It's the first time I have ever hit a player behind play, but I'm not ashamed. I draw the line at what happened to me. I'm entitled to protect myself. I've whacked a few players in my day but I've always done it openly. Too many South players have been "stopped" and somebody has to look after them. Our good players have taken too many knocks and the side has suffered. I'm one of the few big blokes who can protect them.'

It was a searing, sensational admission, Boyd being ordered

to front a special investigation before being suspended for 12 matches. Earlier in the year, also against Carlton he'd received eight weeks for striking Nicholls and rover John Heathcote. He never played League football again.

Boyd continued his football career in the Ovens and Murray Football League and steered the Wangaratta Rovers to premierships in 1964 and 1965.

'JACK, LET ME LIVE . . .'

St Kilda's jockey-sized rover Alan Killigrew says he would have liked a pound for every time he was knocked over during his 78-game League career.

'About the one big bloke who didn't hit me was Jack Dyer,' said 163-centimetre (five feet, four inches) Killigrew in an interview in 1980. 'We were old St Ignatius boys. Once when they were telling me I was too small to play football, Jack said, "You'll play football and you'll play well too."

'A few years later I was playing for St Kilda against Richmond at the Junction. I came out of the pack with the ball, looked up and there was Dyer zeroing in on me at 100 miles per hour. He was going so fast had he hit me he would have killed me. I would have landed in the [Albert Park] Lake. But he let me live. Thanks goodness for old St Ignatius!'

THE DEMON DRINK

Normie McDonald was a speedy and sublimely skilled two-time Essendon premiership half-back with one weakness: his love of an ale. Even on match days he was known to hide a cold one in the cistern of a dressing-room toilet so he could have a 'refuel' at half-time.

The club's legendary coach Dick Reynolds loved Normie and was like a father to him, but even he grew tired of Normie's waywardness.

One Friday night a message came through to Reynolds that

Normie had over-imbibed and was lying flat out in a park near Windy Hill. He arranged for a taxi driver to pick him up and take him home. On the following day, match day, Reynolds looked pointedly at Normie and said, 'You'd better play well today, Norm.'

He did, turned up to training on the Tuesday and having completed a full workout was walking off when Reynolds stopped him: 'Righto Norm, two [extra] laps.'

Having watched him complete those two laps, Reynolds then ordered two more and two more again. Halfway through the fifth, Norm said to Reynolds, 'Listen Dick, I was drinking bloody beer the other night, not petrol.'

OLD SCHOOL VALUES

Tommy Lahiff may have been pint-sized but coming from working-class, rough-and-tumble Port Melbourne, he didn't take a backward step. Ever.

He was playing at Hawthorn during the war years when teammate Andy Angwin was downed, the culprit jumping on Angwin for good measure. An enraged Lahiff squared up immediately and standing over the culprit with his fists raised was ready to go on with it, only to hear the umpire call to him, 'Tommy, wake up to yourself. You've already been rubbed out three times.'

'And this'll be the fourth,' said Tommy, about to unleash before Angwin jumped in front of him and settled him down.

Years later, Lahiff was famous for his dressing-room crosses to Harry Beitzel on 3AW. 'Are yer there, Harry?' he'd ask.

Once when the players were locked away and no immediate interviews beckoned, Beitzel asked, 'Who else is in the room right now, Tommy?'

'Just the Prime Minister [Mr Fraser, a Carlton fan].'

'Well, go and interview him.'

'Me interview him, a bloody Liberal? No way. Come and do it yourself,' said Tom.

7
Laughs

'Wadda I get if I can do it?' asked Bill.
'Free grog, mate ... as much as you want.'

A LIVING LEGION

No one could embellish, enhance and downright butcher the English language like 'Captain Blood' Jack Dyer. But no one cared. Jack was a lovable legend and a Richmond immortal. In 50 years in press, radio and television, Jack was responsible for some of the greatest of all one-liners, quotes and prognostications. Jack called himself a 'living legion in my own lifetime'. He particularly championed the incident-makers, the risk-takers, the headliners.

Jack also authored a best-selling book, *Captain Blood*, one of the finest early Aussie Rules autobiographies.

Of all the mediums, Jack loved radio the best. 'It's just like playing the game,' he once said. 'You're always with it and you can abuse the umpire.' He built a large Saturday listenership not only for what he said, but how he said it.

On the *World of Sport* football panel, Jack made sure he was always at the opposite end to Lou Richards – for Lou's own safety ... 'Just in case I feel like giving you a backhander,' Jack would say.

'You big lug,' Louie would retort. 'Like all ruckmen you've got cabbage ears and nothing in between them.'

Rarely did Jack even try to get his tongue around the longer

ONE-LINERS FROM THE 'LIVING LEGION'

Whether he was commentating on 3KZ, writing in the Melbourne *Truth* or interviewing rookies on Channel 7's long-running *World of Sport*, Jack Dyer was entertainment with a capital E, as shown by these little gems:

- 'Don't go where the ball ain't.'
- 'His arms stretched out like giant testicles.'
- 'If you don't mind, umpire.'
- '[Les] Bamblett made a great debut last week and an even better one this week.'
- 'Fitzroy just copulated to the opposition.'
- 'I won't say anything in case I say something.'
- 'He looks like Tarzan but plays like Jane.'
- 'He couldn't fire on Guy Fawkes night.'
- 'He's so scared he sleeps with the light on.'
- 'I think it was a deliberate accident.'
- 'An Essendon supporter is a Collingwood supporter who can read and write.'
- 'It's as dark as the black hole of Dakota.'
- 'If you're not in bed by 12 o'clock, go home.'
- 'Don't wake up Grumpy. Creep out of the room.'
- 'Retaliate first.'
- 'I only have two words for you men: believe in yourselves.'

names. Richard Radziminski was 'that Richard fella' and Carl Ditterich 'Dietrich' (as in the actress Marlene Dietrich). Collingwood's Fatui Ataata was a tough one. Jack called him 'Fatal Ta-Ta' and he didn't even bother with Robert Di Pierdomenico. He was simply 'Dipper'.

'I'm told there's a fella in the seconds at Collingwood named Pappy-doppo-lous or something,' Jack announced one day. 'Hope he never gets a [senior] game. It'll take me five hours to say his name!'

When his beloved Tigers plunged down the ladder one

year, he said, 'If Ray Dunn [the Tiger's long-time secretary] was alive today, he'd turn in his grave.'

Jack was at World of Sport one afternoon when the wood-chopping segment started and he heard the familiar voice of his old mate Jack O'Toole counting the axemen in, 'Ready axemen. One … two … three …'

'Haven't seen old Jack for a while … it's good to have him back,' said Jack to no one in particular. 'Hope he comes down for a drink before he goes home.'

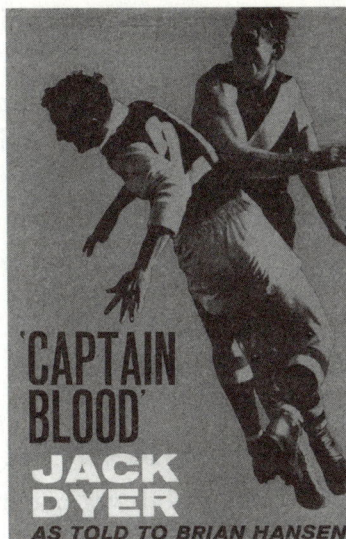

ENTERTAINING: Jack Dyer's autobiography was one of the first released by an Australian Rules footballer

No one bothered to tell him it was all taped and that O'Toole in fact had died several years earlier …

When talking to recruits, Jack would invariably start with: 'and what's your height and weight and how tall are yer?'

If they happened to quote metrics, Jack would quickly interject, 'Tell us in the old, son.'

One time he called Carlton's matchwinning half-forward Peter Bosustow 'a good ordinary player' and still refused to concede any ground even when Bosustow won Goal of the Year, Mark of the Year and played in a couple of Carlton premiership teams.

Channel 7's *League Teams* on Thursday nights was always must-viewing. Occasionally Jack and his sidekicks Lou Richards and Bob Davis would read out a team – but not often. Instead Lou would go with some recipes from wife Edna and they both would bait Jack nonstop.

One night some members of the *Les Girls* cast appeared, one sitting on Jack's knee.

Afterwards Jack said to Lou, 'Geez, that one sitting on my knee wasn't a bad sort.'

'It's a bloke, Jack!' said Lou.

Jack reflected a little and then said, 'I didn't know she was a transistor.'

When Jack died in August 2003, Richmond's match-day banner the following weekend proclaimed: 'Heaven's football team can now take the field because your captain has arrived – Jack Dyer 1913–2003.'

STUCK IN THE MIDDLE WITH YOU

Collingwood was playing in Sydney one day and about eight of the boys took a lift to the upstairs viewing room to watch the reserves, only for the lift to get stuck in between floors. All the heavyweights were on board, including David Cloke, Brian Taylor, Wes Fellowes and Ronny McKeown. They stayed wedged in the lift for a good hour, missing the start of coach Leigh Matthews' team meeting. 'We were hollering and ringing the bell but no one came,' said McKeown. 'It was a hot day and once a few of the blokes began to fart, it became most unpleasant. We didn't get out of there until about 25 minutes before the game was due to start. We all smile about it now but at the time it wasn't much fun.'

'EVER BEEN TO HINDLEY STREET, FISH?'

Nineteen-year-old Paul 'Fish' Salmon was on his first State trip to Adelaide and feeling blessed and honoured to be mixing with the likes of icons such as Dougie Hawkins, Wayne Johnston and Jimmy Buckley. Having won a close game, the players were out celebrating, Johnston paying for the taxi and the Hawk paying Salmon's entry into one of the nightclubs down Hindley Street.

While they downed their mixers at a great rate, Salmon sat on his Cokes and happily listened to the legends, hoping to learn. At one stage he suggested to them that his Coke tasted strange but they said it was all to do with the Adelaide water. It transpired that they'd slipped the barman $20 to lace Salmon's drinks with generous hits of Bundaberg rum and when they arrived back to the team's hotel, Salmon was shirtless, moneyless and starting to feel decidedly seedy … gotcha!

CONGRATULATIONS … 40 YEARS LATER

It was a not-so-distant late September night when Don Scott answered his phone. It was his old coach John Kennedy snr.

'Don,' said Kennedy. 'You played very well.'

'What?'

'The '71 Grand Final. You played well.'

'Fuck,' said Scott. 'It only took you 40 fucking years!'

Rarely had the legendary coach ever complimented Scott before. And he'd played most of his 300 games under him.

'I've just seen a replay of the game,' Kennedy said. 'I've never watched it before. Just wanted to let you know. Well done.' And he hung up.

Scott was so chuffed, he rang his captain David Parkin.

'Guess who just rang me?'

Parkin, too, had rarely, if ever, had a compliment from Kennedy – and he was one of his disciples.

He immediately rang Kennedy then and there and said, 'Dave here, John.'

'Hello, Dave.'

'Heard you just made a nice phone call to Scotty about the '71 Grand Final … were you going to ring me too?'

'No, Dave,' said Kennedy, 'didn't think you did much …'

NOW THAT'S WHERE THEY WERE …

Melbourne's captain David Neitz turned up late to training at the Junction Oval one morning. 'I couldn't find my [car] keys,' he said. Turned out he'd left them in his car with the engine running all night! 'I wondered what that humming noise was coming from the garage,' he said.

'IT'S NO JOKE, CROCK . . .'

Darren Crocker thought North's rehab expert David Buttifant was joking when he told him to hop into an ice bath under the club's old grandstand at Arden Street.

Seeing his look of utter disbelief, Buttifant said, 'All right, I'll hop into it first ...'

Looking to return from a knee reconstruction, Crocker asked what was in it for him and his knee. 'The Russians have been doing it for years,' said Buttifant, 'and before that ... 2000 years before, the Romans did it too ... it'll decrease the swelling and enhance your recovery ...'

Crocker was still doubtful but once Buttifant had got in – and out – Crocker did too, with a 'you must be mad Butters!'

He was the first 'guinea pig' of the ice baths routine now part and parcel of all big-time sport. His daily treatment allowed his career to extend a further three full years and saw him play in North's AFL Centenary Year premiership in 1996.

BREAKING THE MOULD

Leigh Carlson was coaching the Fitzroy thirds and was far from impressed by their initial efforts this day. Midway through his almighty half-time spray the lights in the rooms suddenly went out. There was total blackness and a titter of muffled laughter from near the door. On they came almost as quickly. There was full-forward Darren 'Doc' Wheildon at the switch delighted by the success of his prank. Speech interrupted, even Carlson had to share Wheildon's smile.

CELEBRATING TOO HARD

Having piloted Collingwood's first premiership in 32 years, Tony Shaw was almost 13 kilograms (two stone) overweight when he finally stopped celebrating and returned for an early pre-season game in the summer of 1991. Wearing jumper No. 48 rather than his normal, celebrated No. 22, Shaw played out of a forward pocket and hardly got a touch. Said one supporter to another, 'That little fat bloke won't make it!'

BARKING MAD

The always-colourful Ray 'Slug' Jordon was coaching Essendon's Under 19s and having his normal verbal fisticuffs with the men-in-white. A dog ran onto the oval and the field umpire caught it and was taking it back towards the fence when Jordon yelled, 'Why don't you come off and leave the dog out there!'

A ROOST TO REMEMBER

It was too irresistible a lure to ignore: free grog for anyone who could do it ... Billy Brownless and some mates were on their way to a wedding in West Wyalong when out of the blue, in the middle of nowhere, they came across a two-storey hotel with a sign: 'COLD BEER'.

'Once the car pulled up, we all thought, "Well, the car's here now. We'd better go inside." Apparently we'd hit Marool, population 27 – or 30 including us. The barman wasn't that friendly initially but got quite animated when we saw an old very-flat footy up high on a shelf. "What's the story with the footy?" we asked.

'Oh, that's for anyone who reckons they can kick a ball over the silo just over there. An Aboriginal fella did it once, but no one has ever done it since ... and dozens have tried ...'

'Yeah?' said Brownless.

'Yeah.'

It was decided that Billy, the famed long-kick champion of Assumption and Geelong FC would have a try first. 'Wadda I get if I can do it?' asked Bill.

'Free grog, mate ... as much as you want.'

'Free frothies?'

'Yeah.'

'Right,' said Bill.

A pump was provided and the party walked across the road to the railway line and the silo. It looked about 15 storeys high.

'I'll give it a burl,' said Billy and with his very first kick, a drop-punt, up, up and up it soared … and cleared the silo!

A kid ran to retrieve the ball, yelling, 'He's done it, he's done it!'

Billy, totally triumphant, accompanied the crestfallen publican back to the hotel and partook in the first of his many free beers, leaving his mates behind.

An hour later back in they came, sunburnt and thirsty and with their dress shoes all mangled. None had got within cooee of Billy's mighty roost.

HAPPY GILMORE RIDES AGAIN

The Collingwood boys were enjoying a little post-season 'r and r' at South Molle Island. As usual they were competing ever so hard, from sculling beers to canoe races and golf challenges.

Shane Morwood thought he had captain Tony Shaw covered in the golf when on one of the late par fours, Shaw skidded a trademark slice behind a small tree just 40 or so metres ahead of the tee.

His second, a 3-iron, was hit right out of the screws and it came screaming towards the green, hit the flag stick and ended up just 10 metres away on the fringe of the green. Meanwhile, Morwood was on in regulation figures and eyeing a 10-footer for the birdie he reckoned would break Shaw's spirit.

The greens were bumpy and somehow Shaw putted in a 30-footer for a birdie and hollered in jubilation, 'YES-YES-YEESSSS!'

So distracted was Morwood that he missed his putt and the match remained alive.

On the next, a par three, Shaw launched another 3-iron and it again went way right and ended high up in a block of units which bordered the green. 'There's no escaping here, pal,' said Morwood, who'd driven just short of the fringe. 'Do you want to hit another?'

'Nah,' said Shaw. "I'll find it' – and he did, four floors up.

'Mate,' he yelled down to Morwood. 'You wouldn't believe it but I've got a shot [room to swing].'

Between him and the green were a small pathway and a mound with a clump of small trees. It was an impossible shot … or so it seemed.

Shaw chipped; it bounced on the pathway, sideswiped a tree and finished within gimme distance a foot from the hole! Again he whooped it up, hands outstretched like he'd won another Grand Final. Morwood matched his par but Shaw, on a roll, won the next and the money and proudly wore his new nickname 'Happy Gilmore' for the rest of the break.

THE BUGGERS

Essendon's Terry Daniher trudged back to his car after the Bombers lost the 1990 Grand Final to find Collingwood stickers covering every inch of his front windscreen. 'The buggers,' he said.

TIT FOR TAT

Craig Davis (Nick's Dad) was rising 34 when he played his last season, after five years' break, with Sydney (in 1988). He'd been the club's chairman of selectors and runner and was given jumper No. 60. 'It was just about the only jumper left by that stage,' said Davis. 'Someone in the crowd yelled out to me one day, "Hey Davis, is that your age?"'

'No dickhead,' answered Davis, 'it's your IQ.'

EXPOSED

West Coast was playing the Brisbane Bears in the first-ever night game at the WACA Ground in 1987. Press-box positions were at a premium and when asked if he'd like his ABC team to be camped indoors or out in the open under the stars on a warm Perth night, Tim Lane opted for outdoors. Within minutes the heaviest downpour Perth had experienced in two years descended, saturating everybody – commentators, equipment, the lot. For the next two and a half hours, Lane, Kevin Bartlett and Co. huddled in their wet clothes calling the game under a tarpaulin. 'KB' has never let Tim forget it!

COMMERCIAL-FREE ...

St Kilda was struggling to win games even under 'Mr Magic', Darrel Baldock.

The Doc reckoned the team lacked skill and strength. One night he stopped training and said, 'Right, 50 push-ups ... now.'

Most huffed and puffed their way through, but ruckman Warren 'Wow' Jones had no idea.

'Wow,' said the Doc, 'what do you call them?'

'Push-ups, Doc.'

'They're shocking, Wow.'

Addressing the players afterwards he said, 'I want you all to go home tonight and during the TV add breaks, I want you all to do sets of push-ups. We'll see how you go with them again on Thursday night.'

Halfway through training on the Thursday, the Doc duly stopped training and called for 50 push-ups.

'Okay boys, show me what you can do ...'

Jones was again shocking and Doc stopped him halfway through. 'Wow,' he said, 'what did I ask you to do ... during the add breaks on the telly – do your push-ups.

'But, Doc,' said Wow, 'I watch the ABC.'

SMITHY

After David Rhys-Jones' opponent Gary Ayres won the Norm Smith Medal in the 1986 Grand Final, some of Rhys' Carlton mates started calling him 'Smithy', a not-so-subtle reminder that Rhys had underperformed in the most important day of the season. Twelve months later he won the Norm Smith on Dermott Brereton and his mates were again calling him 'Smithy', this time for all the right reasons.

HE CAN SMILE ABOUT IT NOW . . .

Among the few to officiate in 400 games, field umpire Rowan Sawers was not having his best day at Princes Park this mid-'80s Saturday. 'Two Carlton blokes pushed each other and I gave one of them a free,' he said, 'and my performance went down from there.' Later in the game he bounced the ball in front of the Carlton Social Club and it went sideways straight into the crowd! He was dropped from the panel the following week.

LUCKY BUCKS

Carlton's champion midfielder Jimmy Buckley had broken his thumb late in the 1982 season against North Melbourne. It was slow to mend and Grand Final week was fast approaching. In desperation he had a special guard designed and picked it up midweek in time for Thursday night's vital, final training session before the Grannie. Trouble was he left the guard in his car in bright sunshine and it melted! Somehow he got through training without it and played in his third premiership team.

PRE-BOUNCE BANTER

More than 80 000 fans had shown up for Richmond legend Kevin Bartlett's 400th game. His opponent for the day was Collingwood's Ray Byrne. As they shook hands, Byrne produced a present for Bartlett: a toothless comb. 'I was thinking of king-hitting you before the bounce but didn't think I'd get out of the ground alive,' he said with a smile.

Running onto the ground, Bartlett had been unable to breast

the banner. 'The banner was too big and too strong for me,' he said. 'I was getting old and I didn't have enough speed up [when I hit it].'

SUDDEN EXIT

Russell Greene's departure from St Kilda to Hawthorn in mid-season 1980 was extraordinarily sudden, Greene not finding out about the transfer until he'd returned home from walking his dog late on the Thursday night. In the car park at VFL Park on the Saturday he was spotted by North Melbourne's Steven Icke. 'Mate, you've come to the wrong ground,' said Icke. 'We're playing Hawthorn here …'

'That's right,' said Greene, smiling.

UNFORGIVING

Giant Fitzroy ruckman Matt Rendell rolled up after one Christmas break a little overweight and was immediately dubbed 'Bundi' after the heavyweight wrestler of the time King Kong Bundi.

EYE CANDY

Kevin Murray had just arrived at Sandringham. It was a hot, summertime evening and one of the lads, Darrel 'Goose' Mackenzie suggested to the new coach that they train down the beach. 'Good idea, Goose,' said Murray following along happily as Mackenzie took the squad straight down to nearby Abbott Street beach, which for a long time had been topless. The boys did their sprints up and down the beach and in between enjoyed the eye candy. With the boys in their speedos and the girls in their G-strings, it was a 'win-win' for everyone. Murray couldn't stop laughing. Coming from the north of the Yarra, he'd never seen anything like it …

RHETT WHO?

So often was Justin 'Harry' Madden found on his favourite couch in the Carlton medical room that one joker made a cardboard plaque with 'Harry's Couch' on it. It stayed there – as did Harry – for years.

Big Harry was watching the reserves from the players' race one day – something he rarely did – when teammate Peter Dean joked, 'What are you doing watching this? You never watch the reserves. You wouldn't know half these blokes' names, particularly the younger ones. For example who's that bloke, No. 7?'

'Arr ... that's Rhett Batten,' said Madden, meaning to say Brett Ratten!

'WHO'S THAT, HARRY?' Justin Madden wasn't always good with names ...
Inside Football

HELD TO RANSOM

Justin Madden wasn't big on end-of-season trips and not seeing any benefit in it for him, he even baulked one year at selling the player's own fundraising raffle tickets. One night, his birthday, he had to appear at the AFL tribunal as a witness and on walking into the Carlton car park found his pride-and-joy Peugeot sitting up on timber blocks with the four tyres neatly chained to a nearby railing. Alongside them was a ransom note to chip in the appropriate monies owed. Not wanting to be late, he found his way to the hearing by other means and returned later to re-fit the tyres in pouring rain. As birthdays went, it was washout ... and he never did go on the trip ...

NOT SO IMPORTANT

Noel Judkins was in Sydney and feeling pretty important. He was on his first interstate recruiting mission for Richmond and keen to assess the form of several young likelies. 'The game was about to start and I was trying to be as incognito as possible,' Judkins said. 'There was hardly anyone else there in the stand and this fella kept on looking at me. Finally he got up and approached. All sorts of things were running through my head. Why would this bloke possibly want to speak to me?

'"Mate," said the man. "We haven't got anyone to run the scoreboard … I'll give you a dozen cans if you can do it!"'

PROUD SON OF AUSTRALIA

Sam Kekovich the football coach made a good lambassador. VFA club Camberwell 'won' two wooden spoons during his three years as coach in the late '80s.

In one game at Oakleigh, his Cobras were three goals down at the first break. A big crowd surrounding his huddle listening intently to his words of wisdom. 'Fellas,' said Sam, throwing his arms around, loving the theatre of it all, 'what did I say about building the wall? C'mon, let's build the wall. Don't let 'em score.'

At half-time Camberwell trailed by six goals. Undaunted, Sam said the team needed to stick to their disciplines and build the wall. At three-quarter time they were 12 goals down and Sam was fed up. 'Forget the bloody wall,' he said. 'How many goals are we down? Twelve. C'mon we can still win this …'

Even his old coach Ron Barassi would have been impressed by Sam's positivity. Alas, Camberwell lost the game by a huge margin and failed to win a game all year.

But, as the loquacious Sam said, it was an unmissable experience, involving quality sons of Australia, in the greatest country of all …

LONGEST EVER

Even into his 80s, Carlton legend Harry 'Soapy' Vallence was claiming the longest goal ever kicked. 'We were at Glenferrie and it was raining cats and dogs but I really got onto this one. It soared over the grandstand and into a passing goods train,' he said. 'Apparently it ended up in the shunting yards at Warragul!'

THE MEAN MACHINE

So close-checking was Essendon half-back Garry Foulds that teammates nicknamed him 'Vault'. They reckoned he was so mean he wouldn't even give his grandmother an easy kick.

THANKS, PETER!

Dermott Brereton was working for the VFL as an office boy. One of his jobs each August was to post out complimentary Grand Final tickets to the Brownlow Medallists. The 1956 winner, Footscray's Peter Box, was proving hard to contact and after the tickets were returned for a third time with a note: 'NOT AT THIS ADDRESS', Dermott pocketed them and gave them to his parents Jean and Dermott snr, who had quality seats at the '83 grand final!

WHALE'S WOES

Brian 'the Whale' Roberts had put in a shocker against old foe Carlton, one of his rare touches coming right at the end when he took a mark on the siren. Coach Tommy Hafey was inconsolable. Going down with hardly a whimper in such a big match was simply not on. He sprayed every player as they came in, saying it as it was.

The Whale hated letting Tommy down and hated being criticised. When Hafey eyeballed him, Roberts got in first: 'You can't blame me, Tommy … you can't blame me!'

'Why bloody not, Whale?'

'I was just starting to come good when the siren went on me!'

BUCKLING AT THE KNEE

Hawthorn was playing Richmond in a practice match at Drouin, home of the Abletts, when Richmond's runner Peter 'Grub' Grant sprinted out to deliver a message only to suddenly buckle at the knee and have to be helped off.

Later that same season in a fair dinkum game, on he came again to assist Michael Roach who had hurt his knee only for him to again break down. 'Instead of helping Roachy off, Roachy helped him off!' said eyewitness, Hawthorn's full-back Kel Moore. 'It was impossible not to smile.'

SEEING TRIPLE

North Melbourne's Homebush Hotel did a roaring trade in the '70s, catering not only for the blue collar tradies and workers but also for those who wanted a few bells and whistles on their night out. Mine hosts Brian Hansen the football writer and Kevin Morris the footballer had one golden rule throughout the pub: No drunks.

This particular hot night, one of the most notorious local drunks wandered in where Morris was serving in the public bar. 'Give us a beer, mate, will ya?'

'No way – get out!'

The drunk wandered off back the way he'd come, found another door and again asked for a drink, only to be served by Morris for a second time.

'Mate, I told you ... get out!'

Off he went again, this time to a third Homebush door. Morris, always the most tenacious of footballers, had anticipated his move and put himself behind the upmarket bar.

'Give us a beer, will ya mate?' the drunk started and then

seeing Morris said, 'Good God, how many bloody pubs do yer own?!'

WILD TIMES

On Sunday nights in Melbourne in the '70s, it was impossible to get a beer anywhere after six o'clock – except at Caulfield's famed Bear's Cave.

Each and every Sunday, up to 400 testosterone-charged girls and boys would crowd into the clubrooms and party, prance and play-up like in the iconic Prince hit '1999'. There was drinking, sex, strippers and general mayhem. My mates glamour Saints Trevor Barker and Michael Roberts would walk in with two or three girls on their arms. Beer sales in four hours often matched those taken for a whole week at the local pubs. While it was all illegal, the local police would often drop down and have one or two themselves in the back room. It was all very convenient …

There were no rules at the Cave. At the end of a night, some of the girls would take their tops off, jump onto the shoulders of their boyfriends and joust. Once a well-endowed Tongan girl took *all* her clothes off and was promptly pelted with tomatoes.

I was working at the pink paper the *Sporting Globe* at the time and had interviewed Collingwood's madcap rover Ronnie Wearmouth for his 100th game. Right on edition day, there was a phone call. It was Ronnie, tipping me off that he wouldn't be playing after all. His hand was in plaster, the result of a very late night jousting session at the Cave the previous night. He'd straddled a mate's shoulders and come down straight on his wrist! Wild times, indeed.

NO TOUCH, PERC!

Ron Barassi had called a team dinner at the Lyndhurst Hotel. Boom recruit Peter 'Perc' Jones was just finding his feet and implementing the first raft of practical jokes he was to be famous for over the next decade and more.

Finding himself seated next to man-about-town John 'Ragsy' Goold, noted for his expensive imported suits and trademark cravats, Perc planted a greasy pork chop in Goold's pocket. Looking at his soiled suit in disgust, Goold turned to Perc, and said he didn't mind a joke, but PLEASSSSE, in future, could he leave his clothes alone?

THINKING ON HIS FEET

Tiger ruckman Mike 'the Swamp Fox' Patterson was aghast at a decision that had gone against him and roared at the umpire, 'You bloody idiot, Crouch!'

'What did you say, Mike?'

'Bloody good decision, Jeff.'

A GLENFERRIE ARGEE-BARGEE

Johnny Birt lay prostrate on his back in front of the old Hawthorn Stand as Essendon and Hawthorn players warred around him. Making his way officiously through the angry throng, umpire Ron Brophy demanded, 'What's going on here?'

'Nothing's wrong here, Ron,' said Hawk John Peck. 'It's a lovely day, perfect weather for football, tremendous game and your exhibition cannot be faulted … but I think the heat has got to this poor little chap [Birt] – he's fainted!'

LAMB ROAST ON SUNDAYS

Collingwood's unchallenged king of recruiters, long-time secretary Gordon Carlyon would do anything to get his man. The game's first fulltime secretary, appointed in 1950, Carlyon's signings included George Hams, Jack Hamilton, Lerrel Sharp, Jack Fink, the Twomey brothers, Frank Tuck and Ray Gabelich through to Wayne Richardson and dozens more. Everywhere he went he would reinforce Collingwood's proud record, its player provident fund *and* his wife Vivian's country-style home cooking …

Often in March and into April the Carlyon family would host five or six would-be-champions at their Northcote home. On Sundays, Mrs Carlyon would serve the traditional lamb roast, complete with the spuds that had been cooked next door as the Carlyons' cooker wasn't big enough. 'We had only a very small gas stove,' said Carlyon, 'so Mrs Munro, our neighbour, would cook the spuds and other vegies in her cooker for us and pass them through the back fence when they were ready. It was the only way we could possibly feed the likes of "Gabbo" [Gabelich] and Graeme Fellowes who were both six-foot-plenty. Boy could they eat! We'd play cards afterwards, the losers having to do the wash-up.'

Invariably, as the hopefuls assembled, the Carlyons would run out of beds. 'Lerrel Sharp arrived from Tassie and I told him he could stay but he'd have to sleep on the floor. We found some old chaff bags down the back and he wedged himself in between Gabbo and Graeme – who were both giants – but about three o'clock the following morning there was all this screaming. One of the boys had to go to the toilet in the middle of the night, had forgotten Lerrel was there and stepped on him!'

At the time of my meeting with Gordon in 1991, football was changing rapidly. One of his bugbears was that football training started too early and coaches and administrations were asking too much of their players. 'Old Jock McHale used to say players didn't recover

COLLINGWOOD
CENTENARY PREMIERS 1958

GORDON CARLYON
SECRETARY

ONE OF THE GREAT SECRETARIES:
Collingwood's Gordon Carlyon
Tom Mahoney

from a Saturday game until the following Thursday,' Carlyon said. 'He believed everyone should do what they liked – tennis, cricket, whatever – until March; then it was football season from March to September. Now they give them only six weeks' break. The players will pay for this later on with arthritis and all that. In our day we built grandstands through careful planning and saving. Now they spend the money and then worry about paying it back. Football is totally controlled by money.'

TALES OF THE GALLOPING GASOMETER

Few were as wholehearted from April to September as heavyweight country boy Mick Nolan, famously nicknamed 'the Galloping Gasometer' by Lou Richards. Mick reckoned running on the ball all day in-season gave him the licence *not* to have to train overly hard in the lead-ups.

Mick's ballooning waistline was a complicated issue, the tyrannical Ron Barassi finding it ever-challenging dealing with big Mick's range of explanations and excuses on just why he needed to stay in Wangaratta rather than come to Melbourne for pre-season. For several summers running, Mick told 'Barass' that his grandmother had just died and he had to stay in 'Wang' to look after his family. When he tried the same excuse for a third pre-season in four, Barass erupted: 'Just how many grandmothers do you have, Mick?' he asked.

It's true that Mick had a big family. He was one of nine from the tiny outpost of Tarrawingee, just outside Wangaratta and there were relatives everywhere.

Despite a barrel stomach which hung over his belt-line, he was surprisingly light on his feet and ever-so-skilful with his ability to pinpoint his rover with expert palming of the ball, especially at the boundary throw-ins.

After he won Tarrawingee's best and fairest as a 17-year-old in 1967, his 'signature' became the ultimate prize between

arch rivals Wangaratta and immediate neighbour Wangaratta Rovers.

Trevor Steer, who'd played in the '66 Grand Final, was coaching 'Wang'. On his way back from his schoolteaching duties in Beechworth, he'd often pop into the Plough Inn, one of Mick's favourite local watering holes – just to keep the lines of communication open.

Ernie Payne, secretary at the Rovers, soon heard of Steer's friendship missions and thought he'd better keep on Mick's hammer too. 'Every night for a week I spent socialising at the Plough. Mick set a hot pace and was starting to wear me out. In the end, I said, "What about it, Mick … will ya sign?"

'"Yeah, no worries Ernie. I was always going to play with you blokes, anyway!"'

Big Mick wasn't one to worry overly about team meetings and the like. Invariably he'd be late on match days and would nonchalantly saunter into Finlay Reserve shortly before 2 p.m. wondering why everyone looked so worried.

It was the same on training nights. Arriving after everyone else, he'd open his battered bag and take out his ankle bandages, carefully roll them up, fasten his ankles and only then put his gear on. It was an elaborate process, which seemed to take the best part of half an hour leaving no time for the compulsory warm-up laps. Having ambled a slow half-lap, he'd blend in with circle work. Despite the oft-proclaimed lack of fitness, he amassed 100 games with three senior clubs: Rovers, North Melbourne and Mayne in the Brisbane League. He also played 40 with Tarrawingee – and was loved everywhere he went.

Wangaratta sporting legend Kevin Hill had some business in Tarrawingee one Friday evening and stopped off at the 'Tarra' pub, 'just to be sociable'.

Inside as usual were the Nolans, including Mick who was yet to begin his League career in the Big Smoke but was very much part of the furniture at the Rovers.

Mary, Mick's mum, was on one side of the open fire, beer in hand, winding down after a long day. Pete, his dad, was operating the bar. Mick, cigarette in hand, had just drained yet another cleansing ale and motioned to his dad for a refill, only to be rebuked by Mary. 'Michael,' she said, 'you'll never be able to play football tomorrow if you keep smoking ...'

Mick never forgot his old mates and come the '75 Grand Final he'd organised tickets for just about every family member, country cousin and mate. Arriving early at Mick and Nettie's place on the morning of the game, his mates noticed half a dozen empty long necks on the servery. When questioned, Mick admitted to having had 'a few' with his neighbour the night before.

They all hoed into breakfast with the lot, Mick having his usual match-day serving of six sausages with three eggs. Later that day, he told a 3AW interviewer that he was 'pretty toey' about the Grand Final and hadn't 'been able to sleep or hardly eat' in the lead-up to the game!

He played all 26 games that special year for North. The only one to also play every match in 1975 was club captain Barry Davis.

PARTY TRICKS

For a policeman, Emmett 'Plod' Dunne had a wicked sense of humour. His favourite, printable, party trick was leaving smoke bombs in the locker of Richmond teammate Barry Rowlings.

'ERR ... SORRY, SAM, I'M ACTUALLY PLAYING TOO ...'

No one used more ankle-strapping than Sam Newman, especially in his final years of AFL. His dicky ankles rarely allowed him to train more than once a week and given he was in his early 30s, he was 10 years older than the majority of the senior list and didn't always socialise with the younger players.

During the '77 season, one of the rookie Cats blooded by Rod Olsson was a young bloke from the thirds in Gerard Fitzgerald (now coaching the North Ballarat Roosters) who had overcome knee injuries and, after four years, finally been selected in the seniors for the first time.

Fitzgerald was in the medical room, still in his civvies, about to get ready. In barged Sam, saw Gerard standing there and said, 'Mate, [head trainer] George Clarke is busy. Can you help put some tape on my ankles?'

Fitzgerald introduced himself, saying how pleased he was to meet him, but in actual fact he was also playing that day ...

It was at the after-matches at Kardinia Park, following the official speeches, where Sam first developed his hilarious routines, grabbing the mike and giving his view of the world. 'He was always hilarious,' said eyewitness Kevin Sheehan, 'a true larger-than-life character.'

OOPS, I KNEW I'D FORGOTTEN SOMETHING ...

Australia's 1984 Gaelic representatives were at the Bronx in New York at the start of their overseas tour. A team picture was due to be taken, but there was a delay and Gary Pert and a few of the other players pulled on some tracksuit bottoms to stay warm. 'Finally we got the okay and trooped outside,' said Pert. 'I took my tracksuit off only to realise I'd failed to put on any shorts whatsoever and was naked from the waist down! "Roosy" [Paul Roos] thought it was hilarious. I don't think I have ever blushed a darker shade of purple!'

EMBARRASSED: Gary Pert

MR MAGIC: St Kilda's heartbeat of the '60s was its import captain Darrel Baldock from Latrobe. He wasn't quick and wasn't tall – yet in one-on-ones he was well nigh unbeatable

LEGENDS ON EVERY LINE: One of the greatest of all Essendon teams was its 1950 line-up which overpowered North Melbourne by 38 points in the Grand Final. Back row, left to right: Ted Leehane, Bill Snell, Bob Syme, Bob McClure, Wally May, Jack Jones, Roy McConnell and Bert Harper. Sitting: Jack Collins, Ron McEwin, Les Gardiner, Dick Reynolds (captain-coach), Cr. W. R. Crichton (president), Billy Hutchison, Norm McDonald and Harold Lambert. Front: Chris Lambert, Noel Allanson, John Coleman, Alan Dale and Bill Brittingham. Coleman kicked four goals and the fleet-of-foot McDonald was best afield

FIRST EVER: Hawthorn captain Graham Arthur with the 1961 premiership cup, with teammates Graham Cooper (left), Martin Browne and Cam McPherson. My Dad, Ken snr was very, very happy about the result ...
Gold'n Brown Jubilee, the story of the '61 Hawks, Richard Allsop and Peter Haby (Hawks Museum, Hawthorn Football Club, 2011)

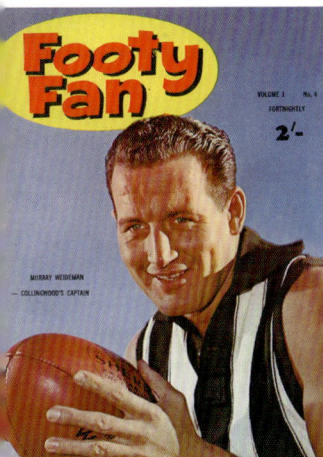

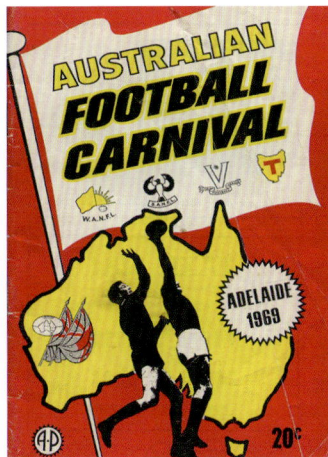

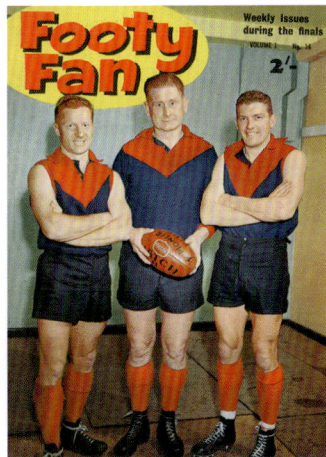

Left: THE WEED: Murray Weideman was a premiership player at 17 and five years later captain in the famous 1958 Grand Final when against all odds, Collingwood stopped Melbourne

Centre: RARE BOOKLET: North Melbourne premiership player-to-be John Burns was one of the 1969 Australian carnival stars in his first year out of country football

Right: 17 FLAGS BETWEEN THEM: Red and Blue legends Bluey Adams with coach Norm Smith and Brian Dixon. Adams and Smith were each involved in six Melbourne premierships and 'Dicko' five. He was stood down from the 1955 flag team after playing in a mid-week Grand Final against orders

Left: GLENFERRIE DESTROYER: Demon Hassa Mann's goal in time-on of a thrilling 17th-round encounter cost Hawthorn a place in the finals in 1964

Right: THE FATMAN: Doug Wade played a practice game for Melbourne before being 'pirated' by Bob Davis and Geelong

Tom Mahony collection

THE BEST VIEW OF ALL: Glenferrie Oval's railway wing offered an unparalleled view of the game. From 1963 on, I was a regular. This picture is from the 1969 Hawthorn-North Melbourne game. The players left to right are: Frank Dimattina (31), Des Meagher, Daryl O'Brien, Mick Porter (9), Peter Crimmins, Sam Kekovich (with ball), and a very young David Dench (44)

Drew Payne/Ken Piesse Collection

ELUSIVE: Goal-kicker extraordinaire Peter Hudson made a habit of giving his opponents the slip. John Kennedy often had him standing alone 60 yards clear of anyone else at the head of the goalsquare. Here Demons David Hone and Paul Rowlands chase 'Huddo', who has Gene Chiron for protection in a 1969 encounter at the MCG

Drew Payne/Ken Piesse Collection

The Blues staged a fantastic finish to snatch the 1970 Flag from the Magpies in a real thriller grand final at the MCG today.

Left: THE FLEA: Dale Weightman figured in two Grand Finals in his first five years of VFL football, but never played in another final for the rest of his career. He was best afield five or six times in his 20 matches for Victoria, his lightning handball and precise field kicking always a highlight. He was brilliant company off the field too
Inside Football

Right: TIME TO PARTY: Don Scott was a powerhouse in three Hawthorn flags in the '70s and later helped save the club from merger in the mid-'90s. This picture of 'Scotty' in celebration was taken after the 1976 win against North Melbourne, when the Hawks dedicated their victory to seriously-ill ex-captain Peter Crimmins who was to die just 72 hours later
Don Scott Collection

PETER DAICOS **RON WEARMOUTH** **TONY SHAW**

FOOTBALL **RECORD** 70c

Registered by Australia Post
Publication No. VBG 1012. Copyright

April 20/21, 1985 — Vol. 74, No. 5

Essendon

Collingwood

Autographs

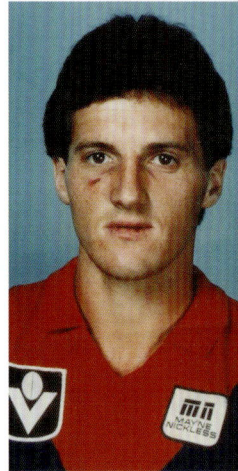

LIVING IN THE EIGHTIES: Top: Woven badges were all the rage in the '70s and '80s and would be sewn on the old duffle coats then in vogue. *Above left:* A VFL *Football Record* from 1985 with Footscray coach Bobby Rose featured. Bobby may have been employed for a time in the west but his heart never left Collingwood. *Above:* Journeymen Gary Shaw and Brian Wilson. Gary was incredibly expensive —and under-performed and Brian, then a Demon, a Brownlow Medallist at 20. Also: Doug Nicholls' autograph from a Fitzroy reunion. Sir Douglas was a trailblazer for his people and a wonderful ambassador for Australian Rules. *Right:* Stephen Kernahan celebrates Carlton's 1987 Grand Final triumph. His rendition of Tammy Wynette's classic *Stand By Your Man* on 'Mad Monday' is still a favourite on You Tube. Pictured with him is David Rhys-Jones, the Norm Smith Medallist

No.31 October 2, 1987

Footy
WEEK

SOUVENIR EDITION

1987 GRAND FINAL

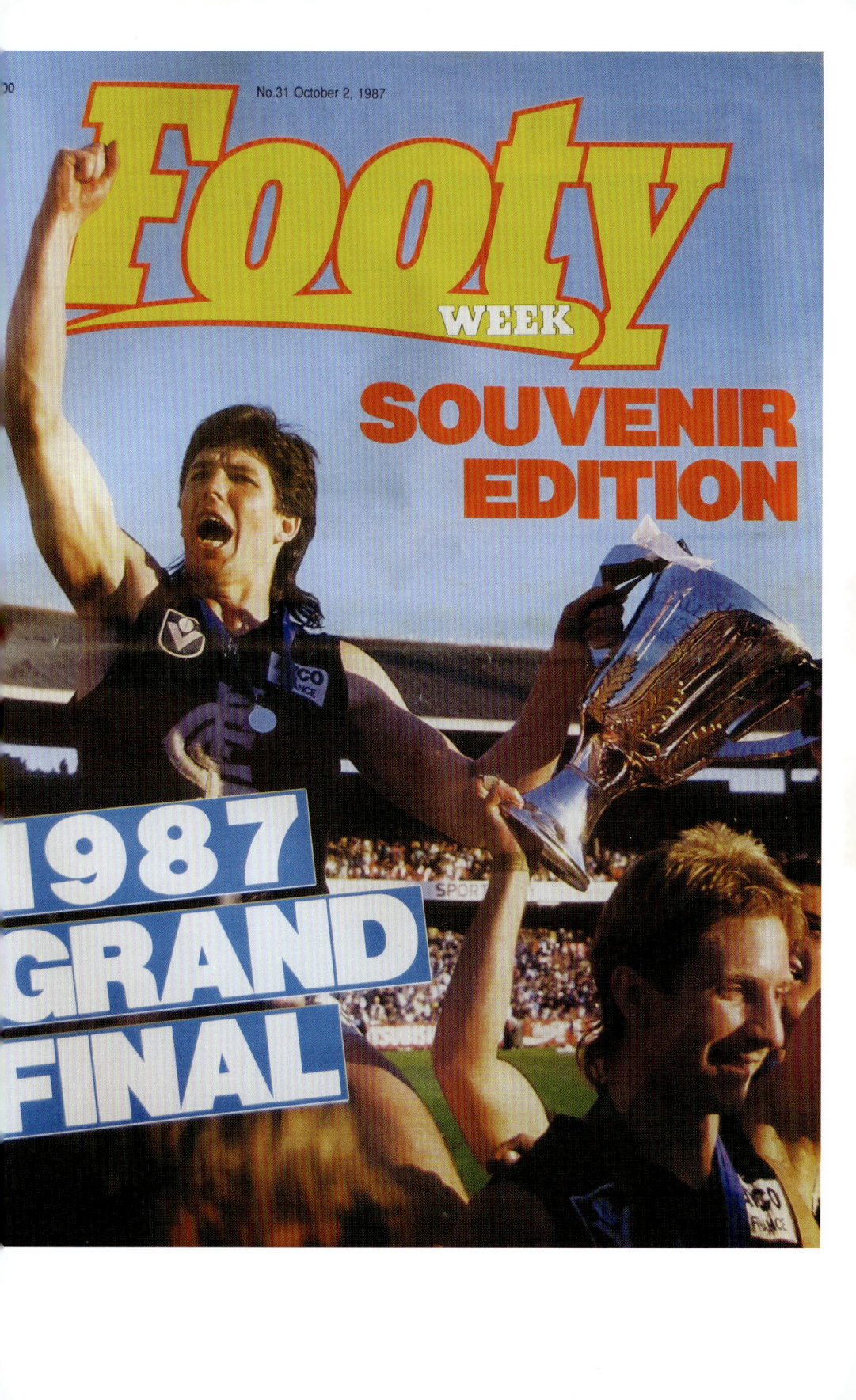

WISE-CRACK: Bomber loyalists Simon and Mary Madden and family in the late '80s. Simon joked once that he'd told Mary he was going down the street to buy the bread and rang again from Germany saying he was on the Essendon tripaway! But he was only joking. 'I would have been in real trouble if it had been true!' he said
Inside Football

THE MOTH

One of Caulfield's recruits in the '70s was a lad named Ned Gerard from Prahran who was soon dubbed 'the Moth' as he would train only on the half of the club's home ground that was floodlit!

LAUGHTER IS THE BEST MEDICINE

Fun-loving Dermott Brereton was always one of VFL chief Jack Hamilton's favourites. 'The Kid', one of the League's five office boys in the early '80s, could do no wrong and around the inner sanctum corridors was known as 'the Pet'.

But even Jack's tolerance could be tested and out of his big corner office one morning came a 'DERMOTTTTT!'

In Dermie ambled with his normal happy smile and said, 'Well, Mr Hamilton, so it's now got to the stage where it's no longer Mr Nice Guy!'

None of the other office boys, Hughie, Chopper, Patto or Toss could have got away with it. Jack burst into laughter and the issue soon dissolved.

WHALE TALE

Only two aspects of life ever ruffled Richmond prankster Brian 'the Whale' Roberts: flat beer and footy training in summer.

As was his habit, he'd had a big few days on the slops and just wasn't in the mood to run laps this hot February night. Donning a dinner jacket and black tie, he walked solemnly into training and threw down his bag next to coach Tommy Hafey. 'What's wrong, Whale? You look bleak,' said Tommy.

'A death in the family, Tommy.'

Hafey excused the Whale from training. Later he found that the 'death' had been 100 whales washed up on the beach at Shoreham!

WHAT ARE YOU DOING HERE, CHARLIE?

Human headline Mal Brown (Campbell's dad) had just one year at Tigerland but was the centre of all sorts of mischief, on and off the field. The club's veteran property steward Charlie Callender was renowned for riding his bike everywhere and one night after training he couldn't find it. Mal was very helpful and suggested that maybe it could be across the road at the local massage parlour! Charlie trooped across Punt Road and was knocking on the front door when out of the bushes sprang a photographer from *The Herald* who duly snapped him entering a place of ill repute. Somehow the print found its way home to Charlie's bride, Theresa. 'She said just two words: "Mal Brown" and she was right!' said Charlie.

A LETHAL CHARGE

Leigh Matthews flattened Peter 'Perc' Jones with one of his trademark charges one day. Having tested his jaw and counted all of his teeth, Big Perc finally picked himself up from the mud and stuttered, 'Di-di-did anyone get the number of that bloody t-t-truck?'

A DIFFERENT TIME ...

Frontline rookies these days can make almost $200 000 a year and are treated like royalty. When five-time Richmond premiership hero Francis Bourke first arrived at Tigerland in the mid-'60s, he lived in Melbourne three nights a week and back on the family's farm in Nathalia for four.

Part of his Richmond apprenticeship on Fridays was to weed the terraces at the Punt Road Oval. 'Richmond hadn't played any games at Punt Road since 1964, so the outer bitumen terraces were a mass of weeds,' he said. 'Graeme Richmond gave me a hoe and said, "Start there, Cocko, and keep going until you get to the other end." That was my job each and every Friday. I got to the end just as the season was finishing.'

THERE'S ONLY ONE ROYCE HART

Every premiership coach has a champion player pivotal to their team's premier performance. Among the crème de la crème are Smith/Barassi, Davis/Farmer, Pagan/Carey, Sheedy/Hird and Clarkson/Hodge – to name just five ...

Tommy Hafey's favourite was Royce Hart. Originally from the Tasmanian Midlands and signed for a suit and six shirts, Hart was destined for a rare celebrity status at Richmond from the time he unleashed the sealing goal with just seconds to play in the reserves Grand Final in 1966.

Tommy's pre-match talks tended to have a familiar theme: 'Kick it to Royce – and keep out of his bloody way.'

At Bronte Beach one year, the players were frolicking in the surf when seven or eight were caught in a rip, including Hart, who was a poor swimmer. Out to sea they were dragged and broke into two groups. Defender Tony Jewell raised his arm for help and Tommy, who had been sunning himself on the beach, sprinted into the water and began swimming through the breakers like he was Johnny Weissmuller. 'Thank goodness,' thought Jewell, 'Tommy's seen me.'

Hafey got to Jewell, stopped only momentarily and kept swimming towards the main group of players another 50 metres out to sea. An exhausted Jewell only just made it back to shore. Later he caught up with Hafey back at the team's hotel. 'What happened, Tommy?' he said. 'You saw me and kept going.'

'Tony,' said Hafey, 'half-back flankers are a dime a dozen. There's only one Royce Hart.'

ROLLS ROYCE: 'There's only one Royce Hart ...'

THE BULL

Richmond premiership ruck-rover Alan Richardson – Matthew's dad – suffered from asthma but it didn't stop him from pushing himself to the limit in the finishing sprints at Punt Road. He'd end up puffing and panting and making so much noise that he was nicknamed 'the Bull', a nickname set in concrete after he sang 'The Little White Bull', a popular song at the time, at an after-match function and ran around the room with his head down and two index fingers up.

A PRELUDE TO THE REAL THING

Neil Kerley thought he must have been late, as on entering South Australia's rooms for the State match against Victoria in 1963, he could hear coach Fos Williams in full flight, banging his fists into a locker, urging and demanding a supreme effort: 'I want you to go in hard … never stop working … take it right up to them until the last dying minute …' Turned out he was merely geeing-up the trainers and had more in store for the players!

JUST CHECK THE SUN, BARRY ...

Barry Cheatley hated conceding goals to anybody and when his opponent Tony Ongarello was given a goal which he believed to be a point at Brunswick Street one day, he blew up. Approaching the goal umpire Steve Stevens, he said, 'That was lucky to be a bloody point – no way was it a goal.' Ignored him totally, Stevens theatrically recorded the goal on his card before finally addressing Cheatley: 'Barry, just check Monday morning's *Sun*. If you're not sure it was a goal, it'll be in there.' Even the shirty Cheatley had no answer to that one.

HELLO, OCIFER

Hawthorn had just won the '61 premiership, their first ever and my father, delighted by the proceedings and waxing poetic about Brendan Edwards' superhuman display in the heat, had arrived home in the company of two policemen. They'd seen his car lurching down Brighton Road, stopped him and confiscated his keys. Dad *had* tied one on, but as he explained to the police, it's not every day your favourite team wins the Big One for the first time. So good-natured were the boys in blue that they taxied him the rest of the way to Beaumaris – and Mum, who was furious. Now 91 not out, she still remembers it like it was yesterday …

GET FEROCIOUS

Geelong's master coach Reg Hickey once told defender Russ Renfrey to get ferocious. 'What number is he?' asked Renfrey.

WORDS OF WISDOM

Having finished last in 1952, St Kilda had sacked more than half its senior list for 1953. It was tradition at the player's pre-season dinner for the captain to speak. 'Normally at this time,' began Keith Drinan, 'I congratulate all the new players on making the list and wish them the best of luck. On this occasion, I'd like to congratulate the older players still left here. May we all have good seasons!'

RED LIGHT ALERT

Percy Beames was new to the Big Smoke. He'd just arrived from Ballarat, Melbourne having organised a job for him at the Vacuum Oil Company and accommodation at an old boarding house in Jolimont, directly adjacent to the Melbourne Cricket Ground. It was the Friday night before his first game

SURPRISE, SURPRISE, SURPRISE: Ballarat boy Percy Beames found himself bunking in a house of ill repute on first arriving in Melbourne

(1931) and Percy was kept awake for much of the night by people giggling and laughing. 'Gee, they're happy around here,' he thought to himself. Turned out he'd been bunking in a house of ill repute!

NO FUSS

Albert 'Leeta' Collier was up a ladder painting the old *Herald-Sun* building in Flinders Street when a mate yelled out, 'Hey Leeta, you've won the Brownlow [Medal].' It was the first he knew of it. There was no pomp and ceremony back in 1929.

8

Legends

Tommy Hafey transcended club loyalties. He was loved and admired by all. When he died in 2013, it was like a death in the family ...

ALIVE AND WELL

From the age of 14, Steve Johnson's mission to be drafted saw him play two games of football in and around Wangaratta most wintertime weekends. But try as he did, he kept missing the elite squads. Finally he was asked to play a trial match or two for the Murray Bushrangers, coached by former North Melbourne premiership centreman Xavier Tanner.

At the conclusion of the trials, Tanner told each of the boys he'd ring them the following morning if they were being cut.

Exactly on 9 a.m. the next day, Johnson's phone rang. Johnson's immediate reaction was 'oh no'. He hadn't slept all night worrying that he may not have played well enough when it counted. His heart sank when he heard his mother answer, 'G'day Xavier.'

Johnson came to the phone, fearing the worst – but instead of Xavier Tanner it was his golfing mate Xavier, wondering if he wanted to play pennant later that day. He was still alive!

MODRAAAAA!

Adelaide teenager Lance Picione was just a boy amongst men; the excitement of being in the big time gave him such an adrenalin surge he just couldn't stop running.

'It was one of my first games [of AFL]. I was still 17. We were playing West Coast and I came on midway through the first quarter to a forward flank. With the rotations it worked out that I lined up against John Worsfold who was one of the most imposing and intimidating footballers ever to play. I was so excited to be playing, and I ran around like a headless chook before Worsfold grabbed hold of me off the ball, pushed me in the chest a couple of times and, somehow managing to dislodge my mouthguard, gave me a left directly to the chops. "Welcome to AFL, you little prick," he said. "Now stop running so much."

'In a state of crapping my pants I punched him in his ridiculously huge chest and replied, "Thanks ... seeya," before running off again as fast as I could.'

Few were as ambitious as Picione who would deliberately pair himself off at training against the Crow's mightiest running player Andrew McLeod. 'I thought it was the only way to improve myself. This particular session he won 10 contests and I won one. There was one more to go so I really steeled myself for a big effort. There we were one-on-one, camped under a high ball with me jostling for the front position. Somehow I lost body contact, then from nowhere whilst I was in midair I felt someone's knees on my shoulder and there was a shout from the boys watching, "MODRAAAAA"... the great Tony Modra had seen an opportunity and taken another of his speckies. "There you go," said Tony as I picked myself up from the ground, "you can go and tell your mates that Tony Modra just took a hanger on you."'

JONNO'S MONDAY-NIGHT SECRET

Monday-night recovery sessions were never meant to be this competitive, especially in summer.

Brisbane coach Leigh Matthews was blissfully unaware of the night-time shenanigans many of his premiership heroes were indulging in the inner suburbs of Brisbane – until they all appeared on TV.

Cricket-loving premiership pair Jonathan Brown and Tim Notting were the ringleaders of the day-night street cricket 'Tests', played for weeks each and every summertime Monday in the early 2000s.

A mate gave Brown a powerful spotlight and from using it initially to light up his driveway, he and Notting expanded their game into the street, erecting a row of temporary lights and expertly marking creases 18 yards (16 metres) apart with spray cans of white paint courtesy of their local Bunnings. 'I've always loved cricket just as much as footy,' Brown said in an interview with the ABC's Quentin Hull, 'and our games just got bigger and bigger. Martin Pike would roll in with his leggies and "Vossy" [Michael Voss] and "Leppa" [Justin Leppitsch] would also have a go. "Possum" [Notting] could bowl pretty fast and didn't mind pinging them in short. It was full-on.'

The local police arrived a few times, one of the ladies whose front yard was at long-on being unimpressed by the constant intrusions of ball-fetchers in her garden.

'We used electrical tape on the balls so they'd really move around and zip off the bitumen,' said Brown. 'Everyone had to take a detour around Harris Street. It became a neighbourhood phenomenon.'

If coach Matthews had been unaware of the street cricket battles, he wasn't any more when Channel Ten's *Before the Game* did a live cross one Saturday night, Brown talking of his love of cricket and how he'd always dreamed of 'opening the bowling for Australia on Boxing Day'.

A left-arm tearaway once rated among the most promising 16-year-old fast bowlers in the country, Brown said he always wanted to play professional sport. It was easier being one of 720 playing in the AFL compared with one of 11 representing Australia in Tests.

Before turning 22, Jonathan Brown played in three premierships for Brisbane. His father Brian and uncle Billy Picken played League football as well, Picken also playing cricket in summer with Collingwood Cricket Club.

YOU WIN SOME AND LOSE SOME

Recruiting can be so hit or miss. For every success story there are a myriad tales of those who got away.

The AFL's long-time National and International Talent Manager and former 100-game Geelong rover Kevin Sheehan was among those responsible for the first intake of scholars to the prestigious AIS-AFL Academy under the keen eye of head coach Kevin Morris. A tour to Ireland at the end of the Academy program was also on offer. It was a finishing school of dreams for every footy-mad teenager.

Morris and Sheehan were assisted in their choices by a handful of AFL club recruiting officers. They were assembled in July 1997, in Darwin, for the second annual Under 16 National Championships where in the last game, an unknown red-headed teenager with a big frame, a great set of hands and a beautiful left-foot kick snagged eight goals.

The 30-strong Academy squad had virtually been selected, but so impressive was the little-known kid from St Joseph's in Geelong that Sheehan and Co. went with him as their 30th and final player. His name? Cameron Ling!

'We didn't have detailed information on all the kids and their backgrounds,' said Sheehan. 'A lot of the time back then you had to go on gut instinct after assessing what you observed. There were no interviews with the player or fitness test results. Until he kicked that bag on the final day of the carnival, Cameron hadn't really been on the radar. He ended up going to Ireland in April the following year where he was so outstanding as a player and a leader that he was appointed Australia's captain for the International match against the Irish. Perceptions changed, too: by the end of his time in the Under 18s, he was doing a 14.5 beep test [an enduring multi-stage fitness test] so instead of him being considered [just] a lead-up forward, he had the potential endurance of an elite midfielder, the proverbial big tank, which he was to show so often with Geelong.'

AFL clubs overlooked drafting Ling as a 17-year-old but he was selected the following year, 1999, at No. 38, Geelong coach Mark Thompson saying that if two potential draftees were considered 'equal' the club would always pick a local. Ling was to become a frontline player and captain in a champion team. The Level 1 Medal of the now flourishing NAB AFL Academy is named in his honour and Sheehan never tires of telling the story of the unfashionable redhead who made good.

But in the same Under 16s championship in Darwin, as he readily admits, there were some big 'misses', too. 'We learnt as we went along,' Sheehan said. 'We identified them on talent to win and use the ball, as well as their athletic ability but it sometimes was difficult to read as some of the 16-year-olds might have been born in January and some in December. At that age, an 11–12-month age advantage makes a huge difference. The older ones can be physically stronger which helps them win the contested ball yet they may not have the same improvement in them compared with those born later in the year.

'The couple we missed that year included a 188-centimetre [six feet, two inches] kid with a ponytail who played down the back but could also move forward. He was a thumping kick but compared to some he was harder to handle. The Vic Metro coaching and management had to chase him to get him to training on time; he was late for meetings and would eat the wrong foods. Having spoken to one of the coaches, we decided to overlook him. It was Brendan Fevola. We should have taken him. Looking back now, he did drift at different times with his attitude and performance, but had he been part of the Academy early on, it may have had an impact on how he went about things. We now pick on talent and back our program to make a difference in shaping that potential.

'Another one I also regret was [the non-selection of] a kid from South Australia in that same very first year of the Academy. He was well built at around 190 centimetres [six feet, three inches] and had huge thighs on him. We noticed he didn't turn 16 years until 31 December that year. He was the youngest at the championships. He was mobile and while he didn't get a lot of the ball there was certainly something there.

'We didn't dig deep enough on this one. We went to his South Australian coach and after speaking with him about his playing group, we overlooked the tall forward, a kid named Matthew Pavlich. The coach of the team was Stephen Pavlich, Matthew's father! He wasn't one to push his own son too hard so we went with a more mature player already playing at senior level in the SANFL. This kid ended up being selected as an AFL rookie but he wasn't an icon of the game like Matty … if only we'd pushed harder … Matty became and still is a champion of the game.'

LONGY THE LEGEND

Essendon had just won the '93 flag and Michael Long, the hero of the day, was being lauded by a sell-out crowd at the premiership celebrations at the Hilton. Finally when the cheering subsided, he said, tongue-in-cheek, 'Gees … I played well!' It brought the house down. Again.

WORDS OF WISDOM

Those privy to Leigh Matthews' speech before the 1990 Grand Final have never forgotten it. Having reiterated Collingwood's game plan and how they had to start like there was no tomorrow, Matthews paused and said, 'Whatever happens today, I'd like to thank you for what you have done throughout the year. I respect each and every one of you for what you have been able to achieve. Go out, have a good day and enjoy it.'

'ARE YOU LISTENING, SON?'

Darren Jarman was as gifted a player as any to wear the brown and gold stripes at Hawthorn. This day at Waverley he was being closely tagged. Paul Dear was rucking and in the pre-bounce huddle it was decided to block Jarman's opponent and allow 'Jars' space in which to run. 'We want you to get clear, take two bounces and kick a goal,' said Dear. Jarman did, miraculously evading all oncoming traffic and drilling a laconic 60-metre drop-punt straight through the high-diddle-diddle before being followed back into the next huddle by his tagger. Turning around, Jarman said, 'Now are you listening, son?'

ESSENDON THROUGH AND THROUGH

Simon Madden always said, 'You can take the boy out of Essendon, but you can't take Essendon out of the boy.' But in the summer of '86, it got very, very close.

Dr Geoffrey Edelsten threw copious amounts of money at rebuilding Sydney's list. Madden was targeted alongside the likes of Greg Williams, Gerard Healy and the tough-as-teak Bernard Toohey.

Madden, the most decorated ruckman in the game and then only 28, fielded all sorts of inducements amidst the Edelsten spending spree: $100 000 cash to sign plus $450 000 a year for three years – more than any other player at the time.

When Madden told Edelsten he had just started a new job, as a schoolteacher, Edelsten said he would arrange a similar job for him in Sydney and even buy him a school if necessary! Madden was to remain at Essendon with his mates because it was easier – but the extra cash would have been handy …

ONCE BITTEN, TWICE SHY

Bruce Doull was the shyest and most silent of champions. Nothing seemed to disturb him, except the time Hawthorn's Kevin Ablett sprinted off with his headband one Tuesday night match at Waverley. 'Never ever had any of us seen Bruce so animated,' said eyewitness Geoff Southby. 'That headband of his was like a security blanket. Bruce chased after Ablett, who could really run, threatening to kill him. It was like a lion chasing a gazelle. Luckily the umpires got to him first and were able to restore order.

'The following Saturday we were playing out at Waverley again, this time against Essendon. The Bombers had obviously worked out that Bruce's Achilles heel was his headband. It might be a way to upset and out him off his game. There was a boundary throw-in early on. I was just a few yards away from Bruce and saw little Tony Buhagiar jump up, grab Bruce's headband, run to the fence and toss it into the crowd. Everyone erupted. We waited for Bruce's response. Would he again go crazy? Would he clock "Budgie?" What effect would it have on the game? It seemed every eye was on Bruce. But instead of even remonstrating with Budgie, he leaned down to his sock, pulled out a spare headband and on he and the game went. It was classic. He'd done his homework, too!'

THE NO. 1 TIGER

Few supported football and cricket so passionately as businessman and philanthropist David Mandie, who was a saviour at both Richmond FC and Prahran Cricket Club.

Mandie was Richmond's patron and No. 1 ticketholder for decades. From the 1950s, he was the most active employer of footballers and proudly believed his James Richardson 'team' at its very top would have taken some beating.

In 1982, he penned his all-star team of footballers he'd employed over three decades at his furniture duty-free emporium:

GENEROUS: Lifelong Richmond supporter, businessman and philanthropist David Mandie at the unveiling of the Jack Dyer statue he funded at the Punt Road Oval.

Backs: Wayne Harmes (Carlton), Barry Richardson (Richmond), Grant Allford (Richmond)

Half-backs: Michael Bowden (Richmond), Jim Jess (Richmond), Gary Cowton (North Melbourne and Footscray)

Centres: Dick Clay (Richmond), Bill Barrot (Richmond), Graeme Bond (Richmond)

Half-forwards: John Northey (Richmond), Mark Maclure (Carlton), Neville Roberts (Richmond)

Forwards: Mark Lee (Richmond), George Young (St Kilda), Trevor Barker (St Kilda)

Rucks: Michael Green (Richmond), Bruce Monteath (Richmond)

Rover: Chris Pavlou (Carlton)

Interchanges: Rod Galt (St Kilda and Carlton), Mark Hegarty (Carlton)

Emergencies: John Wise (Collingwood), Gary Smith (Footscray)

Coach: Charlie Priestley (Richmond)

In 2003, Mandie commissioned a bronze statue of the greatest Tiger of all 'Captain Blood' Jack Dyer, which was unfurled just months after Dyer's death. Mandie had a key involvement in the establishment of the Jack Dyer Foundation and the redevelopment of the Punt Road Oval, Richmond's home since 1885.

He was also chairman of the VFL committee in the 1980s, which was pivotal in the establishment of a national competition. His daughter Evelyn, granddaughter Georgia and grandsons Andrew and Matthew remain staunch Tigers.

T-SHIRT TOMMY

No football octogenarian was as tanned, taut and terrific as Tommy Hafey. The Richmond legend thrived on his daily routine of a dip at St Kilda beach followed by 600 sit-ups and push-ups. His fitness was his byword. Asked how he was, he'd always say, 'Sensational ... and getting better every day.'

Even into his late 70s, Tommy possessed the fitness reserves, the 'pecs' and the 'six-pack' the rest of us could only marvel at. On the coldest days, he'd still walk around in shorts and a T-shirt.

He was a father figure to the players he coached, involving himself in their lives, rejoicing in their births and grieving alongside them when loved ones passed.

Kevin Sheedy, one of his disciples, said there'd been no finer human being than Tommy. 'There was just something about him. You wanted to win for Tommy, not just for Richmond ... if I ever got ahead of myself, Tommy would say, "You're not that good, Kevin. Remember, you're just a back-pocket player and the world's got plenty of those."'

The first time Tommy invited the team back to his home in Beaumaris one Saturday night, he told the players it wasn't compulsory ... just they wouldn't be selected again if they didn't show! The players hid their longnecks in the garden and excusing themselves at regular intervals, trailed outside, not wishing to upset evangelistic Tommy who frowned on any of his players partaking in the demon drink.

Once Tommy sprung a group moonlighting at a St Kilda pub, just days before a particularly big match. 'You so-and-so's,' said Tommy looking around. Everyone had pots of beer except for Tony Jewell who was drinking stout. 'What did I tell you all,' said Tommy shaking his head. 'Well, at least Jewell has the sense to be drinking Coke.'

He left Richmond only after believing he'd lost the support of the Tiger's long-time powerbroker Graeme Richmond. In his first year at Collingwood in 1977, Tommy took the team from last into a Grand Final. Late in his career, legendary Tiger Kevin Bartlett was seriously considering joining Hafey at Victoria Park, but was dissuaded by Tommy himself. 'I still think you may regret that if you look back in time and leave the Tigers,' he was told.

So loved and admired was Hafey that at 79 he became an ambassador for Jeep, a Chrysler Australia spokesman saying, 'Tommy Hafey's inspirational and remarkable work ethic and fighting-fit physique clearly embodies our Jeep "Don't Hold Back" mantra. We couldn't find a more fitting ambassador to help celebrate 70 years of Jeep in Australia.' Tommy did a series of TV campaigns, typically in shorts and runners, showing off a frame men half his age would have been proud of.

He remained a role model to the young and old alike, even into his 80s regularly visiting schools and clubs encouraging young people to get the best out of themselves. After one school visit, he received a Christmas card from a teenager who said he had been contemplating suicide until being inspired by Tommy's message, passion and zest for life.

On arrival at Tigerland for the 1966 pre-season, Tommy was as fit as any of the club's most-feted senior players. 'All of a sudden,' said Kevin Bartlett, 'we had this coach who was beating everyone around the Tan and beating everyone in the 400s and the 200s. It was quite remarkable.'

BESOTTED: No one loved football as much as clean-living fitness-disciple Tommy Hafey

Other than his habitual fish and chips on Wednesday selection nights, Tommy was the ultimate fitness fanatic, his idea of fun to go marathon running. He and wife Maureen lived at the Mentone end of Beaumaris and each morning Tommy would sprint up the steep pathways criss-crossing from the Charman Road cliffs to the Mentone beach walkway followed by another round of sit-ups on the headland before heading home.

One fine summer Sunday, Tommy announced his intention to run to their holiday shack 65 kilometres away in Sorrento. 'Come down in the car with the kids later,' he said. Maureen Hafey picked her exhausted husband up on the side of the road at Dromana. 'He was so dehydrated, he'd run nearly 40 kilometres – and he was 38 at the time … looking back on it now, it was a pretty silly thing to do, as it was so hot, but we never doubted that he could do it.'

In 11 years at Richmond, Hafey won four premierships and coached the Victorian State side. He always believed himself privileged to be coach of the club he'd barracked for all his life. For years his parents had run a milk bar in nearby Bridge Road, just down from the ground.

Hafey was universally loved and admired among the playing group. He'd ring each of his players on a Friday night, reinforcing his confidence in them to play an important team role. 'It's true that we wore the Richmond colours and were called Richmond, but ultimately we played for him,' Bartlett said. 'If we lost, we felt we'd let him down.'

Tony Jewell, also a Richmond premiership coach, said Hafey was 'totally obsessed' by football and would talk it, if he could, '24 hours a day, every day'. 'Once I stayed down with Tom and Maureen at Sorrento. On the front page of the morning paper was a story about Russia invading Czechoslovakia and I said so to Tom. "What?" said Tom. "Can they make the four?!"'

For a time St Kilda's Trevor Barker was dating Tommy and Maureen's daughter Karen and would come down to Sorrento to stay.

They'd have some late nights and Tommy could never understand why Trevor wasn't up at first light to share a cuppa with him. 'No thanks, Tommy,' he'd say. 'I might sleep in a little longer today …'

'The kids would have only just come home an hour or so earlier!' said Maureen. 'They were such fun days. All the footballers were like family with us. They'd come to us and we'd go to them. It still happens now. There's such a great fraternity amongst everyone.' Maureen was known to cook for the entire football team. 'And they took some feeding,' she told me.

Once, when organising a reunion, Tommy even placed an advertisement in the Hobart *Mercury* asking for the much-travelled Alan 'Bull' Richardson to contact him. The Bull had to field 14 phone calls from former teammates asking him 'to ring Tommy'. He duly made the celebration.

Teetotaller Tommy was a disciple of Percy Cerutty, who trained Australia's 1960 Rome Olympics Gold Medallist Herb Elliott on the sand dunes at Portsea. Never beaten over 1500 metres, Elliott had an incredible last-lap kick that he attributed to the sand sprints Cerutty insisted on.

During the 1967 pre-season, Hafey took his Richmond players down the coast one weekend for two days of hell that they still talk about. He instigated a third night of training at Olympic Park where the players often had to complete ten 400-metre sprints with only a minute or two of break-time in between. Older players fell away and younger, ambitious ones thrived on the fitness demands and the fresh opportunities.

Having just missed the finals in his first year back from the bush in 1966, Hafey had all three of the club's teams in the Grand Final in 1967: the seniors, reserves and Under 19s.

On the eve of Grand Final day, Cerutty wrote a letter to Hafey, which he read to the players pre-match. 'Anyone,' Percy said, 'could keep with the great Herb Elliott for three laps, but he would always draw away in the fourth and final lap.'

'Fellas,' said Hafey with growing excitement, 'Herb Elliott was never ever beaten. Anyone can keep with a good side for three quarters, but not for the fourth … it's no use finishing runners-up. Let's go out there and eat 'em alive.' Elliott was in the rooms before the game. His mere presence was inspirational to the younger ones, particularly a 19-year-old Royce Hart.

At three-quarter time with the Tigers ahead by just two points, Hafey again talked of Elliott's incredible finishing burst which no one in the world could match. Raising his voice, Hafey said, 'This last quarter will sort out the men from the boys … this is the time when all good players rise to the occasion … we can do this. No one remembers who finishes second. Let's burst … let's run 'em off their feet … Come onnnn …'

Geelong had the more experienced team and was being brilliantly led by its legendary captain and No. 1 ruckman Graham 'Polly' Farmer. Play was blisteringly fast and even – the scores levelling four times in the first 15 minutes of the quarter. Where was the famous Elliott burst? On a kick-off, the teenage champion Hart, characteristically jumping from the side, took one of the greatest of all marks on the shoulders of Peter Walker, Geelong's powerhouse centre half-back. Ruckman John Ronaldson, who had replaced the suspended Neville Crowe, kicked a second wonderful goal from the boundary. Almost 110 000 were out of their seats and roaring. It was one of the great finishes.

Deep into time-on, another Tiger tyro, 20-year-old Kevin Bartlett snapped the sealer. Despite several near-misses by Geelong and a mark by Richmond's captain Fred Swift which Geelong fans still claim was taken in the fourth row of the seats at the back of the Punt Road goals, the Tigers had won their first flag in almost 25 years.

It was wild night in Richmond town. Swift was named Lord Mayor for the night, given the keys to the city and the council's drink's cupboard and enjoyed himself fully, repeatedly ringing the

PARTY TIME: Captain Freddie Swift, Francis Bourke (long sleeves) and Bill Barrot (nearest to camera) celebrate Richmond's 1967 flag win over a fast-finishing Geelong. Years later Bourke conceded that the best team of the year had finished second. Ever-honest, he said, 'We pinched it from them.'

Town Hall bell. Meanwhile, Tommy was also happy relaxing – with a cup of tea. It was to be the first of four Richmond premierships in the club's mightiest era. And Cerutty had a hand in all of them, Hafey famously bringing him in pre-match before the 1973 play-off to give the players a 'gee-up'.

'The paint nearly peeled off the walls when Percy let fly,' said one of the players Rex Hunt. 'Percy had come into the rooms ranting that the lady at the Sorrento post office had refused to send his telegram so he'd come in himself to read it. Hafey had obviously set it all up – it was a brilliant ploy involving a man who inspired us all.'

ONE OF THE GREAT MARKS:
Tiger Royce Hart's spectacular mark from the side against Cat Peter Walker late in the 1967 Grand Final

If Richmond was ever beaten, the players knew that Tommy Hafey would take his revenge at Tuesday-night training. A shock loss to unfashionable Fitzroy in the opening round of 1970 saw the reigning premiers given three hours of non-stop running the following Tuesday night. 'We ran so many laps of Indian file we were dizzy,' said Hart. 'Tommy was furious. We'd won the flag the previous year and Tommy reckons we'd all believed our own publicity. If we had, he certainly brought us down to earth that night.'

Tommy loved to remind Kevin Sheedy how he got to live the high life in Sydney in the late '80s after Sheedy had knocked back the head coach role at the Swans. 'Thanks Kevin,' he wrote in a foreword to one of Sheedy's books, 'it was a wonderful experience for Maureen and me, living close to the beach, having club functions at the Bourbon and Beefsteak in the Cross and trying to educate the people of Sydney about our game. There were some pretty good moments, too, especially the time [in 1987] at the Sydney Cricket Ground when we thrashed your Bombers by 163 points ...'

Few made as important a contribution to football. And none remained as passionate, focused and giving. Tommy spoke to our Australian Cricket Society lads at our annual footy launch just a year before he passed. So worked up and involved was he that even the 70-year-olds wanted to run through a brick wall. Long-time Tiger historian Bill Meaklim said oxygen had to be called for once after Tommy went into overdrive at one of his speeches. 'He gave his all, each and every time,' he said.

On the back of Hafey's business card was a message:

Every morning in Africa a gazelle wakes up. It knows it must run faster than the fastest lion or it will be killed.
Every morning a lion wakes up. It knows it must outrun the slowest gazelle or it will starve to death.
It doesn't matter whether you're a lion or a gazelle. When the sun comes up you had better be running.

Tommy Hafey transcended club loyalties. He was loved and admired by all. When he died in 2013, it was like a death in the family.

AHEAD OF HIS TIME

Geelong coach Graham 'Polly' Farmer was way ahead of his time – and just as elite off the field as he was on, according to many lucky enough to have played under him. 'He was so professional in everything he did,' said Kevin Sheehan, who has had a lifetime in football. 'Back in the '70s when he was coach, we were part-timers, training three and four times a week. Polly wanted us to train twice a day almost every day. He was a perfectionist and his skills were extraordinary. Even into his 40s he was still the most skilful on the track. Stab-passes, drop-punts, reverse torpedoes, handpassing … it was all at such an elite level. He didn't drink or smoke. Those who couldn't totally commit or embrace his methods didn't have great careers. They were the dissatisfied ones and would backstab.

'I thought he was a fantastic coach and mentor and while we didn't make the finals [in three years] under him, in 1974 when we finished sixth, he blooded 14 players, more in one year at the club than hardly any other. His ability to coach and

AHEAD OF HIS TIME: Graham 'Polly' Farmer was ultra-professional on and off the field

Ken Piesse Collection

communicate was underrated. It was a pleasure to play under him.'

One day at Geelong, Sheehan was 19th man and not expecting to get a run until well after half-time as in those days, once a player was replaced, there was no coming back on. 'Poll was big on always doing the disciplined, team-oriented things and this day he was unhappy with the way "Ferret" [Paul Sarah] had started,' he said. 'He missed a handpass and the message came to get him off. It was barely 10 or 12 minutes into the game. I started warming up in front of the members in front of what was the AR 'Jack' Jennings Stand and just as I was taking off my tracksuit top, Ferret stood on the shoulders of his opponent as he could do and took a fantastic mark and kicked truly. Within a minute he'd added another. Here was I standing on the edge of the boundary ready to go on and looked quizzically upstairs back at the box with my hands out, as if to say, "Surely, Poll, you can't take him off now?" Polly nodded and indicated to me to sit down again. Paul stayed on. It was the one and only time I ever overruled the coach!'

THE MOST RECLUSIVE MEDALLIST OF ALL

Of all of post-war football's Brownlow Medallists, Peter Box was always the most media-shy and elusive. Centre half-forward in Footscray's 1954 premiership team, despite being just 179 centimetres (five feet, nine inches), Box was gone almost as quickly as he arrived, playing just 107 games in six

League seasons. He went bush, shunning reunions and his old teammates.

My colleague and mentor Greg Hobbs was keen to interview him for his long-running 'Bushwhacked' column in the *Sporting Globe*. Greg would be away for weeks with his photographer Ray Jamieson, chatting with and interviewing old footballers and cricketers all around Victoria, Tasmania and beyond.

Peter Box's story always intrigued him. Greg was in Morundah having a beer with the locals when Box's name came up. 'Doesn't he live here in the Riverina?' asked Greg.

'Yeah, but you'll never get to him. He's so private he hardly talks to anyone.'

They kept chatting and yarning and Greg found out that Box's partner worked at the local high school. When he paid her a visit, she also said that Box was unlikely to talk. 'But Greg,' she said, 'he does have some very promising sons. All three play. One is as tall as Peter already and he's only 14. He could even play Teal Cup [the then national Under 16 championships], he's that promising. That could be a good way to get him talking ...'

Hobbs and Jamieson found Box 20 miles north working in a shearing shed. 'I don't talk to journalists,' he immediately said.

'That's all right,' said Greg. 'We didn't come to talk to you. We want to talk about your sons. Apparently the eldest is very good ... a real chance ... that must make you very proud ...'

Box looked Greg up and down and said, 'Maybe it is time for a break.' He sat outside telling yarns for an hour. A double-page feature on the most reclusive Brownlow Medallist of all was Greg's reward. 'We

FRONT PAGE: Greg Hobbs tracks the reclusive Brownlow Medallist Peter Box to a shearing shed in the Riverina

must have done 500 'Bushwhacked' columns, from Brownlow Medallist Roy Wright to cricket's Jackie Badcock, and that was the most special one of all,' he said.

Box told Hobbs he hadn't seen a Footscray game in 20 years, and was happier working in a wool shed than at the MCG. 'Fact of the matter is I am a bloke who doesn't mix well with other people,' he said. 'I was like that even when I played football for Footscray.' It was a stellar interview.

THE FOX

Even in his twilight years at South Melbourne, Norm Smith was the hardest of taskmasters. No one was exempt to a Smithy 'cook' – not even the club's champion captain Bobby Skilton. Late one day 'Skilts' aimed a banana kick at the goals from a big angle only to hit the post. Smith thought he was posing and told him so, as only he could. A chastened Skilton arrived home quieter than usual and told wife Marion about the spray. 'It was a good one,' he said, 'as only Norm can deliver 'em.'

Marion Skilton was furious and said she was going to give Smith a piece of her mind that night at the club's cabaret function. One of their boys had been ill and on arrival, Smith made a beeline for Marion and before she could get a word in, asked about him and said how he was terribly sorry to hear that he'd been unwell. Her rehearsed payback went undelivered. They didn't call Smithy 'the Fox' for nothing.

MEETING AN IDOL IN THE FLESH

The Reporters' Room at the now defunct Melbourne *Herald* newspaper in the 1960s was a motley mix of the inspiring, the insipid, the brilliant and the big-noting bullshit artist. It was an afternoon paper with four editions produced under relentless pressure and was a school of experience and university of hard knocks for any young journalist. Mentoring was unheard of. As a place of work it was enthralling, intriguing and frightening.

As a teenager straight from year 12, Ken Davis – one of my long-time colleagues and good mates – reckoned it was a wonderland like no other. Covering law courts, police rounds, state politics mixed with double checking the TV guide, the shipping and the market prices was a heady mix. But for budding Melbourne sportswriters like 'KD' and I, the lure of covering an AFL match for *The Herald*, or in my case the *Sporting Globe*, was something very, very special.

KD's dream was to be part of legendary football writer Alf Brown's Saturday team – in those days there were six matches on each and every Saturday, all starting at 2.10 p.m. A hangover to one of the regular writers and a lack of reserves one wintery Saturday morning saw fate give KD a breakthrough debut game between Footscray and Geelong at the Western Oval. 'Arrange to pick up Rex Pullen from *The Sun* on the way at the Post Office Hotel in St Kilda,' Alf growled down the phone. 'Good luck and stay sober.'

In his tiny Mini Minor, KD arrived at the hotel at 11.30 a.m. and duly left with Rex but not before four quick full-strength beers had been downed. Rex was a lovable guy, who preferred men to women. He took his job seriously and didn't think his sexual orientation mattered one way or the other. Some in football were wary of him. Others just loved him because of his colourful personality.

As could occur back then, the public and the journos could go into the rooms before a game. KD's eyes were out on stilts. Footballs were whistling past at close range. The smell of the liniment was intoxicating. In front of him were some of the big boys: Gary Dempsey, Laurie Sandilands and Freddie Cook bumping and bashing into each other.

Rex strode confidently to the rub-down tables and gave a naked bum a friendly pat. 'Hi, handsome,' he said. With that, the torso turned over and KD was staring at the naked body of his greatest idol. 'Ted Whitten meet Ken Davis,' said Rex. 'He's on Alf's team. It's his first match.'

Open-mouthed and uttering gibberish, KD put his hand

into Whitten's infamous vice-like grip. And lived. 'Delighted to meet you,' he said.

'Mr Football' never forgot Ken's name. Nor anyone else's. He was the ultimate legend.

A ONE-OFF

The hot-gospelling pocket dynamo Alan 'Killa' Killigrew was the father of the fire-and-brimstone speeches featured at almost every club on every wintertime Saturday in the '60s, '70s and '80s.

His sermons to his players were always colourful and passionate and at all times about the team, rather than the individual.

His teams, especially at St Kilda, may have lacked depth and talent, but every week they would go out determined to win. Once he asked his team to win for a former Saint 'whose bones are rotting alongside the Kokoda Trail'.

So powerful and emotive was Killa's address that football writer Alf Brown reported some players were crying as they ran down the race again after half-time. 'Killa' was running after them, slapping them on the back with a 'Win for 'Arold … Win for 'Arold!'

Killa reckoned leaders from the time of Julius Caesar had been inspiring their troops before battle. 'A lot of players can do well for limited periods,' he'd say, 'but they can't keep it up all day. The muscles, sinews, tendons start crying "enough". It is then a coach's job to drown out those distress cries and inspire them to go hard and harder again.' He was a one-off, was Killa.

A LASTING LEGACY

Few championed the play-on game before its time like Len Smith, a quiet, humble man who coached more matches than he played and celebrated the game and those who achieved success like a fond father.

MASTER STRATEGIST: Len Smith plans tactics with four of his most faithful, from left Graham McKenzie, Kevin 'Muzza' Murray, Alan 'Butch' Gale and Graham Wright. He is using Weeties football figurines, now among the most collectible of early 1960s memorablia
Roar of the Lions, Fitzroy Remembered, 1883–1996, *Garry Hutchinson, Rick Lang and John Ross, Lothian Books, Melbourne, 1997*

Allan Jeans was just one to swear by Smith's methods, admiring his tactical acumen and treasuring the many generous letters he received from his rival coach and mentor.

Smith coached the Fitzroy Under 19s for 13 years before becoming the club's senior coach at Brunswick Street in 1958, taking the Lions from 11th into the finals.

His achievements were dwarfed by those of his brother Norman, Melbourne's coach of the century, but as Jeans always insisted, Norm Smith had the players, Len didn't, yet his legacy was just as lasting.

Smith shared his football handbook with Jeans and others. It consisted of more than 50 typewritten pages and included old-fashioned football sense still relevant today. He spoke in simple, easy-to-understand terms and often used tiny, plastic footballers he'd collected from cereal packs to illustrate positioning and set plays. He was a trailblazer with vision who lived, ate and breathed football.

WORDS OF WISDOM

Included as part of Smith's much-thumbed football notes were several dozen of his favourite proverbs, so applicable to football:

- Success consists of getting up once more than you fall down.
- The past is a springboard, not a sofa. Be more interested in the future. This is where you must live your life.
- No really great man ever thought himself so.
- He that nothing questions, nothing learns.
- Nothing is more unjust or capricious than public opinion.
- As long as I have a want, I have a reason for living.
- Men easily believe what they wish to believe.
- He that never changes his opinions never corrects his mistakes.
- The best way to make your dreams come true is to wake up.
- Nobody can give you wiser advice than yourself.
- A winner never quits and a quitter never wins.
- Your teammates can win this game for you if *you* give them the opportunity.

Among Smith's 'Golden Rules' were to attack from the half-back line and avoid packs or crushes to help encourage peak teamwork.

He rebelled against the mark-and-kick game. He wanted tall running players on every line and tough engine-room players to trap the 'inside' balls and look for a handball to the outriders so they could use their speed and anticipation to run clear of the opposition. 'Getting the ball out of the packs allows for "Play On" which is attacking, attractive and goal-scoring football,' he wrote.

He championed the flick pass which had been in vogue especially in Tasmanian and South Australian football between-the-wars and used it as a vital weapon of his running game. He also favoured playing a seventh defender as a loose man to help launch attacks and for his forwards to mix and match and swap positions – anything to create some confusion for the opposition.

While Fitzroy lacked the depth of talent, especially up forward, to take full advantage of all of Smith's axioms, other teams like the Reg Hickey-coached Geelong teams developed a fast rebound game, with an emphasis on handballing. One of the Cat's golden greats Fred Flanagan told me how he and the rovers Neil 'Nipper' Tresize, Peter Pianto and Bob Davis would arrive early to training and practise their drills before Hickey even arrived. It made Geelong one of the most potent and attacking teams of all in the '50s, the team playing three Grand Finals in a row and winning back-to-back flags in 1951 and 1952.

Len Smith (1912–67) played 95 League games (19 with Melbourne and 76 with Fitzroy) from 1934 to 1945 and coached 107 games (92 with Fitzroy and 15 with Richmond) from 1958 to 1965. He suffered the first of his heart problems just when he was unravelling a star squad at Richmond destined to win four flags in a decade under Tommy Hafey.

BATHING WITH A HERO

It was a young Jack Dyer's first night at Tigerland and having trained, he was tip-toeing around when confronted by one of his idols – big, strong and strapping George Rudolph, who was basking in a huge, hot bath, full of sodium to help heal the aches and pains.

'G'day son,' said Rudolph. 'What's yer name?'

'I'm John Dyer sir … I'm here to play football … I hope.'

'Well, hop in and we'll have a yarn,' said Rudolph, easing himself up a little to allow Dyer to squeeze in at the other end.

Dyer said the two of them were as snug as two gorillas in a fish bowl, but they chatted away happily and Jack never did forget Rudolph's kindness in making a rookie feel comfortable.

TICKET TO FLY

Racial prejudice and vilification was a cruel reality in football in the '20s. Tiny Douglas Nicholls had his heart set on a League career but after six weeks at Carlton walked out without having played a game. He'd been shunned by the players and even the trainers who refused to rub-down a black man. One said he smelled. Several of the players said they couldn't see him because he wore black shorts.

There was no such colour bar as a teenager growing up in Cumeroogunga in northern Victoria, where Nicholls had become known as 'the Flying Abo' with his acrobatic leaping and scintillating speed. He was short, but could run like the wind and had exceptional ball skills which were to be his ticket to a new life. Joining VFA club Northcote, he played his first game in late May 1927, prompting one Melbourne *Herald* writer to comment:

> The ten-stone Hercules had the spring of a rubber ball, the speed of an emu and the strength of a giant. He could flash between followers, bounce higher than a six-footer and squirm through a pack. His kicking and passing on the run, his speed of turn, his spectacular leaps – like a little frog with spread legs – set the crowd roaring. They knew they were seeing as good a footballer as they were ever likely to see.

So impressed were his teammates that they had a 'whip-round' for him after the game. He played in the club's 1929 premiership at the Melbourne Cricket Ground, being one of the most outstanding afield. For two years running he was the Brickfielders' best and fairest player. Despite his popularity among his own, rarely would he play a game without being abused by opposition players and supporters for his colour and race. His brother Dowie also joined the club for a season, the brothers being nicknamed 'Chocolate' and 'Cocoa'.

After five years, Nicholls crossed to Fitzroy where he earned Big V selection and finished third in one club best and fairest behind Brownlow Medallists Haydn Bunton and Wilfred 'Chicken' Smallhorn. The club also gave him a job sweeping out the stands.

On his very first night at Brunswick Street, Nicholls was changing by himself in a remote corner of the room when Bunton walked across. 'What's the idea?' he asked. 'Why aren't you with the others?'

'You know how it is.'

Bunton bought his gear across the room and changed beside Nicholls, a ritual he repeated every Tuesday and Thursday.

Nicholls was one of the first Indigenous Australians to play 50 League games. Football gave him fresh status he could never have had back home at Cumeroogunga. 'I was quick on my feet and quick of eye,' he told one interviewer. 'I got it from my ancestors. They needed it to get out of trouble.'

For him, football was more than a game. It was his salvation. 'How I look forward to each Saturday's play,' he once said. 'The roar of the crowd is music. I revel in the tense atmosphere of the game and the preparations for it. So keen am I on football I'd go anywhere for a game. Once on a football field I forget everything else. I'm playing football and I never take my eyes off that ball. My aim is not only to beat my opponent but also to serve my side. I realise than in football, as in other things, its teamwork that tells.'

At just 157 centimetres (five feet, two inches), Nicholls conceded height to almost all his opponents, but possessed electrifying pace and could outrun them all. Before joining Fitzroy he'd won the Nyah and Warracknabeal Gifts. Embarrassed Carlton officials always claimed it was Nicholls' height that prevented selection, but it was purely a smokescreen. A couple of lines in *The Ballad of Haydn Bunton* by Ken Mansell and Peter Bell are particularly poignant:

When little Dougie Nicholls came down from the scrub,
football was a white man's game, at Carlton he was snubbed;

Just an Aborigine, they would not let him in. No one saw his
blinding pace just the colour of his skin.

One of Nicholls' proudest moments came when he was selected
for Victoria in 1935. He was the first Indigenous Australian to
be so honoured. Such was his popularity that during his time
with the Victorian side, police in Perth exempted him from the
after-dark curfew normally imposed on Aboriginal people.

On the train bringing the Victorians to Perth, Jack Dyer,
then 21, came into Nicholls' compartment. 'How are things
going, Dougie?' asked Dyer.

'I don't like you, Jack Dyer.'

'Why? What have I done?'

'You called me "nigger" on the football field.'

'I don't remember, Doug ...'

'Fitzroy was playing Richmond ... last year. We jumped for
the ball together. You pushed me: 'Out of the way "Nigger" –
that's what you said.'

'Doug, I've got a big mouth ... I'm sorry.'

Nicholls immediately accepted Dyer's apology, grinned and
said, 'Bet I was flying high, when I should have been down.
Can't help going after the ball. Coach gets mad at me.'

It was on that long train trip across the Nullarbor that
Nicholls saw and met Aboriginal people begging for money and
for tobacco at several of the stops. Their clothes were filthy. The
young ones wore nothing at all. The train guards weren't even
allowed to give them water. The authorities wanted them out of
sight and out of mind. Nicholls made a promise to himself that
he would do everything he could to improve their circumstances.
He wanted black and white to work together and in time he was
to become one of the most revered of all Indigenous Australians,
a lay preacher and pastor and a champion for his people.

More than any other Aboriginal sportsman of his era,
Nicholls helped to break through the white man's colour bar.
In 1957, he was the first Indigenous Australian to receive the
MBE and in 1972 the first to be knighted. He served as the

governor of South Australia from 1976 to 1977. He was also Father of the Year in 1962, the first Aboriginal justice of the peace in 1963 and even became the king of Moomba.

At his funeral in 1988, well-wishers lined Bell and High Streets almost all the way to Campbellfield. It was a fitting farewell.

A WIZARD OF ORGANISATION

Percy Page was one of the first of the great football secretaries and recruiting officers. His CV included the signatures of Hall of Famers from Melbourne and Richmond including Brownlow Medallists Stan Judkins and Dr Don

VISIONARY: Doug Nicholls the footballer

Cordner through to the likes of Ron Barassi snr, Norm Smith, Jack Mueller, Ron Baggott and Kevin O'Neill.

Most football staffs back in the '30s consisted of a part-time secretary and a once-a-week typist. Having worked a normal 40-hour week in his Queen Street printing business, Page, who was single, would work another 30 or 40 in football.

He was secretary at Richmond from 1924 to 1931 and secretary at Melbourne from 1933 to 1941, his partnership with the great between-the-wars coach Frank 'Checker' Hughes resulting in seven Grand Final appearances including three premierships, all in a row.

In mid-1980, after weeks of phone calls and being told that Mr Page didn't give interviews, he finally relented and out I

went to see him. 'You know, this is the first interview I have ever given,' he told me. Our conversation was included in the sports pages of the *Sunday Observer* and remains a favourite early interview of mine.

Mr Page said he followed the example and methods of Collingwood's Ernie Copeland, who was a backroom power for years at Victoria Park in the very early days. 'Ernie told me if I gathered the right people around me and worked hard I'd be a success,' he said. 'I was fortunate enough to have two great assistant secretaries, Jack Smith at Richmond and Pat Kennedy at Melbourne. I missed many matches while on recruiting missions, but I was able to as I knew everything would be all right in my absence.'

Other than the basic wage, Page never promised any money to recruits. At Melbourne, in particular, he was always able to offer employment opportunities, Melbourne Cricket Club membership plus the lure in September of playing on the 'Grand Final ground', the MCG. 'I never had favourites,' he said. 'They were all members of a team, whether they had to be dealt with or disciplined, it made no difference. I might have been hard but I never discriminated.'

Page started his football work at 6 a.m. each and every day. He regarded it as a relaxation from the worries of business. 'I had a lot of contacts in the bush and would go and see a lot of country games,' he said. All my information came from officials, umpires and former players.'

When he first worked at Richmond the disparity in payments staggered him. Some were receiving eight pounds to play, others 10 shillings. 'We [then] followed the Collingwood system of a flat rate of three pounds a player – there was a bit of unpleasantness over it and we had to clear some very good players, but it turned out all right. We were runners-up that year [1924].'

When Richmond slipped from the top four for two years in a row in the mid-'20s, Page took his annual holidays and without telling even his mother where he was going, headed to

Tasmania and the north-west coast to Ulverstone where one of his old mates from his Richmond 'cub' days, Checker Hughes, was captain-coach.

'I got my three weeks leave to coincide with their finals,' Mr Page said. 'I didn't tell anybody about what was on my mind. I didn't want to tip off any of the other clubs. I wanted to find out how Checker had progressed. The whole place was in raptures about him and at the end of the three weeks I said to him, "How would you like to coach Richmond next year?"

'He did and then when I went to Melbourne, he came too. I went to Melbourne on the condition I could choose my own head trainer and my coach. Checker had all the attributes of a great coach. He was a disciplinarian but he spent a lot of time with the players, treating them and their problems on a personal basis. He would go with me on our recruiting trips when he could. We built a terrific friendship.'

Richmond made five Grand Finals in six years under Hughes. At Melbourne, where he changed the club's nickname from the Fuschias to the Demons, he finished with three flags in a row, from 1939 to 1941, each of his teams having up to a dozen players from the bush directly targeted by Page. His last game as Melbourne's senior coach – as a fill-in for the great Norm Smith who had been sacked – came in 1965. Checker was 71.

Jack Dyer once said of Percy Page: 'He was the greatest. He'd give you nothing and take you nowhere. One Saturday one of our greatest players came up to him and asked for some new socks. "Take them home and get your sheila to darn them," he said. The player ripped them up and was refusing to play. The dispute wasn't resolved until about 1.30 p.m. on match day. Can you imagine that happening today?!'

While the recruiting of Jack Mueller remained Page's proudest moment as a 'bounty hunter', among the other prize signatures he was responsible for were Echuca's Kevin O'Neill who was part of the revered Richmond full-back line of Maurie

Sheahan, Martin Bolger and O'Neill – the Three Musketeers – and another champion Tiger defender, Rochester's Basil McCormack.

'O'Neill was coming down to Melbourne on an appointment to see Jack Irvine, the secretary at St Kilda,' said Mr Page. 'Somehow I was able to criss-cross him and met him outside Hartley's, the sports store people in Flinders Street. I knew he was a carpenter and had arranged a job. He signed with us.

'Basil McCormack was keen to play at North Melbourne. They were only just joining the League and had finished bottom the year before. Basil thought that would be the best place for him to get a game. I stood at Spencer Street on the platform arguing our case to him for a good 30 minutes if not longer. In the end I convinced him and he became a very great player for us. I don't think he was dropped even once [in 12 years].'

Page had left school at 13 and remained a bachelor until he finished with football. 'One thing which helped me was that I was single through all my Richmond and Melbourne secretary days. I still say that a secretary of a football club these days should be a single man. Recruiting is all important. The success of a football club depended on the quality of players you could assemble. It still does now.'

The Page system of finals was named in his honour.

9
Loves

'You are the girl that I want to
marry and have children with ...'

I JUST CAN'T TALK RIGHT NOW ...

So upset was Lenny Hayes after St Kilda's narrow loss in the 2009 St Kilda Grand Final that he failed to ring his girlfriend and wife-to-be Tara for a fortnight. 'The poor girl didn't know what to think,' said Hayes. 'It had been the best year of football in my life, but it had ended in such agonising fashion ...' He proposed 12 months later.

THE ONE

When Anthony Koutofides met Spasa Angeloski, the mother of Susie, the girl he intended to marry, in no-nonsense Macedonian style she immediately said, 'You're too tall [for her]!'

Smiling, Anthony put his arm around her and gave her a hug. 'I

GLAMOROUS: Susie Koutoufides with her footballing husband Anthony on Brownlow Medal night, 2006
Anthony Koutoufides, Kouta (Hardie Grant Books, Melbourne, 2007)

don't think I am,' he said. Daughter *and* mother were now both convinced. Yes, he was the one!

WILL YOU MARRY ME?

Jo Bailey was sure that this was the night her long-time boyfriend Stephen Silvagni was going to propose. They'd been together five years and she wanted their relationship to grow. Steve asked her to have dinner with him in Chinatown, but he still couldn't pop the question. She left the restaurant, devastated and took off to Noosa for a fortnight to be with her parents, refusing all his calls.

Not long after her return, he lobbed again, this time with flowers and said, 'Here we go,' and this time asked her to marry him. 'It was simple – and beautiful,' said Jo.

IT'S NOT THAT HARD, DERMOTT

One of Dermott Brereton's 'ex's' Brooke Morrow was a keen sportswomen and was sitting in the stands with Dermie one day, her beau having broken some ribs.

'She kept saying how she'd love to have a kick,' said Brereton, 'and I kept telling her that they might be a bit good for her.

'At the end of the game, all the kids came out to play and Brooke wanted to go on too. I found a kid who was kicking by himself and asked if we could join in. The kid went back 30 or so metres and kicked it to us and to my surprise Brooke got in front and took quite a nice mark. "Okay then … let's see you kick the ball," he said.

'With a picture-perfect technique, she hit the kid from 30 metres away with a drop-punt which spun beautifully – as if she'd been doing it all her life.

'"See," said Brooke. "It's not that hard."'

CHANCE ENCOUNTER

Paul Roos met the love of his life in a beer garden in San Diego. He and his Fitzroy teammate Brett Stephens had extended their American experience a little and having sampled Las Vegas, hired a car and found themselves at surf haven Pacific Beach.

The pair had dressed up – nice slacks, shirts with collars buttoned to the wrist and dress shoes – only to find that the locals were basically in T-shirts and thongs.

Roos was walking from the inside bar to the beer garden when he saw a lovely young girl sitting at the end of a table surrounded by five blokes. Fortified by multiple ouzos and Cokes, he made a deliberate detour and in his broadest Aussie said, 'G'day.'

Much to his surprise, he wasn't asked to immediately leave. Soon the original five drifted off and Roos was joined by Stephens and another girl.

'So, what do you boys do?' asked the girls.

Looking out at the nearby surf, the lads said, 'Surfers … professional surfers …'

'No way!' the girls burst into laughter.

They neither looked like nor acted like surfers. And if they were, they'd be down at the beach checking the swell … 'Try again, boys,' the girls said.

They got on famously and at the end of the night the girls gave the two a lift back to their hotel and agreed to meet the next day to see a college football game. But there was a complication over times and by the time the boys made it down to the hotel foyer, the girls had already left.

That night they went to a different bar and despite queuing couldn't get in. Apparently they didn't have the right photo ID passports …

Angry at the lack of local hospitality, they returned to the bar they'd been at the night before and ran into the same girls. One of them said she was heading to Australia with a friend for a holiday the following April so Roos gave her the number of the Fitzroy FC and told her to ring once she made it to Melbourne.

The boys kept on partying and thought little of the encounter until six months later Roos got a message to ring a girl named Tami. 'She sounds like an American,' said Fitzroy's receptionist. Sure enough it was the girl from San Diego.

A romance soon blossomed and after many more trips back and forth to the States, they married three years later. 'It was sheer luck,' said Roos. 'If that doorman had let us in at the second pub, we would never have seen them again …'

Tami and Paul have two children. They are a delightful couple. Paul is one of the great coaches and football brains of the generation.

TAMING A WILD BOY

It was the last home-and-away game of 1987 when Raelene Ratcliffe met Dougie Hawkins, king of the Western Oval. Doug bought her a drink and she reciprocated. But they didn't hit it off, not at all. 'I thought he was a real bighead,' she said. 'It certainly wasn't love at first sight.'

Until they met, girls according to the Hawkins 'rating system' came a poor third behind mates and drinking. But there was something about this no-nonsense girl from Daylesford …

'She wasn't concerned with footy or who I was – but what I was,' Hawkins said. 'Until we met, I was a rebel doing whatever I wanted, whenever I wanted. But when I played up I knew Rails would be out raging if we didn't go out together. She wasn't one to be possessive and sulk. And I didn't care for her being out without me. Raelene thought I was pretty rough around the edges, but she must have seen something in me.'

It was Raelene who proposed, via fax. Doug immediately said 'yes' – beginning the greatest partnership of his life.

KNOCK KNOCK

It was first light on this spring Sunday in Adelaide when Stephen Kernahan, having celebrated Glenelg's premiership all night, did a detour on the way back to the club to awaken his girlfriend Jenny. Scrambling in via her bedroom window, he said, 'Jen, I'm going [to Melbourne].' She was the first to know, even ahead of his parents, and after multiple trips back and forth over the ensuing months she joined him fulltime in Melbourne from 1987.

BREAKFAST WITH THE TRIMMINGS

The young, very pretty wife of a Carlton champion couldn't believe it when her hubby said that Ron Barassi had said it wouldn't be advisable to have sex before a game. It was September after all. Sudden-death finals ... his men were going to need all their strength.

'Whaaatttt?!' she said. 'Don't you think Ron is overstepping his jurisdiction ... just a tad?'

'Well ... err ... maybe ... but anyway, I might take the second bedroom tonight.'

The following morning bright and early, in she marched with breakfast in bed for her hubby, naked as the day she was born, except for a single long-stemmed rose held tantalisingly between her teeth.

Breakfast and the footy were immediately forgotten and afterwards at the game, the wife delighted in telling everyone that her husband was so exhausted that he could barely raise a gallop all day!

M ... M ... MATE ... CAN YOU DO ME A F ... F ... FAVOUR?

Peter 'Perc' Jones couldn't pluck up the courage to ask his wife-to-be Jan, then 18, out on their first date. So his mate Adrian Gallagher, pretending he was Perc, did it for him. 'I arranged for him to pick her up,' said Gallagher, 'but that started another attack of the nerves as she lived in Toorak and he had only a rusty old Holden to pick her up in! Fifty years on though, they're still together.'

'ARE YOU OKAY, DARLING?'

Back in the '50s there was no penalty for anyone 'unauthorised' from entering a sporting arena. When St Kilda rover Geoff Jones was downed in a match at the Junction Oval in 1954, his fiancée Dorothy, a trained nurse, jumped the fence and rushed to his side. 'What the &$#@ are you doing here?' gasped Jones, clutching his injured knee.

'Thank goodness there wasn't TV around in those days,' he said. 'I would never ever have lived it down. It'd still be on the repeats [and YouTube – *ed.*].'

'The boys ribbed me about it for years, but I still ended up marrying her!'

HAPPY DAYS

Allen and Marj Aylett were supposed to be celebrating their engagement at Allen's 21st party this particular Saturday night. But Allen, North's star rover, had been knocked out earlier in the day and while the party raged in the old wooden grandstand at Arden Street, Allen was still in the nearby trainer's room sleeping it off. It wasn't until almost midnight that he felt well enough to join the party. By then, Marj had already done all the speeches – 'and most eloquently too', everyone agreed. Sixty years on, they're still happily married.

SIXTY NOT OUT: Allen and Marj Aylett

RITZING IT

Bob and Elsie Rose married on 4 November 1950, intending to have a night at the swishest hotel in Melbourne before heading off to Adelaide on their honeymoon. Bobby hadn't factored in the Melbourne Cup and that every city hotel was booked out. They ended up staying at the Ritz in St Kilda, not the most salubrious of places, but it didn't bother them. Life was sweet whenever they were together.

LOVE AT FIRST SIGHT

Western Districts boy Stuart Spencer was besotted from his first meeting with a teenage Fay Clark at a Hobart ballroom in July 1950. Melbourne FC was in town for a game and afterwards for a dance at the trendy Belvedere. Little did he know that Fay was engaged and was to be married at 21.

'This young Melbourne footballer asked me to dance,' Fay, then 17, said. 'In those days it was common for boys to ask girls they didn't know to dance. I accepted not knowing that this was the moment that would change my life forever. Stuart introduced himself and told me that it was his first year with Melbourne and his first visit to Tasmania. He looked nice. He had auburn hair and broad shoulders and was also a pretty good dancer despite always making left turns which took a bit of getting used to. I told him that I had watched the game and we chatted a bit about the football, I told him that the only player I had heard of was Denis Cordner. When the music ended we both returned to our groups of friends. A couple of dances later Stuart approached me for a second dance. During that dance he asked me questions about my family, my job and where I worked. He told me that he was a country boy [from Digby near Warrnambool] and had come to Melbourne to play football. He worked at the Gas and Fuel Corporation in Melbourne. I remember thinking that he probably read meters, but I later found out that he worked at the head office.

'When Stuart approached me to have the last dance I wasn't

sure what I should do as the last dance was normally always reserved for the person who brought you. I hadn't told Stuart that I was engaged but when my fiancé told me he didn't mind if I danced with Stuart as he was a visitor, I was happy to accept. The memory of that dance was then etched in my mind forever. A popular song of the day, "Jealous Heart" was being played and Stuart said to me, "As another man seemed to have you occupied, I have a very jealous heart!" I knew Stuart was genuine. Then very seriously he said, "You are the girl that I want to marry and have children with." I was dumbfounded and unsure what to say but when the dance ended he asked if there was any chance he could take me home even though he could see that I appeared to have a partner with me. When I told Stuart that I had come with someone else, he said he was very sorry and politely said goodnight. I felt completely unnerved and guilty that I had not been honest and told him I was engaged, but something stopped me. I didn't know it then but as the future would reveal maybe it was really love at first sight for both of us. My engagement ring was on my finger but he hadn't noticed it. My left hand was on his shoulder as we danced. The next day I was aware that Stuart and his words were on my mind but I tried to dismiss it as a footballer just being flirty. I didn't expect to ever see him again.

'I had told my mother about Stuart and a few days later we were listening to a sports session on the radio when the subject turned to the match between Melbourne and the Tasmanian team. We pricked up our ears when Stuart's name was mentioned and he was described as a very young new recruit to Melbourne who was showing a lot of promise, adding he was a very shy boy from Portland who had never seen a tram before he arrived in Melbourne. I turned to Mum and said, "He didn't seem that shy to me."

'A week later I was at home in bed with the "flu" when my fiancé came to see me with a letter in his hand. "This letter is for you," he said. "It was sent over from the Commercial Bank, the name is also wrong ... I suspect that it is from that Melbourne footballer." The letter had been addressed to Pat

YOUNG LOVE: Fay and Stuart Spencer. They met at the
Belvedere, Hobart's swishest nightclub
Fay Spencer Collection

Clark at the Commercial Bank and of course I was Fay Clark
and I worked at the Commonwealth Bank. How about that for
fate intervening?

'In the letter Stuart asked me to send him a photo of myself
as I was continually on his mind and he wanted to keep in touch
with me although he thought I may be occupied by someone
else. I answered his letter without a photo and said that I did
have a boyfriend. I simply couldn't let myself tell him that I
was engaged. I realised that there was a mutual attraction, but I
thought that it would pass and I should be sensible and not turn
my life upside down by continuing this unlikely romance. Stuart
replied a couple of days later and he said he was disappointed
I still hadn't sent the photo, but would really like to keep the

correspondence going. In my next letter to him I did promise that if I was in Melbourne I would ring. He had changed his job from the Gas and Fuel Corporation and was now working with a former Melbourne player Dick Taylor who had taken Stuart under his wing. After several letters had been sent between us, I decided that I couldn't continue to write and Stuart responded saying that he understood but reminded me that if I was to change my mind would I please get in touch with him if I ever came to Melbourne? He enclosed his phone number again and in my last letter to him I did promise that if I was in Melbourne I would ring him.'

In 1951, Clark broke her engagement. Her fiancé was a kind man, but she realised he was not the man with whom she could spend the rest of her life. 'That July, Mum and I went on a holiday to Melbourne staying with friends in Elsternwick. Mum knew that I often thought about Stuart and that I watched his football career through the newspapers, but I was surprised when she produced the phone number that Stuart had given me. She encouraged me to ring Stuart and I was reluctant to do so but the temptation was too much so I headed off to the nearest telephone box. Dear old Mum. What a matchmaker.'

Fay and Stuart were married for 56 years and had three children. After more than 200 games with Clarence where he also ran the family's transport business Green's, Stuart returned to the mainland and became chairman at Melbourne FC. He died in 2011. The limited-edition Stuey, My Life with Stuart Spencer *by Fay Spencer was a virtual sellout within weeks of its release in 2014.*

HONEYMOONERS

Fitzroy captain Frank Curcio was married on the morning of his club's Round 5 game against Geelong at Corio Oval in 1938. After being congratulated by his teammates, he was showered with confetti as he ran out onto the ground. Afterwards his new wife and he continued on to Lorne for their honeymoon.

10
Matches

'I believe they call you the Flying Doormat?'
Bruce just smiled. He wouldn't
talk, even for royalty.

WINNING FROM NOWHERE

It was the ultimate September 'steal' – and one of the greatest all-time solos …

Having lost a cliffhanging first final in the West, Paul Roos' Sydney was teetering on the verge of bombing out of the 2005 premiership race in straight sets.

A purposeful and highly disciplined Geelong had strangled the Swans at their own 'stop-start' game, keeping them to just two goals in the first half before widening their lead to 23 points in the opening minutes of the final term. Most of the 40 000 at the Sydney Cricket Ground bowed their heads. The team had been gallant all season, rising from the canvas against all odds. One more Geelong goal would finish their season there and then.

'[But] we never believed we were beaten [this day],' said Sydney midfielder, Irishman Tadhg Kennelly. 'We never looked at the scoreboard. No matter what the circumstances, we just had this enormous self-belief that something would happen to turn things around. And that something this day was Nick Davis.

'He was possibly the most talented player on our team, which is saying something given that "Goodesy" [Adam Goodes] had won the Brownlow Medal in 2003, "Hally" [Barry Hall] was the best power forward in the competition and "Micky O" [Michael O'Loughlin] was unbelievably skilful. But "Davo" was simply amazing. He could do things on a football field that no one else could. However, the problem throughout his career had been his dedication to the task … he certainly presented a challenge to "Roosy" and the leadership group to keep him on the right track. All that patience and effort paid off in 20 minutes of finals footy. He was sublime.'

Having run onto a beautifully palmed hit-out from Jason Ball and kicked truly in mid-term, Davis somehow found space in a congested forward line and marked in between two Geelong players within close range and added another. Suddenly Geelong's lead was just nine points and the fans – strangely quiet since the opening minutes of the game – were erupting with excitement. 'SYDNEY … SYDNEY … SYDNEY,' they chanted.

Kennelly involved himself in another incredible Davis goal, but the Swans were still behind and 30 minutes had elapsed. There were just seconds to go. 'The umpires had put their whistles away, with players throwing themselves in desperation at the ball, creating a series of stoppages,' Kennelly said. 'We managed to get it into our forward line for a ball-up, with just about every player on the ground inside our forward 50 metres … we needed to clear the congestion around the ball-up so I immediately went to the goalsquare to pull my opponent out with me and my teammates followed suit.

'I will never forget the next 10 seconds. Bally overpowered his Geelong opponent in the ruck and tapped the ball down into the space that had been created on one side of the contest. Running into that space at full speed was Davo. In one stride he got to the ball, which he never really had under control and got it onto his left boot. I was still in the goalsquare and I saw the ball sail off his boot but I wasn't sure whether it had gone through because of the angle I was at until I looked at his face. He'd kicked it! We'd won from nowhere. He'd kicked the last four goals of the game. I bolted over to him and started jumping around. His goal had come with just 10 seconds remaining.

'It was pandemonium afterwards. The crowd went ballistic. The noise was deafening. It was like we'd won the Grand Final. I did a TV interview on the ground and there was no way anyone could have understood anything I said, because not even I did. I was talking at 100 miles an hour. The changing room was abuzz. It was simply amazing.'

Having lost four of their first six matches of the 2005 home-and-away season, Sydney's momentum into September was irresistible. Its 7.14 (56) to 7.11 (53) defeat of Geelong in the second semi was followed by a come-from-behind preliminary final victory against St Kilda. A week later, in the closest Grand Final in 40 years, the Swans defeated West Coast to take their first premiership since 1933. And Kennelly, one of the team's heroes, did an Irish jig on stage as he accepted his premiership medal.

WRONG WAY, YEATA

It was the 1992 reserves Grand Final and Demon Graeme Yeats twisted out of a pack, had a bounce and wondered why no one was tackling him … he kept running before a teammate roared at him, 'Yeata, you're going the wrong &$#@ing way!' Luckily the Demons were 10 goals up at this stage, but it's still a favourite story at reunions.

COPPING IT ON THE CHIN

An out-of-touch David Schwarz was kick-chasing and had ventured beyond the centre line when confronted by Melbourne's runner: 'The coach [John Northey] wants you to get back into position.'

'Tell the coach to get &$#@ed.'

Garry Lyon overheard the exchange and immediately confronted Schwarz. 'Mate,' he said, 'I don't care how good you think you are, [but] if you get a message from the boss, you cop it on the chin and talk to him about it later on.'

NOT TO BE TOLERATED TODAY

An untold story from the 1991 Grand Final was of racial abuse, several leading Hawthorn players vilifying one of West Coast's stars, Aboriginal Chris Lewis. Their behaviour was fuelled by the belief that the volatile Lewis, one of the best players in the competition, could lose focus and be less valuable.

The taunts and abuse saw, in 2011, Dermott Brereton issue a public apology to Lewis, saying if he and his Hawthorn players had the moment again, they would have played football and not entered into the verbal jousts not be tolerated today.

'Lewi was our No. 1 target,' Brereton said. 'He was an extraordinary player, so we thought anything [goes] to curb his brilliance. We were wrong. Very wrong.'

A founding member of the West Coast squad in 1987, Lewis was club best and fairest in 1990 but earlier in 1991 when the Eagles played off, he was suspended for biting an opponent, prompting Hawthorn's Grand Final tirade. Come Grand Final day, when West Coast kicked the first four goals only to be overpowered

DAY TO FORGET: Chris Mainwaring shows the pain of West Coast's Grand Final defeat in 1991
Tony Greenberg/Inside Football

after half-time, Lewis had just five kicks and one handball. He kicked two goals.

TRAINING DRILL

Hawthorn was pumping Richmond during its glory era in the late '80s and after a goal, umpire Peter Cameron was back in the centre and suggested to the Hawk's ruckman Greg Dear that it was little more than a training drill. 'Oh, I don't know,' said Dear. 'There's no witches hats out here.'

YABBIE-ISMS

Hawthorn was at Carrara and changing in tiny portable rooms – not be tolerated today. Coach Allan Jeans was writing the team placements, player by player, on a whiteboard as the players started to whisk a ball around, preparing for the match. As he was writing, he sensed someone was behind him and turning around, he saw a man writing the team on a board of his own.

'What are you doing?' demanded Jeans.

'I'm writing the team down ...'

'Why ... why are you are doing that?'

'I'm doing it for the PA [public address system].'

It was hot and cramped and 'Yabbie' was quite flustered.

'Who's bloody PA?!' he said.

Another favourite Yabbie story came during a match at Princes Park. Long-haired Tommy Alvin had been running riot and at the main break, Jeans demanded, 'Who's on purple? Who's on purple?' referring to the popular Australian movie of the time *Alvin Purple*.

The players all looked blank until Dermott Brereton piped up, 'Do you mean Tommy Alvin, Yab?'

The whole room erupted.

A SPEECH TO SAVOUR

There were just minutes to go before Australia's Gaelic football Test at Dublin's Croke Park in 1984. Coach John Todd asked all the officials – and there were many – to leave the room while he addressed the players.

'We've had a very nice, happy time since we've been here,' he begun, 'but we're not here for sport, WE'RE HERE FOR WAR.'

First-time Australian representative Gary Pert said you could have cut the air with a knife as Todd continued. 'When you're lined up out there and they play the Australian anthem, I want

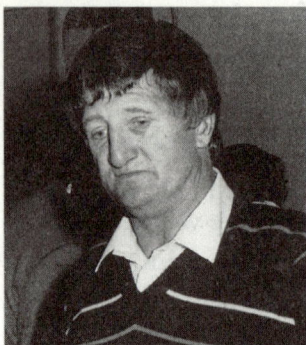

FAIR DINKUM: John Todd

you to think about representing your country and how important it is; not only to you, but to your parents, your girlfriends or wives, your mates, your coaches – everyone who got you here. Don't take your eyes off the Australian flag and think how much everyone back home would like to be in your shoes …'

So pumped were the Australians that follower Mark Lee flattened two of the Irish lads in the first minute. Australia won easily.

TEDDY RIDES AGAIN

The bus carrying the might of the Big V team was late and stuck in heavy traffic eight kilometres from South Australia's Football Park. The scheduled start to the big interstate clash was just an hour away. Everyone was getting fidgety, especially selection chairman Ted Whitten. One of the traffic lights was manned by local police and Ted yelled out to them, in typically colourful language, that if the team bus couldn't get a &$#@ing hurry on, there would be no &$#@ing match.

Several of the police hopped onto their motorbikes and with their blue lights flashing and sirens sounding, led the bus up the wrong side of the road all the way to Westlakes. 'It was an amazing feeling,' said Big V member Gerard Healy, 'belting up the motorway on the wrong side – and with the blessing of the boys in blue. We were all yelling and cheering. It was like Christmas. We got there with 55 minutes to go and won by a kick.'

NO RECOLLECTIONS

So concussed was Essendon's Kevin Walsh after a heavyweight charge from Hawthorn's Robert Di Pierdomenico late during the 1984 Grand Final that he didn't know what day it was. Finally able to make it to his feet, he was assisted to the rooms by head trainer John Kilby and asked, 'Can I wave, Killer?'

'Wave? Yeah, you can wave if you want.'

'I just want to let my Mum know that I'm all right.'

Walsh blacked out again inside and when he woke up, he couldn't work out just which final he was playing in.

AMAZING SCENES

It was the eve of the 1975 Grand Final. North Melbourne had lost the year before, and this year North Melbourne coach Ron Barassi was doing everything possible to fire his players to a first-up premiership. A psychologist had even been flown in from Hobart to speak to the players, one-on-one. Barry Cable and Doug Wade refused to see him. Brent Crosswell pretended he was asleep. 'If you couldn't motivate yourself for a Grand Final, you'd never get motivated for anything,' said Wade.

Wade had always been a renowned final's player. In his first final, the controversial 1962 preliminary final replay in which the Cats lost by five points, he kicked six goals (out of 10). In 1967, when the Cats made the Grand Final before losing in another gripping finish, he kicked eight in the first semi, five in the preliminary and four in the Grand Final.

His last game was the 1975 Grand Final when he kicked four against Hawthorn and Kelvin Moore, one of the best full-backs of any era. 'I had to play him like a backman. Those were my instructions,' Wade said. 'I was to stand down as much as I could, not attempting to mark. I picked up three goals from crumbs and with a little more luck could have had six or seven. That final was by far and away the most exciting of my four Grand Finals. We had lost the year before and while it was disappointing, especially for Ron Barassi, everyone sensed we were a year too soon. Sometimes if you have players who haven't played in finals before, it can be difficult for you. It doubled our resolve to go one better the following year. After we won, the feeling straight after the siren was exhilarating. Going back into the rooms and seeing all those supporters dancing and crying and hugging each other. Many had been waiting 50 years for that moment. [Ex-Kangaroo] Jack Edwards was there with the Channel 7 cameras. There were amazing scenes.'

A CLASSIC MISMATCH

'It wasn't the worst day of my life,' said Sandy Bay's playing-coach Rod Olsson, 'but it was up there.'

Having won every game of the 1973 season, Sandy Bay was the hottest favourite in Tasmanian Football League Grand Final history. The Bay had won the two previous premierships and boasted the competition's No. 1 player, dual William Leitch Medallist Olsson, a John Kennedy disciple from the mainland, whose team-first ethics, commitment and personal example had had a significant impact.

Sandy Bay's opponent was Hobart, a club that had limped into the top four. Somehow the Tigers had survived two heart-stopping finishes in as many weeks to qualify. And it had lost its four earlier games that year to the Bay by an average of 14 goals. It seemed such a classic mismatch that less than 15 000 bothered to attend at North Hobart Oval, the poorest attendance in three decades and in a town that lived, ate and breathed footy like few others.

The Sandy Bay hierarchy had booked an opulent premiership dinner that evening at Wrest Point for several hundred guests. The club's banner read '21 Today! 21 Today!' – forecasting the Bay's upcoming 21st consecutive victory for the season and 29th in a row since the previous July.

'There were no warning signs,' said Olsson. 'We knew if we played our normal handball game, moving it as fast as we could, we could win it again. Maybe we underestimated them a bit, maybe we were a little safety-first – but there was only a goal in it at three-quarter time.'

Olsson's frustrations at his team's failure to produce anywhere near their best bubbled over in the third term and he jumper-punched an opponent – 'a bloke named [Greg] Barnett who was a good strong player, a fly-in from Box Hill'.

'He'd been handing it out to some of our smaller players and I told him to pick on someone more his size. A boundary umpire saw it and ran straight at me but then must have changed his mind. I'd won the Leitch that year, maybe that made a difference. It was the only thing I reckon I ever did I should have been reported for and that includes all my time at Hawthorn. Hobart had the momentum and got a run-on and ended up winning by 20 points, but it was closer than that on the ground.

'Was it my worst day of football? No, the '63 Grand Final when we lost to Geelong was the biggest stage of all and we came second. It's something I regret each and every day as we never got another chance – not in my time anyway.'

Olsson was just 27 and Hawthorn's vice-captain when he left VFL ranks in 1970. The club won the premiership in 1971, but Olsson doesn't have any regrets as Sandy Bay was Statewide premiers and he met the love of his life, wife Elly, later that same year.

MUM'S THE WORD

The Australian All-Stars were playing Carlton in an end-of-season exhibition match at The Oval in London. Afterwards His Royal Highness Prince Charles was introduced to the players. Stopping at the ultra-shy and modest Bruce Doull with his near bald pate and headband, he said, 'I believe they call you the Flying Doormat?'

Bruce just smiled. He wouldn't talk, even for royalty.

BARRACKING FOR THE ENEMY

Having again been relegated to bench-sitting duties for Collingwood, Robert Rose, son of Bob, quietly celebrated each Footscray goal at Victoria Park in '72, willing the team his dad coached to an upset win. The Rose-charged Bulldogs won

11.14 to 7.14. 'That, for all of us, was a most delicious day,' said Peter Rose, another of Bobby's sons.

'YOU MONGREL, PRENTICE ...'

Peter Bedford was playing for South Melbourne when his teenage teammate Norm Goss from Port was flattened by Norm Bussell early in a game at Glenferrie Oval. A series of square-ups and melees resulted, as often occurred in those days. In the third quarter Bussell was chasing down a ball when his opponent, burly Riverina boy Jim Prentice saw his chance and steamrolled him, Bussell running straight off the ground with a dislocated collarbone.

'All you could hear in the next moments,' said Bedford, 'was John Kennedy's booming voice: "You mongrel, Prentice, you mongrel."

'Once John came to speak to us at Port Melbourne [Bedford's "home" club] and [administrator] Barry Kidd asked him if he needed a microphone.

'"Thanks Barry," said John. "But I think I'll be all right ..."'

SORRY RON, WRONG NUMBER ...

Dropped on the eve of the finals in 1968, Carlton's Ron Barassi was strictly a non-playing coach as his Blues qualified for the Grand Final and in a low-scoring thriller won the club's first flag for more than 20 years. The years have lessened Barassi's memories of the game, but he knows winger Gary Crane played a blinder and umpire Jeff Crouch could easily have awarded a late free kick to Essendon's bespectacled full-forward Geoff Blethyn – which may have made the difference.

But over and above the game itself, he recalls the troubles with his radio phone and a 'cross-line' with a local taxi driver. 'I'd be yelling instructions [from the stand] and this bloody taxi driver would be saying, "I don't think that's a good move, Ron!" Boy, did he get some hurry-up!'

WIN AT ALL COSTS

The very first overseas matches involving two League teams was in 1963 when Melbourne and Geelong played exhibition games in Honolulu (13 a side) and San Francisco (18 a side) at the season-end.

The Demons had been beaten by Geelong in the preliminary final just weeks earlier and coach Norm Smith was still livid at an opportunity missed. Having won the first game by a couple of goals, on arrival in America he immediately ordered a curfew on the players. 'He wasn't going to wait until the following season to prove we were better than them,' said Frank 'Bluey' Adams. 'That game [on a huge field at Golden Gate Park] was the roughest and toughest football match I ever played in. Harry Beitzel was umpiring and did his best but he had no powers to report anyone. The locals thought it was the way we played the game all the time. It was win at all costs and we did just that, which satisfied Smithy but didn't prove much else.'

Another of the Demons, key position player John Lord said Smith had insisted the players be in their rooms by midnight three nights before the game, by 11 p.m. two nights before and no later than 10 p.m. on match eve. 'Nobody dared break the curfew – except the night in Honolulu when they told us to get to high ground because they expected a tidal wave. Most of us went down to see it – totally ignorant to the consequences. Lucky for us, the tidal wave never eventuated ...'

Lord had stood on the sidelines at Honolulu nursing an injured shoulder, but played in San Francisco, where he was happy to kick a goal, only to see it disallowed by Melbourne reserves manager George Lenne who was goal umpiring. 'For years I questioned George about that decision, in jest of course, saying he was blind and should get glasses. Sadly he did spend the last 10 or so years of his life blind, but I didn't let up and he gave as much back to me, too ... he was a dear friend.'

BOILOVER OF THE CENTURY

Friday night, 5 July 1963. It was six o'clock and already pitch black. The temperature had tumbled into single digits and a scotch mist illuminated the lights of Melbourne. Wally Clark had called all the Fitzroy players to the Brunswick Street Oval for a Council of War. The bottom-of-the-ladder Lions, without a win all year, were opposing Geelong, prime premiership fancies. With favourite son Kevin Murray away on State duty, Clark was coaching the seniors for the first time. He'd seen all the newspapers. Norm Smith in *Truth*, Alf Brown in *The Herald* and Ian McDonald in the *Sporting Globe* all agreed: it was a Mission Impossible, especially as Graham 'Polly' Farmer, the biggest name in the game was playing club rather than State football. Who could possibly stop him?

Farmer's combination work with his rover Billy Goggin was uncanny. His habit of taking the ball out of the ruck contest and instantly handballing 15–20 yards (14–18 metres) to little Billy standing off the pack was a cornerstone of Geelong's attacks, Goggin's daisy-cutting passes invariably finding Doug Wade or the exciting teenage find from Tooleybuc, John Sharrock. As a pair, Farmer and Goggin were just about unstoppable. The Cats had A-raters on every line. Fitzroy were plodders; totally out of their depth. It shaped up as a classic mismatch. No one had picked the Roys. And much to the club committee's disgust, not one of Melbourne's radio stations, even the racing ones, were bothering to send a commentator.

As they trudged into the cricket club rooms for their meeting, avoiding the puddles after heavy rain earlier in the week, Camperdown recruit Brian Carroll approached Clark. His brother-in-law Geoff Daffy, a racehorse trainer, had tagged along. Could he come in and listen? 'Sure,' said Clark.

For 40 minutes Clark spoke earnestly and purposefully, outlining his expectations. He raised his voice only when reinforcing how everyone considered Fitzroy the rank outsiders, a 100-1 chance. 'But fellas,' he said, 'the ground's a bog. Geelong

Lions have shock win

Delirious supporters carried Fitzroy players off the ground after they had caused the biggest upset of the season by heading Geelong by 36 points.

The young Lions bewildered the Cats from the start and their marking, handball and teamwork shocked the Cats to give them their first win of the season.

Harvey (Fitzroy) won the toss and Fitzroy kicked to the railway end with the breeze. The ground was muddy and soggy.

Clever handball by acting captain Ron Harvey sent the Lions into attack and Beers from a free gave Hayes a chance but he only managed a behind.

They had another chance as they flashed forward with smart play by Sykes, Pert and Beers, but Bahen kicked poorly for another behind.

The Lions' teamwork was worrying Geelong at this stage, and they went forward again through Fry, Eastman and Hayes only to be stopped by a free to Callan.

Then they hit the target when Hirst shot the ball well into attack from a free and Lazarus marked well to boot the first goal of the match.

The Cats' first score finally came when Sharrock kicked the ball off the ground in the goal square for a behind.

SLOW START BY CATS

SCORES

	Fitzroy v. Geelong			
1st	3 4	22	0 6	6
2nd	3 7	25	1 6	12
3rd	8 11	59	2 9	21
Final	9 13	67	3 13	31

FITZROY
B.: Carroll, Lynch, Brown.
H.B.: Pert, Sykes, Beattie.
C.: Eastman, Bahen, Sleep.
H.F.: Hirst, Harvey, Beers.
F.: Miers, Lazarus, McCrae.
Foll.: Fry, Clements.
R.: Hayes.
19, 20: Slocum, Fitzgerald.
Slocum replaced Hayes in last quarter.
Fitzgerald replaced Beers in last quarter.

GEELONG
B.: Callan, West, Watts.
H.B.: S. Lord, Goodland, Devine.
C.: Routley, Miller, Walker.
H.F.: Hamer, Ryan, Williams.
F.: Polinelli, Sharrock, Yeates.
Foll.: Farmer, Wooler.
R.: Goggin.
19, 20: Brushfield, Vinar.
Vinar replaced S. Lord (injured leg) at half time.
Brushfield replaced Ryan in last quarter.

Umpire: Gaudion.
At Fitzroy. — Official

By Ian McDonald

McCrae pounced on the ball after a ball up near the goal square and snapped another goal to have the Cats struggling.

Watts gave a free against Lazarus soon after and the young forward brought a tremendous roar from the stand with a glorious goal to put the Lions 3 points in front.

For the quarter, — Fitzroy 19 marks, 10 frees; Geelong 19 marks, 8 frees. Out of bounds 10.

At three-quarter time. — Fitzroy 8.11.59; Geelong 2.9.21.

Scorers for the quarter. — Fitzroy: Bahen, 0, 2, 0; Hayes, 2, 0, 0; Lazarus, 1, 0; Miers, 0, 1, 0; McCrae, 1 0, 0. Geelong: Wooller, 0, 0; Yeates, 0, 1, 0; Polinelli, 0, 1, 0; Sharrock, 0, 0.

Vinar, Polinelli and Williams all had shots and missed as Geelong fought to try and reduce the lead way.

Then they ran up string of three successful behinds through Polinelli, Farmer and Ryan.

They were attacking hard but they needed an avalanche to catch the speedy Lions.

Geelong bombarded the forward line and they finally broke through from Vinar, who

BOILOVER: A cutout from the Saturday night *Sporting Globe* match report in July 1963 when Fitzroy stunned premiers-to-be Geelong
John Hayes Collection

may have the skill, but we have the desire. And if we jump them early, who knows what can happen.'

He paused and went through the basics, the non-negotiables. It had to be four quarters. No shirkers. No retreat. Plenty of guts and determination. Stick to the team rules. No kicking across goal. Attack down the grandstand side, defend to the boggier woodyard side. 'And fellas,' said Clark, pausing and running his eye back and forth over the whole group, 'everyone has to run and run and run – just like we did out here on Saturday. Tomorrow we're going to use lots of handball. They won't be expecting it. Flankers: at all times you must be positioned inside

| 16 | THE FOOTBALL RECORD | | | July 6, 19— |

FITZROY

GEELONG

(Maroon & Blue) Coach—Kevin Murray	G	B	(Blue & White) Coach—Bob Davis	G	B
1—Sykes, D.			2—Nicholls, E.		
2—Murray, K. (C.)			3—Wooller, F. (C.)		
3—Pert, B.			4—Lord, A.		
4—Powell, I.			5—Farmer, G.		
5—Bond, C.			6—Lord, S.		
6—Eastman, W.			7—Callan, T.		
7—Clark, W.			8—Vinar, P.		
8—Carroll, B.			9—Devine, J. (v.c.)		
9—Fry, R.			10—Sharrock, J.		
10—Williams, B.			14—Scott, I.		
11—Lynch, A.			15—Rice, C.		
12—Beers, B.			16—Eales, C.		
13—Bahen, J.			17—Herrod, D.		
14—Miers, M.			18—Hamer, G.		
15—Hayes, J.			21—Brown, J.		
17—Sleep, C.			22—Goodland, K.		
18—Duncan, S.			23—Wade, D.		
19—Harvey, R. (v.c.)			24—Fox, J.		
20—Campbell, G.			25—Lowe, B.		
22—Haag, S.			26—Ryan, W.		
23—Pollock, B.			27—Rosenow, G.		
24—Doubleday, G.			28—Watts, J.		
25—Fitzgerald, B.			29—Routley, H.		
26—Beattie, R.			30—Brushfield, B.		
27—Slocum, R.			31—West, R.		
31—Lazarus, G.			33—Williams		
33—Dixon, J.			34—Walker, P.		
34—McCrae, I.			35—Goggin, W.		
35—Brown, N.			36—Polinelli, A.		
44—Lovett, E.			37—Miller, W.		
47—Hirst, A.			40—Yeates, J.		

FIELD UMPIRES

1—Andrew, W.	3—Brophy, R.	5—Gaudion, B.	7—Schwab, R.
2—Blew, D.	4—Crouch, J.	6—Nunn, R.	8—Toohey, R.

THE TWO TEAMS: The *Football Record* centre pages from the 6 July encounter

*MCC Library/Ken Piesse/*The Miracle Match

WAL'S BOYS: Wally Clark (right) with some young Lions from '63, Brian Pert (left), John Hayes, John Bahen, Graham Campbell, Ray Slocum and Ian Aston. Four played on 'Miracle Match' day
Ken Piesse, Miracle Match *(www.cricketbooks.com.au, Mt Eliza, 2014)*

your opponents. Push 'em to the boundary. Don't give 'em any room.' He reinforced the importance of every position and how one weak link could be fatal. To full-back Allen Lynch, one of Fitzroy's best all year, he emphasised how dangerous 'young Sharrock' was. 'He's a left-footer, Al, so always attack his right side, no matter what. He'll always turn back into you.'

You could have heard a pin drop. Few were more admired or respected than the crew-cut, roly-poly brick salesman. Having played 100 games, he'd continued to serve the club as playing-coach of the seconds. He was both mentor and mate to dozens, from the March champions on.

Working his way through the lines, Clark came to the rucks and paused. 'Bryan,' he said, addressing country boy Bryan Clements, not yet 21. 'You can win it for us.'

'You have the biggest job of all: Polly Farmer. If we can negate him or just break even with him, we're in this game.'

FIVE OTHER REMARKABLE RESULTS

2001: Few seemed as invincible as Essendon in 2000 and 2001. Having been beaten only once all year in 2000 to win the flag comfortably, the Bombers won 14 of their first 16 games again in 2001 to be three games clear. The Round 16 match against North Melbourne at the MCG saw the Bombers overturn a record deficit of 69 points 10 minutes into the second quarter to win by two goals, 27.9 (171) to 25.9 (159). Only two other teams had also overturned a 10-goal deficit to win: Hawthorn v St Kilda at Waverley in 1999 and Collingwood v St Kilda at Victoria Park in 1970.

1970: Fitzroy's upset of reigning premiers Richmond in the Round 1 'Royal Match' at the MCG, the game the first to be played on a Sunday in honour of the royal visitors including Queen Elizabeth II and Prince Philip. A few of the players including Fitzroy's captain Kevin Murray called for their false teeth before being introduced to the royals at half-time. Having trailed by five points at the main break, the Lions won 16.20 (116) to 14.12 (96). Accusing his team of complacency, a furious Tommy Hafey ordered three hours of non-stop running for his Tigers the following Tuesday night. The Lions had finished 10th the previous season.

He talked of the West Australian champion's expertise in using the angles and his thighs, jumping into his opponents and nudging them away before taking the ball with his right hand, quickly transferring it to his left and shooting off destructive handballs to the will-o-the-wisp Goggin, invariably standing on his own. 'You have to block off Farmer's right-hand side Bryan,' he said. 'Don't allow him any room to move, to free his arms. Use your leap. Don't let him body you. Come in late at him. And always from the right side. Compete. Nullify. Frustrate ... Ronny [Fry] will be around to help too.'

1960: Hawthorn's first-ever win against Collingwood at Victoria Park, 7.16 (58) to 7.15 (57), by one point in Round 13, full-forward John Peck kicking the winning goal after the siren. It had taken the Hawks 35 years to win at Collingwood's long-time stronghold. Coach John Kennedy said it was one of the most significant steps in Hawthorn's history. Just over 12 months later, the club won its first premiership.

1958: Collingwood's Grand Final upset win against Melbourne stopped the Demons from winning a fourth straight flag and equalling Collingwood's proud record of four in a row from 1927 to 1930. In wet and soggy conditions the Magpies won 12.10 (82) to 9.10 (64), the tagging of Demon's champion Ron Barassi by Barry 'Hooker' Harrison pivotal in the shock result. Melbourne had finished three games clear in top place and beaten the Pies by 45 points in the second semi and was at the shortest possible odds before the game.

1929: Having become the first team to win all 18 home-and-away games, raging favourites Collingwood, known as 'the Machine', inexplicably lost the second semi to Richmond, 18.15 (123) to 8.13 (61). Syd Coventry and George Clayden – two of Collingwood's key players – were felled in the first five minutes of the game, Richmond's coach Frank 'Checker' Hughes insisting his players intimidate the favourites. 'They hit us pretty hard,' said one of the young Magpies Harry Collier. 'Maybe we were a little overconfident. It is still very hard to work out how we were beaten in that one.' It did no harm as it meant Collingwood could use its right to a challenge match, giving the players another four pound match fee, very handy with the impending Great Depression. The Magpies had defeated Richmond in the two previous Grand Finals and won both home-and-away contests comfortably, Collier saying, 'We always knew we had the wood on them.' Collingwood went on to win the challenge final and a record fourth consecutive premiership in 1930.

A LETTER FROM A HAPPY FAN

FROM: Alex Risk, Melbourne

At the time of the 1963 Fitzroy-Geelong game, I was working at the National Bank in North Melbourne, on the corner of Elizabeth and Victoria Streets. One of our regulars was Ray, a delivery van driver, who worked for a company which distributed small-goods like coffee and nuts around Melbourne cafes and restaurants. He was always betting on the footy and talking about it afterwards. The TAB was only just new and a bit of a novelty. But you could have a bet on the footy with an SP bookmaker.

After the first few rounds of the new season, Alf Brown, the long-time writer for *The Herald* wrote a piece about an emerging hoodoo: whoever played Richmond was losing its very next match.

I started to take notice of this and, sure enough, the trend was continuing. In Round 9, Geelong thrashed Richmond by 38 points and the Cats were due to play Fitzroy the following week, at Fitzroy. Home-ground advantage was big in those days. And on the Monday I asked Ray to find out from his SP what price Fitzroy was to beat the Cats? He came in the next day and said, 'They're long shots: 33 to one.'

I gave him a pound which was a lot of money for me in those days and asked him to put on a bet with his bookie. He came in the following Monday with my 34 quid. 'If it hadn't been for you, the bookie would have had a skinner [and wouldn't have had to pay out to anyone] on that game,' he said. I don't remember ever having another bet on the footy. I'm more of a racing man. But I can recognise a good hoodoo when I see one!

Eyeing John Hayes – selected as first rover for the first time – he told him how he also had a key role to dim the brilliance of Goggin. 'We can't allow him his run, Johnny. It puts too much pressure on the boys down back. Tackle like there's no tomorrow.'

Clark wished them all good luck and a good night's sleep. 'See yer all tomorrow,' he said.

Carroll was walking out with Daffy when his brother-in-law stopped him and said, 'You know, Brian … if you all do what Wally Clark says, you'll beat Geelong tomorrow …'

And they did, in a boilover: 9.13 (67) to 3.13 (31). The conditions were vile and the hero was Wally Clark, a stand-in who whipped his players into a matchwinning frenzy in the only game he ever coached.

NO FAVOURITES IN THIS FAMILY

It was just days before the 1943 Grand Final and the long-awaited rematch between Richmond and much-fancied Essendon. The Bombers had won two of three meetings for the year and also beaten Richmond in the Grand Final 12 months earlier. They had an edge in form and class.

One of Richmond's new boys building a reputation for his uncompromising attack on the ball and anyone silly enough to get in his way was a teenager from Kew Amateurs by the name of Max Oppy, who had been starring on a wing.

On the Tuesday night before the Grand Final, Richmond's captain-coach Jack Dyer had a yarn with Oppy. '[Dick] Reynolds is their danger man, Max,'

'Yeah, I know.'

'What do you think of Reynolds?'

'I hate his guts.'

'All right, you're on him on Saturday.'

Oppy, 19, was playing only his 24th match and being played out of position against a triple Brownlow Medallist.

Within minutes of the start, Oppy had downed Reynolds in the fearsome opening. 'Dick was the best,' he said years later, 'He was right out of my class, but he wasn't particularly robust. Jack thought I might be vigorous enough to slow him down a bit.'

Reynolds had his forehead cut and suffered concussion in the clash, but continued playing, Richmond winning by five points

SMASHED: Dick Reynolds was downed by
Max Oppy, his second cousin, early in the
1943 Grand Final

in an upset. Later it was revealed that Reynolds and Oppy were
second cousins!

DIFFERENT DAYS

Football was a gentleman's game back in the 1870s. Sporting allrounder Tom Wills, Geelong's most iconic player, lived five minutes from the railway station and would walk down and greet the visiting teams from Melbourne.

MULTI-TALENTED:
Tom Wills was also a
pre-eminent cricketer
of the times
MCC Archives

Geelong played on a nearby expanse of uneven ground which extended from the Argyle Hotel to the Wesleyan Church. Geelong would always host a luncheon in honour of the visitors at the Argyle, where the players also changed. At points in the game, the teams would return to the Argyle for 'refreshments', Mr O'Brien, the Argyle's mine host, supplying liberal quantities of champagne, beer and various local and European wines. Different days indeed ...

11

Memories

'Just before half-time of the seconds game,
Wes Lofts walked past me and shook his head
angrily and said, "You bastards! You bastards!"'

FRANK ADAMS (Melbourne): 'Two hundred yards [183 metres] separated me from playing with the club of my choice, St Kilda, or going to Melbourne. I lived at 40 Chapel Street in Windsor but it was written down as 40 Chapel Street, St Kilda, which was Melbourne's territory. I went there at the start of 1953 looking for a clearance. St Kilda thirds had finished bottom the previous year so I thought my best chance to get a game was with them. Melbourne wanted me to play a couple of practice games with them and I got a game with their thirds, which surprised me. By the end of the year I was in the seniors, which was an even bigger surprise. If I had got that clearance, I would have played League footy for St Kilda and not played in any finals at all!'

Six of Adams' 164 senior games were premierships. He also represented Victoria four times. He was one of the best afield in his last game, the epic 1964 Grand Final. He was also Australia's professional sprint champion (over 130 yards [119 metres]) in 1959-60.

STAN ALVES (Melbourne and North Melbourne): 'I was knocked back by three clubs before I was invited to train at Melbourne – and after just one night was told not to come back

PERSISTENT: Stan Alves was initially told to go away and not come back by Melbourne coach Norm Smith ...

again. [Coach] Norm Smith said I was running around like a headless chook and was mucking up training. They were on a mission to win a premiership and were going to do it without me. "I'd like to wish you all the best wherever it is," Norm said. "But ... it won't be here."

'I trained again the next night. Everyone looked in disbelief at me. No one was more surprised to see me than Norm. I quickly changed and ran out onto the ground. No one spoke to me and no one kicked the ball near me. I felt so small. Afterwards I didn't bother to even shower. I changed into my street clothes and headed for the Richmond station as disappointed as anyone could be. I was in tears as I told my family. Try as I might, no one seemed to want me.

'It was mid-morning the next day when out of the blue I took a phone call at work. It was Norm asking me why I'd come back and trained. I was shaking as I told him how I was sick and tired of people telling me what I could and couldn't do. "You're a great coach, Mr Smith," I said, "but how can you possibly tell after only 20 minutes if someone has the ability to play League football?"

'"Well, Stan," he said, "what are you doing for lunch?"'

Smith took Alves to the banks of the Yarra, handed him a sandwich and told him he liked his passion, but unless he was to add at least five kilograms to his slender frame over summer, he had no chance. He did, and ended up playing 200-plus games and captaining the club.

Alves' only finals, including a premiership, were played at North Melbourne.

GARY AYRES (Hawthorn): 'The '85 Grand Final was the single most disappointing moment of my career. We were thrashed [by Essendon] and I sat on the bench for half of it. The next morning I went for a five-mile [eight-kilometre] run, I quit my job, took six months off and vowed to get fitter than I ever had before. My year in 1986 was a turning point as I'd wanted to be a really good senior player. No longer did I just want to be making up the numbers.'

Ayres won two Norm Smith Medals for being best afield on Grand Final day, in 1986 and 1988.

RON BARASSI (Melbourne and Carlton): 'I only ever king-hit a player once and I've always regretted it. It was 30 seconds in my life I'd like to have back ... Donny Furness was a strong Fitzroy player and when you tackled him he had a habit of raising his forearm straight into your head. He rammed me so hard on the throat one time I could hardly breath. Two years later, the same thing, this time my nose. I was livid and picking myself up – he was a good 15–20 yards [14–18 metres] away from me by then – I ran straight at him and downed him. The only reason I hit him from behind was because he had his back to me. Kevin Murray evened up with me and there was hell to pay. I worked with Len Smith at the time. He was coaching Fitzroy and on the Monday he called me over. "I know what happened on Saturday, Ron," he said. "I've spoken to Kevin Murray and I've got to say the same thing to you because what you did was not right."

'"Sorry about that, Len," I said.

'Thinking about it later, fancy getting a blast from the opposition coach at work and on a Monday for goodness sake … who would cop that! But Len had such a lovely way about him. I'd never want to upset him.'

KEVIN BARTLETT (Richmond): 'I'd finish school and go straight down the park. We'd kick anything from a paper footy to a sock. If somebody occasionally brought down a new footy we'd kick that for an extra hour, just for the fun of it. At home I'd play my own backyard games, complete with the commentary. I liked to snap goals over my shoulder. It was always more fun kicking the impossible goal than lining one up from 30 yards [27 metres] dead in front.

'Playing my first game was really something. I'll never ever forget it. We lived only 600 yards [550 metres] from the Richmond ground and I bowled home to Mum and Dad and said, "Guess what. I'm playing against St Kilda."

'"No," said my mum, and I assured her Len Smith had told me I was in the side – as 19th man. "You must have heard him wrong."

'We stayed up that night and listened to the teams being read out on the radio at 9 p.m. Lou Richards, Ron Casey and Allan Nash had their own show. I was in – and boy was I excited!'

CRAIG BRADLEY (Carlton): 'Mots [Peter Motley] and I got lost on the way to our first game – I'll never forget that. We were playing at Waverley Park and we looked it up in the Melways and followed the directions. Unfortunately when we "arrived", all that was there was this big green expanse and an old lady sitting in the middle with her dog. We had the wrong Waverley Park!'

LOST HIS WAY: Craig Bradley

DERMOTT BRERETON (Hawthorn, Sydney and Collingwood): 'Alan Joyce liked us to play the toughest brand of football possible [at Hawthorn] and would get quite worked up in his pre-game addresses. Once he told us to "tackle them and drive them into the ground face-first. If they're in your way, run over them, grind them and step them into the ground. Accidentally of course – I don't want any of you to get reported …" That always made us smile.'

ARNOLD BRIEDIS (North Melbourne): 'I was only 16 and playing full-forward in the practice matches leading into my first season [1972]. Ted Whitten, who was going on 39, had been lured out of retirement by our coach Brian Dixon. He was playing out of a forward pocket. He told me to move in the opposite direction to him and it seemed to work. I kept on getting the ball. But they left him out of our opening game of the season proper, against St Kilda down at Moorabbin and he promptly retired. He'd been a mentor to me and had attracted all the attention. My first game ended early. I kicked a goal but went to tackle Big Carl [Ditterich] and broke my arm.'

BRYAN CLEMENTS (Fitzroy): To say that the wind was howling end-to-end at Footscray this 1964 winter's day was an understatement. Twenty-six of the 27 goals scored for the game came at one end, the Bulldogs winning by just eight points thanks to their solitary major against the wind.

Neither team contended for the finals, Fitzroy failing to win even one game for the year but this was a close one – lightly built, beanstalk ruckman Bryan Clements one of the heroes when he kicked one of Fitzroy's 10 third-quarter goals despite having dislocated his collarbone.

'I marked a kick-off from Footscray's full-back David Darcy [Luke's father],' said Clements, 'and came to the ground fairly heavily with John Hoiles [Footscray's centre half-back] and, I think, the rest of the Footscray side on top of me. In those days if a player was unable to take his kick, the ball was bounced. No way they were going to take that ball from me so I tucked my right hand in my shorts and, to the amazement of all, including me, kicked the goal. About 20 years later, John Hoiles' daughter and my daughter were in the same basketball team. He couldn't remember the incident but it didn't stop me from giving him heaps whenever the opportunity arose.'

Long and lean jumping-jack Bryan Clements played 23 games with Fitzroy in the early '60s. The Round 10, 1964, match at the Western (now Whitten) Oval was his last game of VFL football.

JACK DYER (Richmond): 'The Captain Blood nickname? It came from a journo at *The Age* named Johnny Ludlow. We were coming home on the train from a state game in Perth and Johnny told me I'd probably kill somebody one day. He called me "Captain Blood" in one of his articles and it stuck. It kept me going really. People said I was a bit mad and I suppose I was once I crossed the line. Mum tended to worry a lot ...'

ROBERT FLOWER (Melbourne): 'I wrote letters to the club asking for an invite to try out for the Melbourne fourths [the Under 17s] but was rejected because I was not on their talent identification lists and numbers were too numerous to invite just anyone who asked. I kept persisting though, as this was the dream I wanted to pursue. When I did get to play my first game I was virtually straight out of the fourths and didn't know a soul. I had to buy a ticket to get in and when I got to the dressing-room door, the doorman thought I was after autographs. Barry Bourke saw me and looked after me and introduced me around. I called Carl Ditterich "Mr Ditterich" because his wife was teaching me form five English at the time at Murrumbeena High!'

BOYISH: Robbie Flower

DANIEL HARFORD (Hawthorn and Carlton): 'When you're too old or not good enough to play anymore, what you miss most about not being involved at a club 42 weeks a year are your mates. In the AFL fishbowl they were always my strongest and staunchest allies. In the heat of battle when I needed them most, they did their utmost to help and protect. And in return I did the same for them. I missed Ray Jencke's finger-breaking floaters in the rooms before a game. I missed Johnny Platten trying to fire us up even with his mouthguard in and you had no chance of understanding anything he said. I missed seeing Mark Graham with his head in a bin, vomiting with anxiety before every game. And I missed trying to talk myself out of hopping into an ice-bath during recovery ... I was involved for 10 years but gee it went fast.'

GREG HEALY (Melbourne): 'I was trying out for the Under 19s in a practice game at The Slope, just over the road from the Junction Oval. It was January and it was stinking hot. I couldn't have done much early, as at quarter time our coach Raymond Clarence "Slug" Jordon looked at me, said I couldn't play and was wasting my time and his. Actually it might have been a bit stronger than that. It was just his way of testing me. I lasted through that game, was picked again and I was away ...'

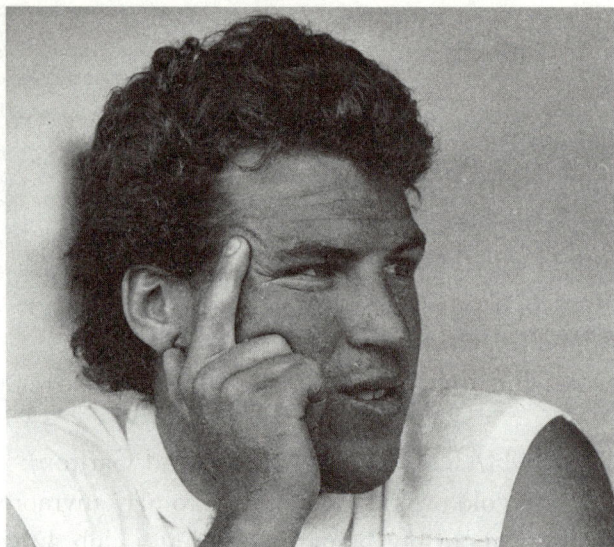

BRAVE: Greg Healy

Healy had a decade at Melbourne and captained the club. He took one of the bravest chest marks I have ever seen against Hawthorn late in the 1990 elimination final, running with the flight of the ball and with the full knowledge that a pack of players was coming at full throttle the other way. 'Either I was going to be a hero or be buried,' he said. He cuddled the ball like it was the Crown Jewels, kicked the goal and the Dees won. A few weeks later, he bumped into Hawthorn icon John Kennedy snr who said, 'That was a great mark, son.'

TONY JEWELL (St Kilda coach): 'We had some poor teams in my time at St Kilda and we were due to play at home against Carlton which was chock-a-block with stars, especially up forward. I joked with [general manager] Ian Stewart how we should hope for rain, but it was a balmy week and come the Friday night, it was obvious the big fellow upstairs was not going to assist.

'Stewie rang me and said, "Why don't we water the wickets [the centre pitch area]? We could turn the hoses on."'

Jewell agreed it would be a good idea but they'd have to be sneaky about it and go down late as the Social Club which overlooked the ground would still be open and elsewhere the cheer squad didn't finish making their banner until after 9 p.m.

'We met after 10 p.m. and headed straight for the curator's office, only to discover that the ground's watering system was controlled by computer. We messed around with it for almost half an hour but still couldn't get it to work. Stewie got a few cans of beer for us and it was agreed we'd hose the ground ourselves.

'Arming ourselves with torches, we connected the hoses out in the middle of the ground and spent a good hour watering. It was nice and sloppy without being unplayable. The next day when we turned up it was like a lake. It was unbelievable. Because we'd messed around with the computer, the water came on and stayed on. You could have played water polo out there.

'Just before half-time of the seconds game, Wes Lofts, Carlton's chairman of selectors, walked past me and shook his head angrily and said, "You bastards! You bastards!" and kept walking. And we won the match, too [16.9 to 13.6].'

That was the day Carlton's fitness advisor told the players to get used to the Moorabbin mud and roll around in it before the first bounce. Fun-loving Justin Madden went a step further, finding some horse manure and rubbing it up and down his arms.

JACK JONES (Essendon): 'I was one of the lucky ones: seven Grand Finals in a row and every one of them under my all-time idol Dick Reynolds. Growing up in the Depression years he was as big as Don Bradman in my eyes and suddenly [after the war] here I am playing with him. Simply amazing. We won three flags in those years and could have won more had John Coleman remained fit. Having good players around you made you look better. John was the ultimate star – the biggest and brightest of them all. We felt invincible when he was firing. And the crowds flocked to see him. In the '49 Grand Final which we won, there must have been 90 000 there. It was the biggest crowd I'd ever played in front of and many spilled over the fence and sat around the boundary line. In the first quarter I remember running near the boundary and was bumped over the line by Carlton's Jimmy Clark. I went straight into the crowd and heard a voice saying, "What are you doing here?"

'The voice was familiar. I looked up and said, "What am I doing here? What are *you* bloody doing here?" I'd landed right on top of my own brother.'

JUSTIN LEPPITSCH (Brisbane Lions): 'My first game was Matthew Clarke's first game as well. He got injured early and I found myself rucking against [North Melbourne's] Alex Ishchenko. The first one I jumped up, a little higher than him and tapped it out. The second one he ran straight at me and kicked me right in the nuts. You tend to remember things like that.'

MATTHEW LLOYD (Essendon): 'We were sitting around the dinner table once when Mum asked us not to discuss the football, just to give her and my sister Kylie a break from it. "Can we have just one dinner where football is not discussed?" she asked. Given my dad played and so did my brother, that was pretty tough. Everyone was silent for about two minutes when Mum spoke again, "Okay that's enough. Back to normal," and away we went again.'

Matthew Lloyd is an Essendon great whose habit of throwing up tufts of grass to ascertain the wind direction continued even at Etihad Stadium when the roof was closed. In all, he kicked 926 goals in 270 matches and was a five-time All-Australian.

LEIGH MATTHEWS (Hawthorn): 'There must have been 150 hopefuls there at Glenferrie my first night. I was 15 and totally overawed. We were all stuck outside the main dressing room. The senior players we had seen and read about all seemed about 10 foot tall. I lasted only that first night and went back to Chelsea wondering, "If this is what League football is all about, what chance have I got?"'

Kicking almost 70 goals from a forward flank, 16-year-old Matthews won the Mornington Peninsula goal kicking that season. One of the games was witnessed by John Kennedy who reported back to the club that Matthews was tough, talented and could play. He came to Hawthorn the next year, 1969.

SHANE MORWOOD (South Melbourne and Collingwood): 'We won the night Grand Final in 1982 [at South] and went back to the social rooms. It was free drinks for an hour and then they made us buy our own! I thought, "Hang on, we've just won the flag here!" At Collingwood you would not have had to pay for anything. There the players got everything on a platter.'

KEVIN MURRAY (Fitzroy): 'I'd never have played the games I did [breaking the League record] if it wasn't for my Dad. He treated all my injuries and kept me going. Once or twice a week I'd go down for tea, we'd eat and then Dad would clear the kitchen table, throw a blanket over the top, boil the kettles and treat my back with olive oil and hot towels, the old-fashioned method he'd learnt when he was a player. Not only was he my father, he was my best mate.'

Kevin Murray aggregated a record 333 games with Fitzroy and remains the proudest of old Lions. His dad, Dan, was 19th man in Fitzroy's 1944 premiership team. I spent one pre-season under him at Sandringham. He was too nice to say I wasn't good enough.

SIMON O'DONNELL (St Kilda): Michael Tuck was reported only once in his 426-game career, for striking St Kilda's first-gamer Simon 'Scuba' O'Donnell. 'I was an absolute smartarse,' O'Donnell said. 'Tucky was found guilty but got off with a severe reprimand because of his good record.'

Asked about his 24-match two-year career, O'Donnell said,

'I was inadequate for the role they were asking me to play, defending against men like Malcolm Blight, Roger Merrett, Terry Daniher and Brent Crosswell. I was scared. I thought Crosswell was mad ...'

O'Donnell had been signed by St Kilda under the father-son rule as a 17-year-old, having kicked 96 goals in nine games with Assumption College. He played almost all his VFL football in defence. His nickname 'Scuba' came from his teammates who reckons he took a dive one day at Arden Street.

DENIS PAGAN (North Melbourne and South Melbourne): 'I was just a kid playing in the park for the fifths at Carlton. My dad [Don] was watching on. He never missed a game. I came off this day feeling pretty pleased with myself when he said to me, "Do you think you went in as hard as you could have today, son?" It was a real turning point for me. It was something that never left me each and every time I played.'

Having played almost 150 games with two clubs, Denis Pagan became a noted coach, first at North Melbourne Under 19s where his teams played off in nine consecutive Grand Finals and at AFL senior level, where he won two flags. Among the teenagers he mentored were Wayne Carey, John Longmire, Corey McKernan and Glenn Archer. After every thirds game, he'd offer constructive advice to the emerging youngsters. If what he had to say wasn't positive, he'd invariably talk to the player one-on-one, in private.

LOU RICHARDS (Collingwood): 'The '53 Grand Final was particularly special for me as I was captain and we knocked off Geelong which was going for three flags in a row. That day was one none of us will ever forget. I had a hotel in North Melbourne and [brother] Ron was working with me. We drove from the pub to the ground, got there, opened the boot and no gear! I'd left it behind. Ronny was furious. It was his first Grand Final and he was already nervous-as. There was a policeman on a motorcycle near us and I got him to give us a special escort to the pub and back. When we finally arrived back at the ground the bloke on the gate wouldn't let us back in. I told him how I was the captain and we're putting on the bloody show but he wouldn't listen. We ended up parking right down near the Richmond ground and had to walk back to the rooms. Afterwards when we won, a fan told me he'd put me on his shoulders and walk me back to the car. He lasted about three or four paces before we both went head over heels. There's nothing quite like a premiership, especially when Collingwood win!'

JOHN RONALDSON (Richmond): 'Kicking three goals on Grand Final day [1967] was a dream come true for me. I'd played only nine or 10 games that year and most were as 19th or 20th man and in those days they'd only make a change if someone was injured or if it was very late in a game just to give you a run. I really felt for Neville Crowe as he was out

ONE OF THE GREAT GRAND FINALS: The front page of the Melbourne *Herald* after Richmond's surging finish to down Geelong in front of almost 110 000 MCG fans

suspended. Royce [Hart] handballed one out of the pack for my first goal and the other two were from drop-kicks close to the boundary. They tend to get bigger and bigger over the years but one was from in front of the old cigar stand – a [60-yard] drop-kick which I was trying to get to the goalsquare for Paddy Guinane to take a screamer. Barry Richardson had passed it to me deep on the boundary line and as I was kicking it, Tommy's runner, Barry Stanton, was in Bones' ear abusing him for not playing direct football!'

John Ronaldson played two winning Grand Finals among his 59 senior games in six years with the Tigers from 1965 to 1970. His son Tony represented the Australian Boomers in two Olympic Games.

PAUL ROOS (Fitzroy and Sydney): 'There was nothing quite like being on the end of a David Parkin spray. We were playing Footscray at the Western Oval and had been soundly beaten. My opponent Max Crow was at the end of his career yet still kicked four. He gave me a bath. Having started on a few others, "Parko" came to me: "And you, Roosy, all you wanted to do was take mark of the year, while your opponent was giving you a bath." He then proceeded to give me the most theatrical performance I have ever seen from a coach, talking as he went. "You took one of these – no two of these." And showed the entire team and support staff how I'd jumped on my opponent's back and stuck my knee in to take the mark. David was just so animated. Everyone wanted to laugh but dared not. His conclusion was classic Parkin: "You're nothing but a loose, kick-chasing non-contact centre half-back!"'

BOBBY SKILTON (South Melbourne): 'I was captaining South for the first time, standing-in for [the injured] Ronny Clegg. We were playing Footscray at home and Teddy Whitten was their captain. I tossed the coin as high in the air as I could and before it had even landed, Teddy ran back to the centre, saying, "We'll go down [the ground]." By the time I got back to the centre, spluttering and complaining, all the players were in position and the game was ready to start!

'Teddy tried the same trick another time at South, but I was awake this time. We both ran back to the centre while the ball was flipping in the air, pointing our teams in the same direction. The umpire Don Blew was non-plussed and scratching his head wondering what to do before Teddy relented and grinning at me said, "We'll go this way."'

ROOKIE SKIPPER: Bobby Skilton

DON SCOTT (Hawthorn): 'Playing on Polly Farmer was quite an experience. It was my first year and his last year [1967]. He gave me an absolute football lesson. I beat him in the first contest and never got another touch. He altered his game, working me out in an instant. I had spring but back then knew nothing. It took him an instant to work it all out and there was nothing I could do about it.'

GRAHAM TEASDALE (Richmond and South Melbourne): Having kicked almost 100 goals with the reserves and Under 19s, Brownlow Medallist–to-be Teasdale kicked six on his debut match against South Melbourne at the old Lakeside Oval in 1973. 'In hindsight, my first game became even more special because of all the great players I lined up with. Royce Hart was in front of me at centre half-forward, Ian Stewart was in the middle and there were guys like Kevin Bartlett, Kevin Sheedy and Francis Bourke all running around. I feel proud to have played my first game with guys like that.'

MAX WALKER (Melbourne): League football can be a hard school not for everyone. Remembering the words of his coach Norm Smith to play in front no matter what, Tasmanian teenager Max Walker was elated on his debut [Round 12, 1967] to win a couple of early hit-outs against North Melbourne's much-celebrated captain and No. 1 follower Noel Teasdale. After he won a third, Teasdale sidled up and threatened Walker with a whack to the earhole if he kept getting in his way.

Thinking it was merely gamesmanship, Walker went to take the front position at the next boundary throw-in only for Teasdale to land a round-arm haymaker. 'I thought the old head had been torn loose,' said Walker. 'I landed about four metres outside the boundary. All the umpire did was call "play on".

'At the next boundary throw-in I again got in front and copped one under the other ear ... all of a sudden my enthusiasm for the front position had evaporated.'

Not wanting to lose the faith of coach Smith, whom he idolised and realising he need to change tactics, Walker bounced in from the back, leapt higher than Teasdale and with his elbow crunched Teasdale squarely to the top of his head, so enraging the veteran that he spent most of the day trying to square up with Walker. Melbourne won the game by a kick.

MURRAY WEIDEMAN (Collingwood): 'I played my first season of VFL in 1953. It was a year I'll never forget. I played two games in the Under 19s, 12 in the reserves and the last four in the seniors. I had the flu and missed the second semifinal day but Jack Hamilton broke his arm that day and I got back in for the Grand Final. They read the teams out on 3DB and it was a huge thrill for all of us to hear my name. I rode my bike to Fairfield station and caught the train into the game, getting off at Jolimont and carrying my Gladstone bag down the hill to the rooms. I was 20th man and being so young [17] I didn't think I'd even get a run. But Pat Twomey was injured in the first quarter [19th man] George Hams going on and

WHAT WE MISS

- The Junction Oval's peanut man, John Boyd, shuffling up and down the terraces yelling: 'Peanuts … shilling a bag. Peanuts …'
- Pie Park, the spiritual, long-time home of the Collingwood FC
- The Arden Street elephant – one of the more madcap marketing ideas was to have an elephant appear at North Melbourne during a game against Collingwood in the late '70s. The ground was packed and the crowd roared when one of the teams ran onto the field, badly scaring the elephant. He was lurching towards the crowd and was only just stopped by his handler before trampling those nearest to the fence
- The 'Animal Enclosure' at Moorabbin, those who stood between the races at the old Moorabbin ground
- 'Long Bombs to Snake' and other classic one-liners from Ronald Dale Barassi
- Dermie's strut
- Lou, Jack and Bob on *League Teams*, a not-to-be missed comedy show in the guise of a footy show
- Teddy Whitten at just about every State match saying how the Big V 'had stuck it up 'em!'
- Channel 7's Peter Landy saying how he'd like to buy some real estate from the umpire, so extravagant were his 15-yard penalties
- Three Grand Finals on the same day from 8 a.m. at the 'G
- Bigs, Chick and Doug on Harry Beitzel's *Footy Show*
- Mickey O, the sublimely gifted Swan Michael O'Loughlin
- Twenty-two rounds when everyone played everyone else twice …
- Stan Alves doing cartwheels after North Melbourne's premiership in 1977
- Brent Crosswell's columns in *The Age*
- Phil Carman's white boots
- Floggers, the coloured streamers on sticks the cheer squads would wave up and down to signal a goal
- The Lake premiership (matches between neighbours St Kilda and South Melbourne)
- The G-train, Fraser Gehrig
- Helen D'Amico, the shapely Grand Final streaker

THE WEED: Murray Weideman captained Collingwood in the 1958 Grand
Final and fulltime for four years from 1960. This is the 1960 team:
Back row, left to right: Harry Sullivan, John Henderson, Kevin Pay,
Mick Twomey, Graeme Fellowes, Kevin Rose, Peter Rosenbrook,
Alan Wickes. Sitting: Ray Gabelich, Ron Reeves, Bill Serong, the
Weed, Thorold Merrett (vice-captain), Brian Beers, Bill Thripp, Bert
Chapman. Front: Ken Turner, John Carmody, Brian Gray and Des Field

just before three-quarter time Arthur Gooch was also injured
so I got the nod from Phonse Kyne [Collingwood's coach].
Everywhere I went the ball seemed to fall into my arms. I must
have had eight or nine kicks in that last quarter and we won. It
was an amazing feeling.'

*'The Weed' was the youngest footballer to play in a winning Grand Final
side. He captained the club to the 1958 premiership, and then quit at 27
before returning later as senior coach.*

DALE WEIGHTMAN (Richmond): 'The '80 Grand
Final was one of the great days. My whole family and
many of my mates were there. Apparently when I kicked the
first goal my brother Kent jumped up and said, "That's my
brother!" One of my best mates from Mildura, Peter King, was
a one-eyed Collingwood supporter and had begged me to get
him a ticket. I did – it turned out to be right in the middle of
the Richmond cheer squad! Later he somehow got himself into
our rooms and was one of many to drink from the premiership
cup that night. Country boys know how to have fun.'

*Richmond defeated Collingwood by 81 points, the most one-sided Grand
Final to that time.*

12
Quotes

'David had a face only a mother could love. His face had a look that challenged others to hit it ...'

'That's right. A dog bit me and I bit it back. I was only three at the time but Dad and Mum assured me it happened. Not that it was a bulldog or an Alsatian or anything like that. Apparently it was just a little tich of a thing.' – Brisbane legend JONATHAN BROWN to Fox's Mike Sheahan on *Open Mike*, 2015

'Good luck trying to catch Jack Gunston. It's like trying to catch a thoroughbred.' – Footscray's ROB MURPHY, 2014

'I think the public has probably got this perception that I am just this pure party animal that doesn't care about the footy. Footy means more than anything to me.' – the Cats' STEVE JOHNSON, 2011

'I've been lucky enough over the course of my career to give a lot of speeches. This is one I've dreamt of all my life.' – Collingwood president EDDIE MCGUIRE heralding Collingwood's 2010 premiership

'You weak dog. Don't you retire. Because we're coming at you [next year].' – Hawthorn coach ALISTAIR CLARKSON to Matthew Lloyd after Lloyd in his last game had flattened Brad

Sewell shortly after half-time in the Round 22 match at the MCG in 2009

'Afterwards a lot of people at Geelong tried to cram in 44 years of celebrating.' – JIMMY BARTEL (in 2007) after Geelong's first premiership since 1963

'David Neitz was one of the toughest footballers of my time. Before the 2005 finals he hurt his leg and we thought it was just a corky, but x-rays showed that he'd broken the bottom part of his leg. But he still wanted to be available and lead his team into September. We did a secret fitness test at the MCG. The longer it went, the worse he got and he missed out. But to see him try to get through the session without showing any pain was really something.' – NEALE DANIHER on David Neitz

'A cardboard cut-out would offer as much as John Worsfold does in his post-match press conferences.' – leading football writer MIKE SHEAHAN, 2004

'Brace yourself for a tough ride. You will be dealing with an alien dressed up as Ben.' – West Coast club doctor ROD MOORE to Ben Cousins' father, Bryan, at the height of his wild child's drug addiction

'When I took drugs, I thought I was being clever, hiding in full view.' – BEN COUSINS

'They [the Wakelin twins] both sleep with the lights on and in bunk beds. For them to have a crack at [Alastair] Lynch, everyone in the football world knows they are weak pricks and if they want to have a cheap shot, well come here [to Brisbane] and have a cheap shot.' – Lions' premiership specialist MARTIN PIKE responding to criticism from the Wakelin brothers of the Lions' vigorous style of play.

'Mate, if you don't play in a premiership, captain a League club and nearly win a Brownlow, you won't have reached your full potential.' – MICK TURNER on the emerging Luke Hodge, 2000

'I was so skinny when I first got to Sydney that I often joked I put on weight just by walking through the door of the gym.' – Irishman TADHG KENNELLY on his formative times with Sydney in the early 2000s

'I was just a spoiler, really.' – BRUCE DOULL in a rare utterance about his exulted career

'The full-back is not always the best kick in the side. Jamie Shanahan who played full-back for 140 games without ever scoring a goal, was banned from kick-in duties by three separate coaches: Ken Sheldon and Stan Alves at St Kilda and then Neale Daniher at Melbourne.' – author and journalist NATHAN JARVIS, 2006

'My apologies Paul … I thought you were here purely for your superannuation.' – JOHN KENNEDY SNR to Hawthorn Team of the Century member Paul Salmon on his initial shift from Essendon to Glenferrie

'It breaks my heart every day.' – 138-game ex-Fitzroy centreman ALAN THOMPSON on the demise of his old club, 2014

'There are a lot of people in high places who don't want North Melbourne to be strong, don't want them to be successful.' – DENIS PAGAN after winning the '99 premiership

'Footy would be a whole lot more fun if you didn't have to run so much.' – BRENDAN FEVOLA

THE BIG FISH: So successful was Paul Salmon at his adopted Hawthorn he made the club's Team of the Century. He is pictured with Hawk-to-be Stevie Greene

'He used to demoralise teams, not just the player he was playing on, he'd demoralise the guy I was playing on.' – GLENN ARCHER on the impact of Wayne Carey

'Every father who has played League football and his son has [also] played will tell you they play the game again. So I haven't played 239 games. I've played 500-plus!' – SERGIO SILVAGNI (father of Stephen Silvagni)

'Libba [Tony Liberatore] scratched me with his fingernails, sledged me, elbowed and scragged me and did everything he could to put me off my game. He wasn't there to play football.' – BEN COUSINS on close-checking opponent Tony Liberatore

'I was in hospital alongside a bloke who stuttered and he asked me, "W-w-w-what are you in h-h-h-here f-f-f-for?" I told him, "Because I pee the way you talk!"' – TED WHITTEN SNR

'I was born to play Grand Finals.' – ROBERT DI PIERDOMENICO

'Gary Ablett [snr] has changed more games than any other player I have seen … he could really turn it on.' – MALCOLM BLIGHT

'It was good to get the four points.' – the ever-guarded ALAN JOYCE, refusing to let his guard down, even after his Hawks had come from behind to win the 1991 Grand Final

'Sometimes you spectated when you played alongside him. I was there shouting, "Go Gazza, go," and then I remembered I was actually playing in the game too.' – BILLY BROWNLESS on Gary Ablett snr and his 1989 Grand Final heroics

'The Sydney Swans just forgot about me.' – Wagga's WAYNE CAREY, 2006

'When North Melbourne arranged to see me and [coach] John Kennedy walked into the restaurant, my dad [Fred] and I almost fell off our chairs. I was rapt that a bloke of John's stature had made the extra effort to come all the way to [Corowa] to see me. I was virtually theirs from then on.' – JOHN LONGMIRE on a very special dinner, in 1987

'We're thieves. We did it at Geelong and again today [against Melbourne]. Unbelievable mate, unbelievable.' – ROBERT DI PIERDOMENICO after Hawthorn's last-gasp entry into the 1987 Grand Final courtesy of a goal after the siren from Gary Buckenara

'He was one of those rovers who was born great.' – KEVIN BARTLETT on Dale Weightman

'You are playing for your jumper and playing for your teammates. There is a gentle and friendly chiacking among players. When the crunch comes, each player stands together. You know that your mate will stand by you no matter what.' – Hawthorn's PETER CURRAN

'There'd be 20 or 30 of us kicking from pack to pack at lunchtimes at school [Loxton High in the SA Riverland]. I'd get down the back and try and take speckies.' – TONY MODRA on how he learnt to fly in the '80s

'I couldn't tell you where the Coleman medals are – think Mum has them at home somewhere.' – TONY LOCKETT

'I was a dad first and a chairman of selectors second.' – FRANCIS BOURKE explaining his decision to stand down from Richmond's match committee on the drafting of son David

'No wonder they call him "the Diesel". He goes at the same pace and just doesn't stop all day.' – St Kilda's NATHAN BURKE on Sydney's running man Greg Williams, 1986

'At one stage I was bigger than Elvis – I had so many marks of the year I could have started my own car yard.' – WARWICK CAPPER, 2001

'If the umpires made as many mistakes as you blokes, you'd have something to whinge about.' – some old-fashioned footy philosophy from Hawthorn coach ALLAN JEANS

'I left school on my 15th birthday. My reports weren't flash: Pretty destructive in class … Using the classroom as a cross-country field. The only subject I got good marks in was PE!' – Bulldogs great DOUG HAWKINS

'If anyone thinks Hawthorn is going to be easy meat this year, they are in for the shock of their lives. We have a magnificent team with a goal to goal line that is loaded with young talent.' – RON COOK, Hawthorn president on the eve of the 1986 season when the Hawks played off for a fourth consecutive year

'Four points and a place in the five. What more is there?' – a satisfied Footscray coach MICK MALTHOUSE, 1984

'You're not one of us and you're not part of us … get over there.' – Geelong coach MALCOLM BLIGHT excluding an out-of-favour Austin McCrabb from his three-quarter-time huddle

HOW SWEET IT IS: A young Mick Malthouse

'People don't forget you. You always know you're at home when you're at Collingwood.' – BILL TWOMEY

'Aren't you the bloke who ran over the mark?' – an Australian travelling in France who saw JIMMY STYNES on a train in Paris in the summer of '87

'Last year Stewart [Loewe] progressed from the Under 19s to the reserves to the seniors in three weeks. I've never known that before.' – long-time St Kilda administrator IAN DRAKE, in 1987

'David had a face only a mother could love. His face had a look that challenged others to hit it.' – JUSTIN MADDEN on David Rhys-Jones

'Some can speak nice and quiet and slow. But I find I can't. I tried but I can't!' – Under 19s coaching guru, the hot-gospelling RAY JORDON

CHALKIE: Having transferred States, Stephen Kernahan's first job in Melbourne was working as a 'chalkie' at the Melbourne Stock Exchange
Geoff Poulter/Inside Football

'Bruce Doull here. I hear you're interested in Carlton. It's a great club. I'd like to have you over here.' – the normally taciturn BRUCE DOULL in a telephone call to a 16-year-old Stephen Kernahan, 1980

'Growing up, Justin and Simon weren't easy on the furniture. They all liked World Championship Wrestling. I came home one day and they'd wrestled their way through a plate glass door.' – THELMA MADDEN, the only footballing mum to have two 300-game sons

'I'm just amazed Justin has lasted so long. He's the most uncoordinated player I have ever seen.' – TIM WATSON on Justin Madden

'Most taggers are dumb stooges. They're just robots.' – DOUGIE HAWKINS

ABUSED: Champion West Coast Eagle Chris Lewis was racially targeted in the 1991 Grand Final, behaviour not to be tolerated today
Inside Football

FIERY: Among those who verbally assailed 'Lewi' was Dermott Brereton, no stranger to a fracas or two. Alongside him is Hawthorn's runner George Stone no doubt telling Dermott that the finals are about to start and whatever happens, don't get reported!
Inside Football

LOU AND JACK: Lou Richards (far right) and Jack Dyer (far left) were the lifeblood of Channel 7's World of Sport Sunday lunchtime panels for years. With them are Bruce Andrew, Alan 'the Baron' Ruthven, Neil 'Coconut' Roberts and Kevin 'Skeeter' Coghlan

Left: LEGENDS: Lou and Jack with fellow Media Hall of Famer Ron Casey
Greg Hobbs

Above: MATES: Ted Whitten (left) with Neil 'Knuckles' Kerley before an interstate challenge match in Melbourne. Fiercely loyal to their own States, they were the closest of buddies off the field
Inside Football

POPULAR: Trevor Barker was a darling of the Moorabbin crowds – and everyone else for years. It was tragic that he died so young

Ken Rainsbury/Football Fan

IMMOVABLE: Carlton's Justin Madden owned the front position on the boundary hit-outs. His arms seemed to stretch to the clouds. He and brother Simon both played more than 300 games

Ken Rainsbury/Football Australia

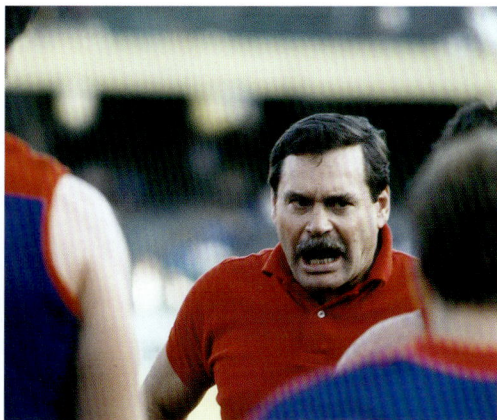

eft: JEZZA: Alex Jesaulenko the coach could be mellow one minute and absolutely
nbending the next. He transferred to St Kilda after a fallout with Carlton's club
*resident George Harris

ight: BARASS: Ron Barassi's return home to Melbourne had long been anticipated
ut the Dees never finished higher than eighth in his five years as coach

ONGY: 'Boy I was good,' said Michael Long after the 1993 Grand Final ...
he crowd erupted, again

en Rainsbury

Left: NEITA: David Neitz was not only brave, he was a super talent and a linchpin of many a Melbourne victory in the '90s and into the early 2000s. Here he marks ahead of Collingwood's Michael Christian and Damian Monkhorst
Ken Rainsbury/Football Australia

Right: BIG GAME SPECIALIST: Paul Dear won a Norm Smith Medal ahead of all his big name teammates in the 1991 Grand Final. He may have been undersized for a follower but he could seriously play
Ken Rainsbury/Football Australia

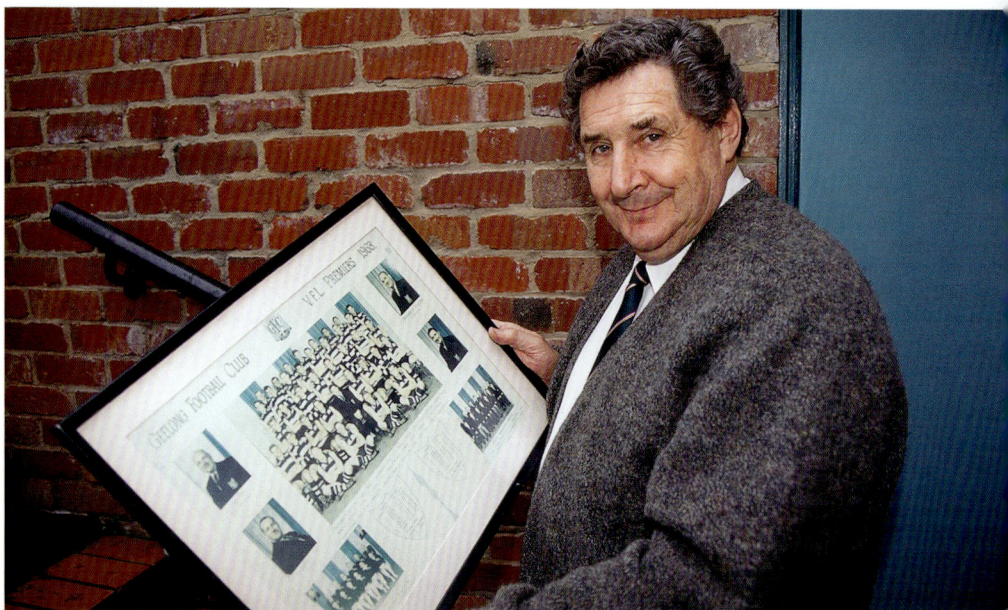

THE GEELONG FLYER: Bob Davis had so many happy memories from a lifetime in the game, playing, coaching and commentating
Davis family collection

MODRRAAAA!: Tony Modra, Adelaide's prince of goal kickers, could jump tall buildings with a single leap . . . Crows' fans dubbed him 'Godra'

Stephen Laffer

Left: REBUKED: During his time at Fitzroy David Parkin reserved one of his great blasts for Paul Roos ...
Ken Rainsbury

Right: MICKY O: Few could baulk, charm and dazzle like Sydney's champion forward Michael O'Loughlin. We still miss him ...
Ken Rainsbury

BARGAIN BASEMENT: Wayne Carey breasts the banner before the 1999 Grand Final. Alongside him is fellow country boy John Longmire. In one of the bargain deals of the Century, they cost North Melbourne just $70000 ... peanuts today
North News/North Melbourne Football Club

'I actually got a letter from a Colac farmer with a $20 cheque in it, congratulating me on what I did [breaking Leigh Matthews' nose]. I sent the cheque back to him and thanked him for his best wishes, but I couldn't accept his money.' – Geelong's STEVE HOCKING after the Matthews-Neville Bruns behind-play incident (1985) in which Bruns had his jaw broken and seconds later Matthews his nose, by a revengeful Hocking

'Normally I don't say anything about the umpires and today I'm particularly not going to say anything about them.' – an angry JOHN KENNEDY SNR treading a fine line after a North Melbourne match, 1985

'As long as you have success, people are happy with you.' – ALLAN JEANS on his longevity as a coach

'The moral of that story is that you can only take so much shit from people for so long.' – KEVIN SHEEDY having shown *First Blood* to his players on the Thursday night leading into the 1984 Grand Final

'The Kid's just a kid.'– ALLAN JEANS refusing journalists access to first-gamer Dermott Brereton after his five-goal debut for Hawthorn in a final in 1982

'What's better than beating Collingwood by 10 goals in a Grand Final? Beating them by five points!'– a not-so-generous Carlton president GEORGE HARRIS after the '79 Grand Final

'Too many Grand Finals got away from us. I'm still haunted by them all. [The year] 1980 was no problem. We were outclassed [by Richmond] but the others [two in 1977 and 1979] were all close. They were there to be taken and we just didn't win them. My kids and I sit down watching them sometimes and they'll say to me, "Where are you?" If you don't produce on the day or do that one thing to change the direction of the game when

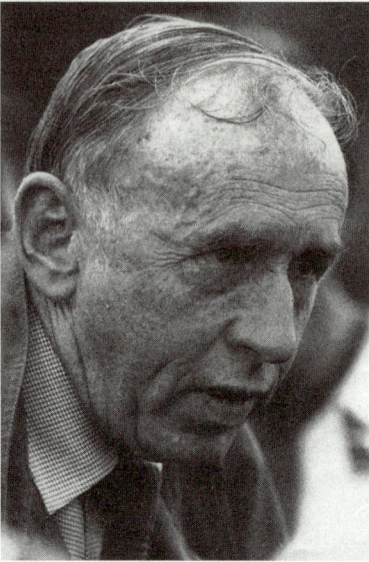

TACITURN: John Kennedy snr

THE KID: Dermott Brereton

it counts, you regret it – always.' – Collingwood's RONNY WEARMOUTH

'He may look like Rasputin the Mad Monk but as far as Carlton is concerned, he is a knight in shining armour.' – RON BARASSI on Bruce Doull

'You're older than you think.' – JOHN KENNEDY SNR'S oft-used line warning his players how careers pass in an instant

'I go off for a second. They do intimidate you. I lose my temper like a lot of blokes, but I wouldn't go out of my way to hurt someone.' – North Melbourne's rover JIMMY KRAKOUER

'I'm loving it so much that I wish I was young and it was all starting over again. That's the difference playing for a good club makes.' – JOHN CASSIN, the ex-Bomber and 1977 premiership Roo

'As you think back on this day which has been one of the great spectacles in Australian sport, I hope you'll agree that all the hard work and all that shit put on you by the coach was worth it … and I want you to know very sincerely … that I love you.' – RON BARASSI after the '77 Grand Final replay

'I've never had a beer. The only inkling I have about the taste of alcohol is when my wife Maureen makes trifle as a dessert.' – TOMMY HAFEY

'No one has ever died on me yet, son. Go harder. It won't kill you.' – ALLAN JEANS to a young Jason Dunstall on arrival at Glenferrie, 1985

'He's as good a player as I have seen and as good a player as I have coached.' – DAVID PARKIN on Leigh Matthews

'Anything I did was on instinct, on the spur of the moment. In my desperation to get to the ball I was probably more ruthless when I was young … I wouldn't have liked to have played on myself in the early days.' – LEIGH MATTHEWS

'A man is too long retired. I've lost between one yard and 10 yards in pace. I didn't get off the ground at all and the only time I could bend below my knees was to pick up my drink at three-quarter time.' – Saint premiership star IAN COOPER on his comeback with Keysborough in 1979

'It bothers me that blokes like Des Tuddenham and Kevin Murray will still be bothered by football injuries at the age of 40.' – Fitzroy great JOHN MURPHY

'Give me 90 000 people at the MCG and I was Hercules. Give me a grey, windy day at the Western Oval and I wasn't worth a cracker.' – BRENT CROSSWELL

'Ron Joseph rang me and the 10-year-rule was happening and when it passed through the League he would like first option on speaking to me. I said, "Yeah." Until then I hadn't given a thought to leaving Geelong.' – Geelong captain DOUG WADE who was one of 'the Big Three' to sign with North Melbourne (along with Barry Davis and John Rantall) in 1973

'Neil has made a decision to get his hair cut. He has been very brave about it – he isn't even having an anaesthetic.' – Richmond secretary ALAN SCHWAB on Neil Balme

'What happened in the second quarter at the MCG on Saturday made me sick. We can take a beating, even in a Grand Final, but I for one cannot easily forget the way Geoff Southby was flattened. It was one of the worst things I have seen in football.' – Carlton's DAVID MCKAY on the behind-the-ball round-arm which concussed his teammate Geoff Southby in the 1973 Grand Final between Carlton and Richmond

'Balmey [Neil Balme] suffered probably more than I have over the years. He had a terrible case of white line fever. He was a brutal character – yet so good off it. He's had a remarkably good career in the game. We still interact and speak.' – GEOFF SOUTHBY on his infamous KO in the 1973 Grand Final

'He was a good persuader and most of the time got it right. Ruthless is one way to put it but I prefer to think of him as single-minded.' – FRANCIS BOURKE on the powerbroking Tiger Graeme Richmond

'By crikey boys, you've never played well in League football until you've played well against Collingwood at Collingwood.' – GRAEME RICHMOND

'Peter Hudson was the greatest gate attraction we've ever had.' – long-time Hawthorn administrator RON COOK

'What would you do if Jesus Christ came to Hawthorn? Move Peter Hudson to centre half-forward.' – a sign at a local Hawthorn church at the height of 'Huddo' mania, 1970

'Percy Page was the greatest loss Richmond Football Club ever suffered. It cost us a string of premierships as his combination with 'Checker' Hughes was supreme. He was in a class of his own as a football club secretary. He had two great rules. The first, that all the promises in the world didn't mean a thing until you have the signature; and the second, never trust a man from another club.' – GRAEME RICHMOND on one of his great Tigerland influences Percy Page, 1980

MASTER RECRUITER: Graeme Richmond

'He was a great chaser, a great tackler, he was tremendous on the ground, he never fumbled, he was a beautiful kick and he was a great competitor.' – KEVIN BARTLETT on the incomparable Royce Hart

'Fitzroy offered me $1200 [to sign] which was three years' footy wages in those days. I picked Fitzroy [ahead of Hawthorn] because I got on better with the blokes. I was from the same area and Hawthorn was a bit like the Melbourne Cricket Club. I just didn't fit in.' – JOHN MURPHY on why he chose Fitzroy rather than following in his father's footsteps and playing at Hawthorn

'My personal trainer for 18 months [at North Melbourne] was Ron Clarke, who held 16 or 17 world records. Ron would run backwards and I still couldn't keep up with him.' – SAM KEKOVICH

'Our Geelong team in '67 was better than the '63 side ... we just played a better side [Richmond] on the day.' – BILLY GOGGIN

'It's the biggest thrill of my life.' – FRED SWIFT on captaining Richmond's 1967 premiership team

'The '63 side was so full of champions, all I had to get right were the songs the piano accordionist was going to play and where Harry 'Happy' Hammond [the TV personality and one-eyed Geelong supporter] would run out with the rest of the boys!' – Geelong coach BOB DAVIS

'Happy' was to run out third, after the captain and vice-captain!

'One minute you're obscure, the next you're famous. That first game [against Melbourne in 1963 at the Junction] changed my life. There was no turning back after that and it never stopped until the day I retired [284 games later].' – headlining ruckman CARL DITTERICH

'It's said that Bradman anticipated the pitch of the ball before other batsmen. "Doc" read the play before the rest. He had amazing ball sense.' – ALLAN JEANS on Darrel Baldock

'There's more violence in a Popeye the Sailor Man cartoon than on the footy field.' –St Kilda's hot-gospelling coach ALAN KILLIGREW

CATCHPHRASES

'Pagan's paddock.' – DENIS PAGAN'S tactic in clearing his entire forward line to allow full reign for his champion Wayne Carey

'Long Bombs to Snake.' – RON BARASSI'S instructions to his North Melbourne players to best utilise the high-marking skill of full-forward Phil 'Snake' Baker

'Here comes Billy.' – Collingwood's BILL PICKEN who would often commentate as he flew for marks in his pomp in the '70s

'Kick it long to Royce and get out of his way.' – TOMMY HAFEY in most of his pre-match addresses at Richmond when Royce Hart was in the line-up

'Jezza-lenKKOO ... you beauty.' – Channel 7's MIKE WILLIAMSON after Alex Jesaulenko's soaring mark early during the 1970 Grand Final

'It was fair dinkum unbelievable.' – a favourite one-liner of Geelong legend BOB DAVIS

'John Lord is a stalwart six-footer with a cheerful manner and merry brown eyes ... he claims he is the oldest unmarried League player at 24.' – JOHN LORD'S player profile from a 1963 edition of the *Australian Women's Weekly*

'I hate Collingwood so much I won't even have a black and white TV at home.' – JACK DYER

'I wore the same knee bandage for 18 years. [Our property steward] Charlie Callander wouldn't give me another one. He was so mean he wouldn't even give you a bit of chewy.' – DYER again

'Dick [Reynolds] achieved everything one could in football but it was his demeanour after finishing that further enhanced the wonderful image of the man. His character was exemplary in all facets of life.' – BOBBY SKILTON on Dick Reynolds

'Jack [Titus] is as game as they come and is always in the thick of it. There's not much of him physically [but] his endurance is amazing. Above all, Jack's greatest quality is his fighting heart.' – Richmond coach PERCY BENTLEY on his most durable and relied upon forward Jack 'Skinny' Titus

'He was a beautiful high mark. He would soar like a bird over a pack. He was a wonderful player in all respects and one of the greatest clubmen at Fitzroy.' – Fitzroy stalwart PERC MITCHELL on the passing of 1936 Brownlow Medallist Dinny Ryan in 1980

'Jack Dyer, Richmond's giant, was the greatest bigman in Australian football. He stands supreme. He is the greatest of the great.' – HEC de LACY on Jack Dyer

'You'd play Saturdays even if you had an injury. You'd be too frightened to say you were crook. Someone was always breathing down your neck for your place – and your pay. Three pounds [a week] in the early '30s was a terrible lot of money. It meant everything.' – Hawthorn's ANDY ANGWIN

'I thought it was beaut just being able to hold my place in the side each week. I was one of the lucky ones. Every week some really good players missed out and I always felt for them. Jock McHale had us all thinking and playing like a team.' – Collingwood's six-time premiership player HARRY COLLIER in 1982

'Had we triumphed, we might have given a lead to our national game, which is almost a national institution. We might have pressured its highest ideals. We might have slain the ogre of professionalism.' – The *Melbourne University* magazine on the club's demise from the VFL competition in 1914

13

Snippets

'Why don't you play a man's game, you poofta!'
said one. Twelve months later Beers was part
of Collingwood's 1958 premiership team.

IN THE FAMILY

The impressive emergence of Tom Papley on Sydney's forward line in early 2016 came as no surprise to his proud grandfathers, Max Papley and Jeff Bray, who were teammates with South Melbourne in the 1960s.

ONE OF THOSE DAYS

Surely it was a misprint: Rye 14.8 (92) v Rosebud 0.20 (20) in the Mornington Peninsula League, July 2014. But it wasn't. Rosebud had 12 straight points to three-quarter time and added eight more in the last, each 'miss' being met with rousing cheers. 'It was just one of those days,' said Rosebud's coach and former Sheffield Shield cricketer Nick Jewell. 'We didn't bother to watch the game back, no …'

FAMILIAR FACE

David Parkin thought he'd take the North Balwyn tram to town to watch two of his old teams Hawthorn and Carlton one afternoon at Etihad. He buried himself in a book but having spent 20 years at Glenferrie Oval and 16 at Princes

RYE v ROSEBUD, 2014: 'We don't intend to watch the game back on video,' said Rosebud's coach Nick Jewell

Sam Sangster/RyePixels Photography

Park, he was soon recognised by fans and was asked, 'Just who will you be barracking for today, David?' One gent in Hawthorn colours was so insistent on an answer that after minutes of nodding, smiling and keeping his opinion to himself, Parkin got off the tram and hopped on the one behind – leaving the question still unanswered …

TAKING A STAB

Few could unleash a stab-pass with the precision and power of Collingwood's Hall of Famer Thorold Merrett. Introduced at one club function in 2009, he was described as the man who could roost a ball up a chicken's arse without ruffling a feather!

MIXED MESSAGES

It wasn't until 2001 that Rex Hunt finally found out that Tommy Hafey had wanted him to stay at Tigerland a generation earlier – rather than transfer mid-season 1974 to Geelong … a move Hunt always regretted. 'I'd been told that Tommy was sick of me,' Hunt said. 'And that hurt me … I was near the water urn having a break from broadcasting at half-time of an early season match [in 2001]. Tommy was there too and out of the blue he asked me why I'd made the move to Geelong all those years ago? I was stunned. Looking directly at him, I said, "Tommy, you didn't want me. Schwabby [Alan Schwab] gave me the message."'

'You've got to be joking, Rex,' Hafey replied. 'I desperately wanted you to stay. I was told you had been transferred to the Geelong Police and travelling would make it hard for you.'

GRATEFUL

Mal Michael sent a message of thanks to Collingwood's Jarrod Molloy after the pair had swapped clubs in 2001, Michael ending up in a premiership team – the first of his three consecutive flags with Brisbane in 2001, 2002 and 2003. 'Without you this couldn't have been possible,' he wrote.

IN MEMORY OF A MATE

Geelong's Ben Graham once wore a black armband in a match against Collingwood in honour of his favourite dog Max, a four-year-old Labrador retriever which had just died.

CONCEALED CASH

Guess how much money was on offer to Carlton's 1999 All-Australian ruckman Matt Allan to sign a new contract at Princes Park the following pre-season?

A mere $90 000 … in several large brown paper bags!

PRE-MATCH

West Coast Eagle goalsneak Phil Matera was doing what he always did in the rooms before a match: *'Vroom-vroom. VROOM-VROOM,'* he said before adding in explanation to a startled newcomer, 'Gotta go fast … gotta go fast … like a car … like a car.'

FLY BOYS: Peter Sumich and Collingwood's Craig Kelly tangle during the 1990 qualifying final draw at Waverley. West Coast travelled east six times in six weeks in August and September.
Inside Football

A TWO-DAY MATCH

When the Waverley lights failed just after half-time of the St Kilda-Essendon Saturday night match in 1996, the game was continued on the following Tuesday night, Essendon winning.

UNDERRATED

So underrated was Hawthorn's Mark Graham in Hawthorn's galaxy of stars in the '90s that he won the nickname of 'Alex' – after Carlton's Alex Marcou.

FLY BOYS

The West Coast Eagles had to travel six times in six weeks to the East Coast late in the 1990 season. 'The players were mentally and physically drained,' said coach Mick Malthouse. 'For our sixth game away we faced Essendon at the MCG and were thrashed ... six weeks straight on the road is unheard of in world elite sport.'

EXPELLED

A teenage Michael Gardiner was expelled from the prestigious Hale School in Perth after finding and photocopying in bulk upcoming examination papers and marketing them to dozens of his senior school contemporaries. Six years later he was the All-Australian ruckman and one of the premier West Coast Eagles of them all.

BACKFLIP

Collingwood's premiership hero Tony Shaw once agreed to become reserves coach at Princes Park under David Parkin before meeting Carlton's verbose president John Elliott and doing a complete backflip. 'I couldn't do it,' he said, 'just couldn't do it ...'

PRIORITIES

Signs around Geelong after the collapse of the Pyramid Building Society and massive retrenchments at Ford proclaimed: 'BUGGER PYRAMID, BUGGER FORD, GET ABLETT BACK' ... The enigmatic Gary Ablett snr was to return and become an even bigger star the second time around.

IN DEMAND

Hawk Dermott Brereton was voted Australia's most-eligible young bachelor by *Cleo* magazine in 1989.

PLAYING FOR PEANUTS

Few were as loyal as North Melbourne's Glenn Archer. Early in his career he was offered $145 000 to switch to Sydney. He was on $5000 at North – and stayed.

PAROCHIAL

They were nice and parochial in the early days at Carrara. When Brisbane kicked a goal, the club's theme song was played, but when opposition teams had a shot, a sign on the scoreboard would appear: 'CHEWY ON YOUR BOOT!'

SLEEVELESS

The 1987 Grand Final was played in record 30-degree heat, Hawthorn's captain Michael Tuck wearing a sleeveless guernsey for the only time in his 426-match career.

OOPS

The newly formed Brisbane Bears, described as 'misfits' by some, were preparing for their very first trial game against Hawthorn in 1987. Their new jumpers had been ordered and duly arrived two days before the game. But to their horror, the maroon and gold colours had been reversed and the design was wrong. It was too late to make a change so they wore the jumpers and adopted them as their 'reverse strip' for early competition games against the Hawks and West Coast.

TEENAGE PRODIGY

Aged 14, Altona High student Ronnie James became the youngest player to represent Williamstown in the 1985 VFA Grand Final against Sandringham. The following year, at 15, he played in his first premiership and at 16, debuted with Footscray.

STONY SILENT

Other than a nod and an occasional hello, Hawthorn legend Don Scott went through his final VFL season in 1981 without saying even one word to the club's new coach Allan Jeans. 'It was complicated,' he said years later. 'He wanted to use me as an impact player and if it wasn't working in the first five or 10 minutes he wanted to take me off all the time. I didn't like that.'

TOO MUCH

Having withdrawn from March training, telling Carlton coach Alex Jesaulenko that his pre-season training demands were

EXCESSIVE: David McKay

'ridiculous', David McKay returned closer to the season start and played in a premiership team that very season and again in 1981, his fourth in one of the great careers. Earlier he'd told me, 'The training is far too hard. You work all day then train from 4.30 p.m. to 8 p.m. – or even later – three nights a week. It's too much.'

MARK OF THE CENTURY

Football journeyman Kevin Taylor was only knee-high but he could leap and had a rare goal sense. He had several stints in the east, with South Melbourne and Fitzroy without living up to the high-flying form he had in Perth where with East Fremantle he took one of the finest marks ever captured, by the *Western Mail*'s Barry Baker.

Making his senior debut with East Fremantle at 19, Taylor kicked 100 goals in a season in 1979, including seven in the WAFL grand final when he won the Simpson medal for being best afield.

His VFL coaches frowned on his leaping and this affected his play. While he kicked five goals against North Melbourne at Arden Street, in 1981, he rarely played at his spectacular Perth-best. Back in WA, however, he attained All-Australian status in 1983 – he was truly a remarkable one-State player.

HUMBLE PIE

Jack Dyer's writings in *Truth* were always colourful and comment-provoking. When a wobbly kneed Glenn Elliott attempted a comeback with Melbourne in 1979, Dyer led the charge against his bid, prompting Elliott to say, 'I just hope guys like Jack Dyer have humble pie all over their faces after I play 20 games this year.' At the age of 28, Elliott, one of my old cricket buddies, played 15 and then retired from VFL ranks – this time for good.

MARK OF THE CENTURY: East Fremantle's Kevin Taylor takes one of the greatest marks in Aussie Rules history
*Barry Baker/Alan East/*Western Mail

CLOSE THING

South Melbourne's team manager Greg Miller was in the bush on a recruiting mission one Saturday when there was an urgent phone call from the club. Someone had forgotten to pick up the seniors' jumpers from the local dry cleaners and it had closed. The reserves had played in a second set of jumpers numbered from No. 60 to No. 80. Would the seniors have to also wear the used jumpers? After a couple of frantic phone calls, the proprietor was found and the seniors set, nice and pristine, arrived with just 10 minutes to spare …

STARS IN THE MAKING

No wonder Our Lady's Ringwood was unbeatable among primary schools in the Melbourne east in the mid-70s: its following-division was Paul Salmon, Peter Banfield and Gary O'Donnell. Collectively they were to play more than 700 games of League football.

WISH LIST

Fitzroy legend Kevin Murray was part of North Melbourne's 'wish-list' in the summer of '73 when they recruited such champions as Barry Davis, John Rantall and Doug Wade. 'They said they needed a bit of experience to help them. They had a five-year plan to win the premiership,' Murray said. 'They offered me a bit of money and said how they hoped I'd play a lot of games for them. But I stayed at Fitzroy and in what turned out to be my last year, I broke the games record in the second-last match.'

LOOKING SHARP

Part of St Kilda 300-gamer Barry Breen's pre-game routine was to sneak into the bootstudder's room at Moorabbin and blow-wave his hair with a ladies hairdryer he had hidden.

FIREY HOMECOMING

Play was held up for seven minutes during the second quarter when streamers and banners behind the Essendon goals caught fire at Victoria Park in 1972. Des Tuddenham was coaching against his old team for the first time and there were wild scenes as locked-out fans used crowbars to break down barriers to enter the ground. More than 42 000 attended. Having trailed at half-time, Collingwood won easily.

EARLY FINISH

So bitterly cold and bleak was the weather at exposed Girdlestone Park, Devonport this day that rival captains Darrel Baldock (Latrobe) and Graeme Lee (East Devonport) agreed not to have a half-time break.

LUCKY SHOT

Long-time Melbourne *Herald* photographer Bruce Howard snapped the photo of a lifetime when he captured a leaping Alex Jesaulenko marking over Graeme 'Jerka' Jenkin in the unforgettable 1970 Grand Final. His colleague Dennis Bull from *The Age* was sharing a packet of Minties and Howard was in the process of unwrapping a couple when someone shouted, 'Look out!' 'We looked up and saw Jezza running and the ball coming. I had two Minties in my hand, threw them into my mouth still with the wrappers on, grabbed hold of my camera and fired … and got the picture of Jezza at his highest point actually marking the ball. I was very lucky.'

QUIET NIGHT

The night in 1968 that Bobby Skilton won his third Brownlow Medal, he was at home in pyjamas watching *Combat!* on television, nursing a broken nose and recovering from concussion.

THANKS BUT NO THANKS

Jack Clarke was doing a giant clean-up – filling an old bag with all his Essendon FC trophies, he threw them over the cliff at the bottom of Hutchison Avenue near his Beaumaris home. Months later there was a knock on the door. An old fisherman had found the bag and returned the lot … intact! 'Why didn't you leave them there?' asked Jack.

UNFORGETTABLE

No team keeper ever rang the siren for so long and so joyously as St Kilda's Freddie Farrell after the Saints won their first-ever premiership in 1966. He blew the siren repeatedly, beginning an unforgettable night of celebrations.

Meanwhile that same afternoon a St Kilda Rabbi interrupted prayers for Yom Kippur (the Jewish holiday of the year) to announce the final score – and to ask those assembled to please start concentrating on the service a bit more!

A RARE DAY OUT

So dominant was Port Melbourne teenager Mal Allen in the 1966 VFA Grand Final that he took his boots off in the last quarter and ran around in his red and blue hooped socks. He even kicked one of the match-sealing goals in his socks.

IT'S NO USE . . .

Ian 'Humper' Cooper was a beanpole 'jumping jack' and just about best afield in St Kilda's one-and-only premiership in 1966. Cooper's subsequent battle to add muscle to his spindly frame was totally unsuccessful. 'A teammate suggested that walking more would sharpen my appetite and add muscle,' Cooper said. 'He even sold me a dog to be my walking companion. The dog ran away on our first walk and I lost half a stone searching for the mongrel!'

THANKS, IS THAT FOR ME?

With seven goals on Grand Final day, 1965, Ted Fordham received a garish red vinyl recliner chair as Essendon's best player afield on Channel 7's *World of Sport*. It was soon donated to an auntie.

MIRACLE GOAL

Having kicked the winning goal in time-on of the 1964 Grand Final, Melbourne defender Neil Crompton was celebrating back in the rooms when hardline coach Norm Smith approached, kissed him and said, 'Well done … and don't do it again!' Crompton had found himself up in the centre waiting for his opponent Denis Dalton, but because the Magpies led and there was less than a minute to go, Dalton went to half-back to be behind the ball. Answering calls from the bench to pick him up, Crompton scouted the crumbs after a Brian Dixon kick downfield and kicked his one and only goal of the season. It was the Dees' 12th and last premiership.

KING OF THE FREES

During his final senior years in Perth, so adept was Melbourne legend big Bob Johnson at falling just when an umpire was around that he became known as 'Autumn Leaves' – even among his own East Fremantle supporters. They reckon he should have gone into acting.

'SORRY, WHAT WAS THAT, BOB?'

Talkative Alec Epis, 'the boy from Boulder', was Victoria's 21st man in an interstate match and acting as the runner for coach Bob Davis, was told to ask ruckman Noel Teasdale how he was going and did he want to come off?

Out he rushed to Teasdale who said, 'What's up? What's the message?'

'Sorry, Teasa, I've forgotten!' said Epis and back he ran to the bench to a thunderstruck Davis who told him he'd never, ever, get another job with him!

WIN-LESS

Kevin Murray was appointed Fitzroy's captain-coach when no one else would take the job in 1963. Amid a welter of retirements, Murray wasn't to achieve even one win in 1963 and in 1964 went winless again before heading, temporarily, to Western Australia. The only match the Lions did win in Murray's two seasons at the helm was in Round 10, 1963, when the team was coached by Wally Clark, Murray absent interstate with the Big V team. Ironically, the Lions that day defeated premiers-to-be Geelong.

TRICKSTER

Essendon's 'Gentle Giant' Geoff Leek was desperate to play in the 1962 Grand Final, but remained in severe doubt right up until an hour before the game with a dicky ankle. Essendon's medical staff decided that his 'test' would be to kick a medicine ball as hard as he could for two or three minutes. Leek duly obliged, was passed fit and rucked superbly against John Nicholls. Afterwards he revealed he'd kicked the medicine ball with his 'good' foot – thankfully no one had picked it up!

TEENAGE PRODIGY:
Ian Stewart

BOY WONDER

In only his fifth game of senior football, Hobart teenager Ian Stewart handed Geelong champion Alistair Lord a football lesson on his debut in 1962 for Tasmania against Victoria on a muddy North Hobart Oval. Lord won the Brownlow Medal later that year; Stewart came to Melbourne the following season and became one of the most decorated players in history.

TAKING THE RAP

The year he won the Brownlow in 1962, Alistair Lord was reported for striking, but identical twin Stewart stepped forward and said *he* was the guilty one and that the umpire had wrongly reported his brother. Alistair was cleared, tribunal chairman Tom Hammond suggesting one of the twins grow a moustache to avoid future confusion. Ask the twins now who was actually guilty and they just smile …

INFLUENTIAL ALF

A secret meeting arranged by the Melbourne *Herald* football writer Alf Brown took 'the Geelong Flyer' Bob Davis from playing into commentary duties with Channel 7. Insisting on Davis' silence, Brown also scooped all of his rivals in the Melbourne papers with his story: 'DAVIS SIGNS WITH SEVEN'.

GENEROUS

Before the 1961 Grand Final, Footscray pair Bob Spargo and Bernie Lee carried a young kid with his broken leg in a cast to his seat in the MCG's northern stand. The young man was to always have a soft spot for the Bulldogs. His name? Leading football writer, journalist and commentator and my long-time colleague and mate Mike Sheahan.

HEATWAVE

The 1961 South Australian Grand Final between Norwood and West Adelaide was known as 'the Turkish Bath' Grand Final after springtime temperatures in Adelaide soared to an unseasonal 35 degrees.

LUKE'S LEGACY

Melbourne's John Beckwith was the first winning Grand Final captain to hold the premiership cup high in the air, in 1959. Previously there had been no official presentation. League chief Sir Kenneth Luke imported the concept from England, having seen an FA Cup final.

EVERYONE'S A WINNER...

Big cash awards in football were unheard of until 1958 when the Melbourne *Herald*, in conjunction with petroleum giant Ampol, offered 1000 pounds for the Footballer of the Year. It was big money and leading into the final round, the three leaders Allen Aylett, Brendan Edwards and Neil Roberts met outside St Paul's Cathedral and agreed to split the monies. Aylett was best afield in the last game and ended up winning 500 pounds while Edwards and Roberts, who also polled 'minor' votes, each received 250 pounds. 'We weren't dealing in small stakes,' Aylett said. 'We were all young men, all trying to get ahead and all very much in need of whatever money we could get our hands on. We agreed that first would get the most and the others would equally split the remainder. It was pretty big money for us all back then.'

MULTI-GIFTED

Brian Beers loved tennis just as much as football. And he was good at both. He was at the Brunswick Street Oval one winter Saturday playing a pennant match for Fitzroy. The courts

SPLITTING THE WINNINGS: *Herald* Footballer of the Year contenders Neil Roberts (left) and Allen Aylett

were in a far corner of the ground near the woodyard. Above were the outer-viewing mounds which would invariably be packed on match days. It was half-time and a group of diehards had turned their attention to the tennis. 'Why don't you play a man's game, you poofta!' said one. Twelve months later Beers was part of Collingwood's 1958 premiership team.

CHANGING SPORTS: Brian Beers

271

LATE SWITCH

When Melbourne's *Sun News-Pictorial* controversially printed the player numbers in their 1958 Grand Final edition on Saturday morning, League chiefs, not wanting sales of the *Football Record* to be affected, insisted that both clubs change their player numbers. The only one to wear his normal number was Collingwood's heavyweight ruckman Ray Gabelich who kept his No. 13. It was the only jumper he could fit into! Instead of his famous No. 31, Melbourne's Ron Barassi wore No. 2.

RAPID PROMOTION

Initially selected to play with Collingwood Under 19s, Keith Burns jumped two grades from the thirds to the firsts on the Saturday morning and made his senior debut in 1957. 'They were short of rovers,' he said. 'In those days the Under 19s were played as a curtain raiser to the senior match. They held me back from the first game and told me I was playing in the main event. You don't forget days like that. I was only 17 at the time.' It was the first of his 28 senior games. Later he won a JJ Liston Trophy at Sandringham and also coached Collingwood thirds for more than a decade.

SEEING IS BELIEVING

The day after he'd kicked the most sensational goal of the 1955 Grand Final, a 50-yard (45-metre) running torpedo from the boundary line – having taken several bounces around the southern wing – Melbourne's silky-skilled Bob McKenzie recreated the moment in his civvies and dress shoes after a teammate had suggested it was a fluke. 'Right, follow me,' said McKenzie and the players trooped to the half-forward line in front of the old Southern Stand. 'Watch this.' And he unleashed another torp which sailed through the Punt Road goals almost goalpost high. A young Ron Barassi was witness. 'I couldn't believe my bloody eyes,' he said.

EXPELL THEM

So down and out was Hawthorn in the immediate post-war years that the *Sporting Globe*'s Hec de Lacy called for the uncompetitive Hawks to be expelled. In 1950 they didn't win a game and in 1953 again finished last, rover Kevin 'Skeeter' Coghlan their leading goal kicker for the year with just 19 goals.

AN EXTRAORDINARY MONTH

Denis Cordner played in three Grand Finals in three weeks in 1948: one with University Blacks in the 'A' grade Amateurs and two immediately afterwards with Melbourne, including the Grand Final draw.

QUICK THINKING

During a game at Kardinia Park in the 1940s, Geelong's timekeeper and former playing legend Peter Burns tried to ring the bell, only for the clapper to fall out. He had to use the clapper like a hammer banging on it to start and finish each of the subsequent quarters.

NO FEAR

No one was tougher than Carlton's Bob Chitty, once cast in the lead role in the first movie version of *Ned Kelly*. Chitty lost a chunk of his finger in an industrial accident yet still played days later in the 1945 preliminary final, his mangled finger protected by a steel guard. Soon into the match he tired of the guard, threw it away and kept on playing. 'He had no fear whatsoever,' said contemporary Lou Richards, 'and had a tank-like body which could dish it out and take terrible punishment.'

THE CHANGI BROWNLOW

When Singapore fell to the Japanese in 1942, 50 000 Allied troops were captured and sent to a prison camp in Changi. Among them were 15 000 Australians who were allowed to set up their own wartime football competition. One match between Victoria and the Rest of Australia was said to have been watched by more than 10 000. Peter Chitty, brother of Bob, received the Changi Brownlow after being voted the outstanding player afield. Later when working on projects like the Burma railway, he cared for sick prisoners and carried their kits as well as his own through the jungle and was awarded the British Empire Medal.

A THREE-PEAT

Melbourne's Percy Beames was judged best afield for the third consecutive Grand Final in 1941 after similar stellar performances in 1939 and 1940. The Dees won all three flags. Beames, with whom I worked at the Melbourne *Age*, was one of the few to captain Victoria at both football and cricket.

SUBSTITUTE

Field umpire Bill Blackburn took over midway through the 1940 VFL Grand Final when Alan Coward broke an arm, having been sandwiched between two burly ruckmen, Bervyn Woods (Collingwood) and Jack Furness (Melbourne). 'I didn't pull out quickly enough,' said Coward of his misfortune.

HAIL THE CATS

So heavy were the hailstones at Corio Oval in 1936 that several players from both Geelong and St Kilda jumped the fence to seek shelter, the *Geelong Advertiser* saying the hailstones were of 'cyclonic proportions' and many players complained of headaches after the game. The Reg Hickey-led Cats won the match by 10 goals.

A DOG OF A DAY

Field umpire Bill Blackburn was bitten by a dog that strayed onto the oval during a Carlton–Collingwood game at Princes Park in 1935.

FREE FAGS

South Melbourne's goal-kicking ace Bob Pratt was an 11th-hour withdrawal from the 1935 Grand Final after he was hit by a truck carrying bricks in High Street, Prahran on the Friday before the game. 'I was about to get on a tram and this bloke came along in a truck and his brakes failed,' said Pratt. 'He hit me, ripped the back out of my suit and took the heel off my shoe. I was lucky really – but it still knocked me about a bit. I couldn't walk, let alone play footy the next day. The driver was very upset when he found out who he'd hit. He bought a packet of cigarettes around to me. That was the last I heard of him.' Without its champion goal kicker, South lost the final by 20 points, replacement full-forward Roy Moore from Sandhurst kicking two goals.

ENGAGING: South Melbourne's goal-kicking legend Bob Pratt

SNUBBED

Despite kicking a League record 150 goals in 1934, Bob Pratt failed to poll in the top six in the Brownlow Medal and didn't win even his own club's best and fairest. Complaining later to an official, he was told, 'You were spectacular, Bob, but not very effective!'

GOAL-KICKING DOYEN

Western Australia's unrivalled 'prince' of goal kickers was East Fremantle's George Doig, who kicked centuries of goals *every* year from when he was a teenager in 1932 until the war intervened in 1941. His best in any one season was 152.

PYROTECHNICS

There were wild celebrations in Geelong for the Cat's first-ever premiership team of 1925. As the victorious team arrived by train, drivers of every locomotive in the Geelong railway yards sounded jubilant blasts and 200 detonators were exploded along the railway tracks. Later at the Geelong Town Hall there was a prolonged fireworks display as part of the hometown welcome.

A NEW CATCHCRY

A keen Richmond fan, a Mr Miles, couldn't afford the price of admission to Richmond matches so would camp in a gum tree overlooking the ground and yell, 'Eat 'em alive, Tigers!' The catchcry stuck.

BY THE WAY, THIS IS FOR YOU . . .

It was 12 months before Edward 'Cargi' Greeves, winner of the first Brownlow Medal in 1924 actually received his medal. There was no razzamatazz ceremony for such things in the '20s, Greeves having it handed to him via Geelong's VFL delegate late in 1925.

ONE HIT WONDER

Kyabram teenager Bill James played just one game of League football, the 1920 Grand Final in which he kicked the sealing goal late in the final quarter. After a week of celebrating Kyabram's flag, he'd been lifted into Richmond's team at the 11th hour after regular full-forward George Bayliss was injured. Prior to the start of the 1921 season, James was accidentally shot in the foot, losing two toes. His career ended just as it was starting.

TWO FROM TWO

Dan Minogue won premierships in each of his first two seasons as Richmond's playing coach in 1920 and 1921, a feat unequalled for 70 years until Hawthorn's Alan Joyce also won two from two in 1988 and 1991.

POPULAR

Diminutive Dr Roy Park never played in a winning team in his 44 games with Melbourne University, but was so admired for his talent and sportsmanship that he was once chaired off by Richmond supporters having finished at the top of the goal-kicking charts after the final match of the 1913 home-and-away season. He'd

A. E. V. HARTKOPF (University).
From "THE WEEKLY TIMES," Melbourne.

NOTABLE: The great Bert Hartkopf from Scotch College was one of Victoria's foremost early sportsmen

kicked 53 of his team's 115 goals for the season. Known as 'the University Midget', Park was just 165 centimetres (five feet, five inches) and 55 kilograms (eight stone, ten pounds). Another of University's foremost goal kickers was the taller and rangier AEV 'Bert' Hartkopf from Scotch College who averaged two goals a game in a poor side. Like Park, he also played Test cricket for Australia. A member of Scotch's first XI from the age of 13 and captain in his final two years, Hartkopf mixed cricket with football, tennis, rowing and athletics – and excelled at them all. In his stellar final year, he captained Scotch at both cricket and football, figured in Scotch's Head of the River rowing VIII and created new athletics records over 110 220 and 440 yards as well as winning the shot-put and the long jump. He was also in the tennis four. 'In his 13 years at school, he achieved the greatest eminence in sport ever reached by a Scotch boy,' said Scotch historian Harvey Nicholson in the school's history *The First 100 Years*, published in 1952.

SUPER SPORT

Multi-gifted Frank Boynton had no peer as Melbourne's most versatile Federation Age sportsman. A medicine student from Wesley College, he won a quadruple blue at Melbourne University in rowing, cricket, football and rifle and represented three VFL teams: University, Geelong and Melbourne.

COMMOTION

Champion of the Colonies in 1886, Essendon's Charles Pearson was nicknamed 'Commotion', his athletic leaps into the air to mark the ball stirring shrill shrieks from many ladies in the crowd worried that he may hurt himself. Said one critic, 'This new-fangled idea in marking will ruin the game. People come to see football, not men leaping in the air …'

14
Stats

'I had a few that night,' he said. 'I felt even worse the following week when we lost the [Grand Final] replay ...'

A SPORTING LIFE

Few were fast-tracked like Saint Craig Devonport in the early '90s. Most footballers have a lengthy junior apprenticeship, but in Devonport's case, his 50th game of League football in the early '90s was only the 100th game he ever played. A talented all-sportsman just as keen on basketball and soccer in his teens, he was a natural and once kicked five goals in a quarter against West Coast at the WACA Ground. He also shares a distinction with two other Saints, Stewart Loewe and Simon O'Donnell of playing seniors, reserves and Under 19s – all in a three-week period.

JOURNEYMAN

According to my maths, Collingwood's Bill Picken had more senior coaches than anyone in League football history: 12 in 12 years – Neil Mann, Ron Richards (for one match), Murray Weideman, Tom Hafey, Mick Erwin, John Cahill, Bob Rose, Leigh Matthews (Collingwood) and Ricky Quade, Tony Franklin, Bob Hammond and John Northey (South Melbourne/Sydney).

Also in prime place in the 'most coaches' category are Peter Francis who had 10 in 10 years, and Bruce Doull with 10 in 18 years.

Francis, one of the best afield in Carlton's memorable 1979 premiership had Ian Stewart, Serge Silvagni, Alex Jesaulenko, Peter 'Perc' Jones and David Parkin (at Carlton), Robert Walls (Fitzroy), Mike Patterson, Paul Sproule and Tony Jewell (Richmond) and Kevin Sheedy (Essendon).

Doull's 10 were Ron Barassi, John Nicholls, Keith McKenzie (for one match), Ian Thorogood, Stewart, Silvagni, Jesaulenko, Jones, Parkin and Walls (all Carlton).

SNUBBED

No Hawthorn players were named in the All-Australian team in 1991, despite the Hawks winning the Grand Final by almost 10 goals. Captain Michael Tuck appeared in a record seventh straight premiership team that year, surpassing the record of six held jointly by Collingwood brothers Albert ('Leeta') and Harry Collier and Melbourne pair Ron Barassi and Frank 'Bluey' Adams.

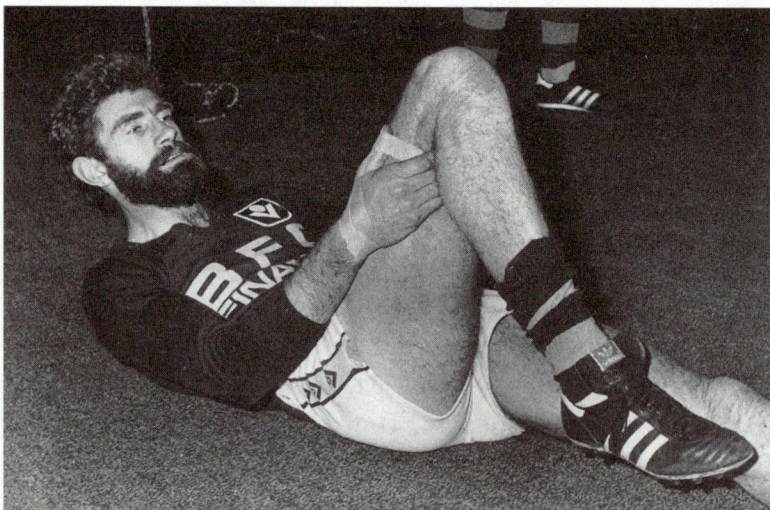

SEVEN FLAGS: Hawthorn legend Michael Tuck

DOUBLING IT UP

Geelong's Murray Witcombe achieved the rare 'double' of reaching 100 senior and 100 reserves games in 1987.

A POOR RETURN

Gary Shaw remains just about the most expensive footballing flop of his generation. So keen was a cashed-up Collingwood to secure his services that they paid his Brisbane club Western Districts 150 000 and Footscray 110 000 and St Kilda 40 000 for bypassing him in the 1983 draft. With a guaranteed playing salary of 40 000 – whether he played firsts or seconds – it made him a half-million dollar investment, yet he played just 32 games in four years and drifted off to Brisbane.

SOLITARY GOAL

Playing his 215th League match, Rod Carter kicked the *only* goal of his 293 match career, against Melbourne at the Sydney Cricket Ground in 1986 – courtesy of a Warwick Capper handpass. He'd spent a lifetime at full-back trying to stop goals rather than score them. Twelve months earlier, having been shifted down forward by coach John Northey, he'd marked well within range, directly in front, only to kick out of bounds on the full.

RARE GOAL: Rod Carter

EXCITING TIMES

No one has ever had more scoring shots in a single game than Kelvin Templeton's 24 for 15.9 for Footscray against St Kilda at Moorabbin in 1978. Included were eight goals straight in the final quarter as the Bulldogs smashed the VFL record for highest score in a game, scoring 33.15 (213) to thrash St Kilda by 100-plus points.

'I'd been inaccurate early and kicked 7.9 to three-quarter time,' Templeton said. 'Late in the third quarter I started to cramp up and didn't even make the distance a couple of times. Don McKenzie was coaching us and at the last break told me if the cramps persisted I'd come off, which was fair enough. We were well ahead in the game. But they disappeared and the game opened up for us. The ball just kept coming down to me and with the cramp gone, so did my inaccuracy. I only got eight possessions in the last quarter but they all resulted in goals. After the last mark, the siren went and the crowd rushed on as happened back then. I was lining it up when the message came if I kicked it, it would be the new League record (for Footscray). I was only 35 metres out and by that stage was very much in the groove. It was a great result for us as a club as we'd been struggling for so long. Being only 21 at the time, it was an exciting time for me, too.'

GOOD MOVE

Having played 12 years and 226 games and captained Melbourne for not even one final's appearance, Stan Alves crossed to North Melbourne, playing in three Grand Finals, 11 finals and 40 matches in three stellar, farewelling years.

THE $2000 MAN

Royce Hart is among an elite band to play back-to-back senior Grand Finals on consecutive Saturdays.

In 1969, he emulated the feat of West Australian Stan 'Pops' Heal to figure in two Grand Finals in two states within a week of each other.

Having helped Richmond to the 1969 VFL premiership, Hart appeared the following weekend in the South Australian

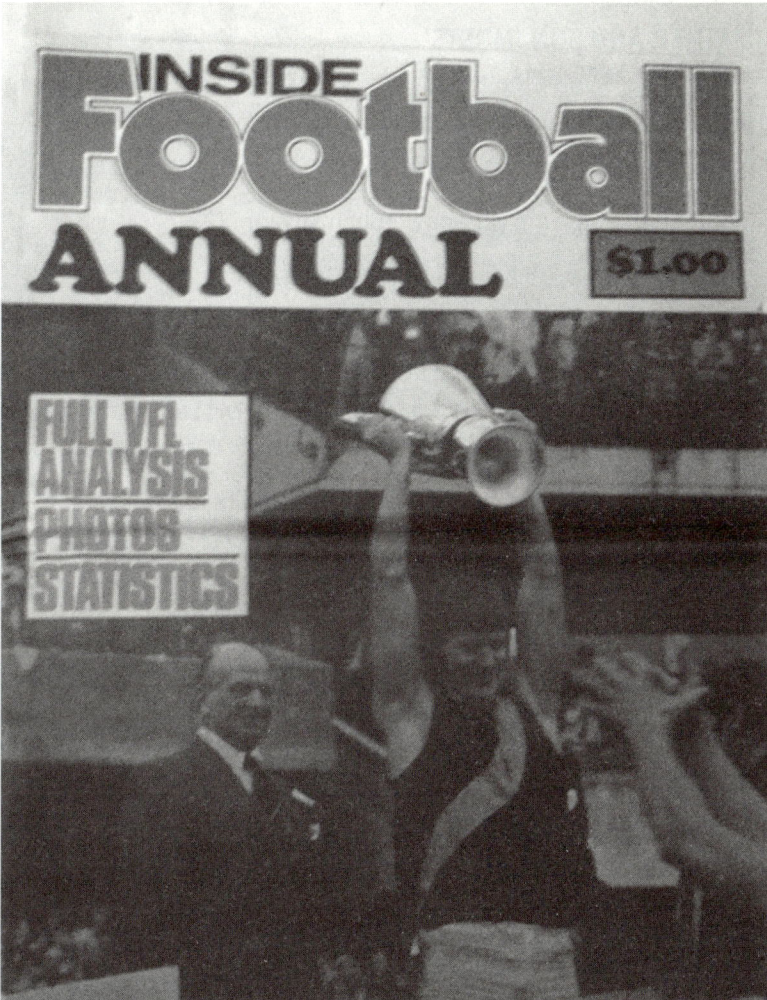

WINNER: Everything Royce Hart the footballer touched turned to gold. He was the biggest name in the game in the late '60s and early '70s

Grand Final, for Glenelg against Sturt on a one-off fee of $2000, a record for the time. He'd been in Adelaide on national service for much of the year and had trained regularly with Glenelg before flying to Melbourne each weekend for Richmond's home-and-away matches.

Within minutes of the start, he was concussed, but stayed on the ground, Glenelg being well beaten.

283

FATHER AND SON 'MOSTS'

Most father-son best and fairests:

Eight: Leo Murphy (2) and John Murphy (6)

Seven: John Murphy (6) and Marc Murphy (1)

Four: Sergio Silvagni (2) and Stephen Silvagni (2)

Three: Brian Martyn (1) and Mick Martyn (2)

Most father-son games:

664: Ken Fletcher (264) and Dustin Fletcher (400)

556: Gary Ablett snr (248), Gary Ablett jnr (274*) and Nathan Ablett (34)

551: Sergio Silvagni (239) and Steve Silvagni (312)

Most father-son goals:

1445: Gary Ablett snr (1030), Gary Ablett jnr (368*) and Nathan Ablett (47)

1206: Peter Hudson (727) and Paul Hudson (479)

Most father-son premierships:

Seven: Ron Barassi snr (1940) and Ron Barassi jnr (1955, 1956, 1957, 1969, 1960, 1964)

Six: Charlie Pannam snr (1902, 1903), Charlie Pannam jnr (1917, 1919) and Alby Pannam (1935, 1936)

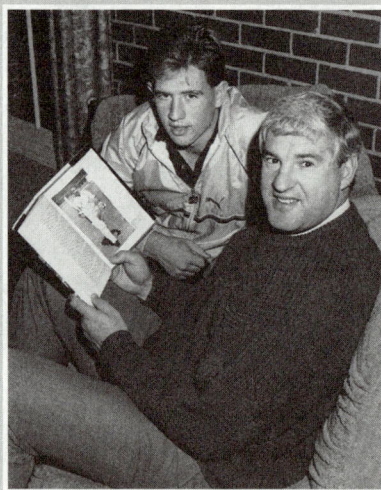

GOALS GALORE: Peter and Paul Hudson

* to the start of the 2016 season

A week later, Richmond met Sturt in the Australian championship final and a Sturt player was knocked out by burly Tiger Colin Beard. Coincidence? Probably not.

STICKY FINGERS

Who took most marks in the VFL in 1966? Maybe John Schultz, Doug Wade or another of the power forwards? No, it was St Kilda's 180-centimetre (5 feet, 11 inches) centreman and Brownlow Medallist Ian Stewart.

WHISTLE-BLOWER

In the 1965 Round 15 match between Fitzroy and Hawthorn at Brunswick Street, field umpire John Gambetta awarded an extraordinary 122 free kicks – 70 to Fitzroy and 52 to Hawthorn. It remains the most ever recorded according to AFL statistician Cameron Sinclair.

UNLUCKY CAT

Geoff Rosenow missed two premierships in a day with Geelong in 1963. Having played in Geelong's senior team in 12 of the 18 home-and-away matches, he was displaced for the finals by interstate import John Watts – but was ruled ineligible for the reserves Grand Final because he'd played too many games at the higher level.

FOUR-IN-ONE FOOTBALLER

Is a young Ted Whitten the only player to win four best and fairests in the same season? It happened in 1950 when Ted won Braybrook Under 17s and the competition best and fairest. That was Saturday football. On Sundays he represented the Collingwood amateurs and was also club and competition best and fairest.

GRAND FINAL NERVES

Essendon full-forward Bill Brittingham had never touched a drop of the hard stuff until Grand Final night 1948 when he kicked 2.12 and the Bombers could only tie with Melbourne, 7.27 (69) to 10.9 (69). 'I had a few that night,' he said. 'I felt even worse the following week when we lost the [Grand Final] replay.'

Upon John Coleman's arrival six months later, Brittingham continued to play out of the goalsquare – at the opposite end of the ground … as Essendon's new full-back!

THE LONGEST KICK EVER

It was the longest recorded kick ever: 116 yards (106 metres) by Melbourne giant Fred Fanning at the MCG in 1939. The kick was verified by a gent from the Lands Department who was called in to do the official measurement.

Jim Cardwell, Melbourne's long-time secretary, was eyewitness to the drop-kick that he said 'just went and went and went … None of us had ever seen anything like it.'

Interviewed by Michael Roberts in 1995, Cardwell said, 'Fred went down and past the centre chasing kicks,' he said. 'He got the ball just one or two paces from the [centre] circle and let go with a kick that went so far it landed about the centre of the green concrete terraces behind the goals [at the western or city end of the ground]. We all signed a statement testifying the fact that it was 116 yards.'

Cardwell said the heavier boots as worn back then allowed players of the era to kick consistently longer than modern-day players. 'Most of them were handmade, very solid and with a heavy toe that contained a metal top. This assisted the flight of the ball, much more than boots of today which are often no better than kicking with bare feet.'

HIGH-FLIER: A late-autumn 1934 edition of the *Sporting Globe* featuring South Melbourne's spring-heeled full-forward Bob Pratt

BOB IN FOR BOB

Having kicked a record 150 goals in 1934, Bob Pratt received a bonus 50 pounds courtesy of South Melbourne's 'bob in for Bob' fundraiser where supporters were encouraged to put in a shilling as a thank you to their star goal kicker. It doubled his monies for the season.

AN EPIDEMIC OF POSTERS

Deep into time-on at Corio Oval in 1928, Fitzroy's scoreline read 1.27 (33) before Jack Moriarty kicked a goal with just a minute to play. The Lions were thumped by Geelong 2.27 (39) to 19.8 (122). The Lions hit the post five times.

SIXTY YEARS, ONE GAME

Richmond's legendary property steward Charlie Callander and secretary Percy Page share a rare record … they are among a select group to represent a League club in an interstate match without ever having played a League game in Melbourne …

It was 1927 and the Tigers were on an end-of-season trip to Tasmania where they were due to play Southern Tasmania in an exhibition game. But one of the players hurt his ankle and two were so seasick from the boat trip that the team was two short.

'Checker Hughes was coach and he told Percy and I there was no alternative than we play so we could at least have 18,' said Callander. 'He put us on the same side of the ground, Percy on a forward flank and me in a forward pocket and gave the players precise instructions that under no circumstances were they to take the ball down our wing. Everything was going well until a ball flew off the side of Frank O'Brien's boot straight to me. I managed to mark it but it

COACHING GREAT: Frank 'Checker' Hughes

had come so hard that it knocked me down and when I got up to kick for goal, I had an air-swing – my moment being caught by a photographer who put it in next day's Hobart *Mercury*. It was my one and only game …'

Charlie was to have more than six decades as Richmond's property steward. He'd begun his career carrying one of the player's bags into the ground so he could sneak in free.

15

Superstitions

'Shit, there is someone there,' ... I jumped out and there was a poor bloke in a wheelchair, completely pinned under the car by all my reversing.'

LUCKY PANTS

So superstitious was Irishman Tadhg Kennelly that he even taped a favourite pair of blue underpants to his body; just to get a few more matches out of them! He also liked to wear a second sock on his kicking foot.

THE DEVIL'S NUMBER . . .

Number 13 has always been controversial. Cricketers say it's 13 from their 'devil's number' of 87, many hotels don't have a 13th floor, some authors refuse to have a chapter 13, while Friday the 13th remains a scary date for many each calendar year.

As footballers go, most prefer not to have it – but some wear it with distinction, particularly the Adelaide Crows captain Taylor 'Tex' Walker and much-travelled Carlton midfielder Dale Thomas.

The most matches by any No. 13 is 265 over 14 seasons by Western Bulldog Daniel Giansiracusa. Melbourne's Adem Yze also played more than 250 games.

Collingwood legend Dick Lee booted 420 goals in No. 13.

NUMBER 13

MOST LEAGUE GAMES

Games	Player	Team(s)	Seasons
265	Daniel Giansiracusa	Western Bulldogs	2001–14
262	Adem Yze	Melbourne	1995-2008
228	Adam Schneider	Sydney/St Kilda	2003–15
217	Rod Carter	Fitzroy/Sydney	1974–90
217	John Law	North Melbourne	1978–89
189	Mil Hanna	Carlton	1986–97
187	Martin Pike	Melbourne/Fitzroy/ North Melbourne/ Brisbane Lions	1993–05
180	Joe Murdoch	Richmond	1927–36
170	Brett Voss	Brisbane Lions / St Kilda	1997–2007

* to the start of the 2016 AFL season

MOST LEAGUE GOALS

Games	Player	Team(s)	Seasons
420	Dick Lee	Collingwood	1906–22
331	Daniel Giansiracusa	Western Bulldogs	2001–14
259	Adam Schneider	Sydney/St Kilda	2003–15
256	Taylor 'Tex' Walker	Adelaide Crows	2009–15*
246	Jack 'Chooka' Howell	Carlton	1942–54
245	Vin Gardiner	Melbourne/Carlton	1905–17
231	Adem Yze	Melbourne	1995–2008
208	Allen Jakovich	Melbourne/ Footscray	1991–96
204	Paul Sarah	Geelong/Richmond	1972–83
165	Alex Ruscuklic	Fitzroy/Carlton	1966–74

* to the start of the 2016 AFL season

MATCH DAY SUPERSTITIONS

KEVIN BARTLETT (Richmond): 'Fish and chips on a Friday night before the game.'

DERMOTT BRERETON (Hawthorn): Insisted on wearing Hawthorn's old-style 'Jason' jumper with the wider brown stripes. 'I'd always have a rub-down with our long-time trainer Johnny Haward and afterwards throw a tennis ball against a wall 40 times and catch it. I always thought marking a footy after that was far easier.'

GAVIN BROWN (Collingwood): 'I'd always have three crumpets with honey on match days.'

PAUL COUCH (Geelong): 'On cold days I'd always stick my feet in a hot bath. It was a trick David Bolton told me about. They always felt better.'

WINNERS: Dermott Brereton with son-of-a-gun Paul Hudson after Hawthorn's 1991 premiership. Brereton won five day and five night flags

BEN GRAHAM (Geelong): 'Always a plate of baked beans before a game.'

RUSSELL GREENE (St Kilda and Hawthorn): 'As a young buck I'd play the loudest possible music: Black Sabbath, ZZ Top and Deep Purple. Later on though I was happy to read a book . . . a favourite was JRR Tolkien and *Lord of the Rings*.'

BRAD JOHNSON (Western Bulldogs): 'I liked to wear the same pair of Speedos and use the same towel each week.'

STEPHEN KERNAHAN (Carlton): 'On match mornings I'd sleep in until 10 o'clock, have some toast, heat up a chicken drumstick and listen to loud music on the way to the ground.'

GLENN MANTON (Essendon and Carlton): 'I'd always tap the end of the race twice with the footy as we were running out. Some players didn't like to have a footy with them, but I always insisted on it. And always beforehand, a banana and a mandarin.'

LEIGH MATTHEWS (Hawthorn): 'Before particularly big games, I always liked to get a new pair of socks.'

MERV NEAGLE (Essendon and Sydney): 'Weetbix with strawberries'.

GREG WILLIAMS (Geelong, Sydney and Carlton): 'A two-kilometre run or swim, just to loosen up.'

ROBERT HARVEY (St Kilda): 'I'd always have a sandwich and listen to the Coodabeens on the way to the game.'

MATTHEW RICHARDSON (Richmond): 'A Mars bar before a game.'

JARRYD ROUGHEAD (Hawthorn): 'I'm always last out and never touch the cheer squad banner'.

Another of the most successful No. 13s was Hawthorn's Paul Dear who was best afield in the 1991 Grand Final. He remains the only Norm Smith Medallist to have worn No. 13. Originally from Jeeralang Junction, near Churchill, Dear says he was grateful to have it. 'Before then I was up from the Under 19s and had No. 58,' he said. 'I wanted to get something closer to my brother who was 14 and as I am still telling him now, the lower your number, the better the player!'

One of Dear's sons, Harry, was drafted to the Adelaide Crows in 2015 and one day may continue the No. 13 tradition – but only when Tex Walker retires!

THE ROSE JINX

Having lost the unlosable Grand Final in 1970 – Collingwood had led by 44 points at half-time – Bobby Rose hosted the players, friends and officials back at his home, his new, ever-so-chic Scandinavian Fler lounge suite collapsing under the combined weight of Denis O'Callaghan, one of his Grand Final teammates and their girlfriends. 'It's the Rose jinx,' said one of the guests. Luckily for him his throwaway line wasn't heard by Bobby, a former boxer.

FRIDAY NIGHT IN CHURCH STREET

Among Don Scott's myriad of memorabilia from a lifetime in the game is a bull's head on a board complete with Hawthorn ribbon around its neck.

'I won our Damn-low Medal for the lowest act of the year,' said Don.

'I was living in Hawthorn and my routine each Friday night before a game was go down to the local laundromat in Church Street and do my washing. I'd load it all in, go back home, have my main meal, return to the laundromat, throw it all in a drier, have my dessert before going to pick it all up again. It's just what I did.

'I had this old EH Holden. It was my first car and I was reversing it back to park. A tram was coming down the hill and was ringing his bell. "I can see you, mate, I'm not going to come out," I said to myself.

'I reversed back and suddenly stopped. There was a clanging noise. The tram conductor was still ringing his bell. "Yeah, yeah, mate," I thought. So I went forward and reversed back again, a little bit harder this time. Same thing. This time there was a muffled knocking noise. "That's unusual," I thought. "No one else is in the car."

'So I went forward again and backed back and this time there was a real hard knocking noise from the back. "Shit, there is someone there ..." I jumped out and there was a poor bloke in a wheelchair, completely pinned under the car by all my reversing. I got him out of there, stood him up and down he went again ... poor fella. His wheelchair was mangled and he was most unimpressed.

'The boys at the club reckoned it was the lowest act of all, said it couldn't possibly be topped and presented me with the Damn-low to keep for good.'

Acknowledgements

It was the last Saturday of spring in 2007, AFL draft day. As I walked my pups up the local beach, approaching from long distance was a man, dressed only in white footy shorts and new runners, running towards me at good pace. He looked familiar. You could tell he'd be running for an hour, if not longer. As we got closer, it was unmistakably my Mt Eliza near-neighbour, two-time Brownlow Medallist Rob Harvey. I said 'G'day,' so did he, and we kept going. At the time, Rob was 36 and gearing for a record 21st season of AFL football – and on a day which was to introduce high draftees and stars-on-the-rise like Jack Watts, Nic Naitanui and Jack Ziebell.

Rob's way of competing deep into his 30s was to run five days a week – even in the off-season – building the best possible fitness base. It was clear just why he was a champion, one of the greatest ever. Sure he had anticipation, rare reflexes and all the football smarts. But along with Don Scott, the inspirational Hawk, he also worked his body harder than anybody I've ever known. I still regularly see him now, early mornings mostly, charging up hills. He's truly remarkable. Given his record and sheer feel for the game, he commands an instant respect everywhere he goes. No wonder Collingwood's Nathan Buckley, who prepares like few coaches I know, has him as his right-hand man.

I'd like to thank Bob for endorsing my latest footy book and contributing the foreword. If he hadn't been so good at football, he was certainly good enough to represent Victoria at cricket.

My long-time Geelong mate Mark Browning again provided extra research and suggestions, as did the ever-encouraging and supportive Geoff Poulter – with whom I first worked at *Inside Football* in Spencer Street, when I was a teenager starting out at *The Age* in the early '70s – and Greg Hobbs, my mentor at the old 'pink paper', the *Sporting Globe*.

I'd also like to acknowledge my wife Susan who worked with me keeping the scrapbooks over a lifetime of writing and reading. Thanks to her, I was able to uncover long-forgotten conversations, some of which – like Percy Page, Jack Mueller, Jack Dyer and Bob Pratt – have been resurrected here.

Collective friends all rallied like Greg Smith/Channel 7, Tom Mahony, Francis Doherty and John and Steven Cominos. Many of the illustrations inside belong to them. Footballers old and young, footy identities and friends also assisted in so many ways and my thanks to them all, in alphabetical order: Stan Alves, Gareth Andrews, John Bahen, Cherryl and Ron Barassi, Peter Bedford, Francis Bourke, Greg Boxall, Barry Cheatley, Evelyn Danos, Ken Davis, Greg and Paul Dear, Dougie Dyall, Simon Fiedler, Ben Graham, Mark 'Heebee' Graham, KB 'Kevin' Hill, Greg Hobbs, Quentin Hull, Col Hutchison, Tim Lane, Rosemary Long, John Lord, Glenn McFarlane, Bill Meaklim, Greg Miller, Drew Morphett, Rod Olsson, David Parkin, Lance Picione, Leon Rice, Tami and Paul Roos, Don Scott, Michael Sexton, John Sharrock, Kevin Sheehan, Cameron Sinclair, Geoff Southby and Peter Walker. Apologies if I have missed anyone.

Over the last months I became a frequent visitor to the wondrous Melbourne Cricket Club library where David Studham and Trevor Ruddell were equally embracing.

My daughter Jessie improved many of the images via her consummate Photoshop skills. The expert team at Five Mile Press/Echo Publishing again excelled, especially Julia, Kyla and Shaun. So did Paul Harvey with his wonderfully humorous and entertaining cartoons. Thanks everyone, again. Hope you enjoy the read. – KP

Bibliography

BOOKS

Alves, Stan with Col Davies, *Sacked Coach, Life ... Football ... Death* (Crown Content, Melbourne, 2002)

Aylett, Allen, *My Game, a Life in Football as Told to Greg Hobbs* (Sun Books, Melbourne, 1986)

Bourbon, Stephen (ed.), *Tales from the Inner Sanctum* (Reclink, Melbourne, 2003)

Brereton, Dermott with Ken Piesse, *101 Favourite Football Stories* (Pan Macmillan Australia, Sydney, 1993)

Capper, Warwick and Howard Kotton, *Capper. Fool Forward* (Bas Publishing, Melbourne, 2005)

Cartledge, Elliot, *The Hafey Years, Reliving a Golden Era at Tigerland* (Weston Media and Communications, Melbourne, 2011)

Cordner, John, David Allen, Paul Daffey, Robin Grow and June Senyard, *Black & Blue, the Story of Football at the University of Melbourne* (Melbourne University FC, Melbourne, 2007)

Eddy, Dan, *King Richard, the Story of Dick Reynolds, Essendon Legend* (Slattery Media Group, Melbourne, 2014)

Fevola, Brendan with Adam McNichol, *Fev: In My Own Words* (Hardie Grant Books, Melbourne, 2012)

Fiddian, Marc, *The VFA, the History of the Victorian Football Association, 1877–1995* (VFA, Melbourne, 1996)

Flower, Robert with Ron Reed, *Robbie* (Caribou Publications, Melbourne, 1987)

Hayes, Lenny with Jason Phelan, *Lenny, My Story* (Hardie Grant Books, Melbourne, 2014)

Hart, Royce with Bruce Matthews, *The Royce Hart Story* (Thomas Nelson Australia Ltd, Sydney, 1970)

Hawkins, Doug with Michael Stevens, *Hawkins: My Story, Both Sides of the Fence* (Double M Marketing, Moonee Ponds, Melbourne, 1991)

Hillier, Kevin, *Like Father Like Son, Legends of AFL football* (Pan Macmillan Australia, Sydney, 2006)

Hogan, P, *The Tigers of Old, Richmond Football Club* (Melbourne, 1996)

Hunt, Rex, *Rex, My life* (Pan MacMillan Australia, Sydney, 2002)

Jarvis, Nathan, *Origin of the Speccies, the Players and Positions of AFL* (Fremantle Arts Central Press, Perth, 2006)

Kennelly, Tadhg with Scott Gullan, *Unfinished Business* (Mercier Press, Melbourne, 2009)

Kernahan, Stephen with Tony de Bolfo, *Sticks, the Stephen Kernahan Story* (Random House Australia, Sydney, 1997)

Klugman, Matthew and Gary Osmond, *Black and Proud* (NewSouth Publishing, Sydney, 2013)

Koutoufides, Anthony with Tony de Bolfo, *Kouta* (Hardie Grant Books, Melbourne, 2007)

Main, Jim, *Our Game, Classic Aussie Rules Stories* (Viking, Melbourne, 2007)

Malthouse, Mick and David Buttifant, *The Ox is Slow, But the Earth is Patient* (Allen and Unwin, Sydney, 2011)

Matthews, Simon, *Champions of Essendon, ranking the 60 greatest Bombers of all time* (Hardie Grant Books, Melbourne, 2002)

Maxwell, Nick with Michael Gleeson, *One Grand Week, a Captain's Tale of the 2010 Triumph* (Weston Media and Communications, Melbourne, 2010)

Piesse, Ken, *The Complete Guide to Australian Football* (Pan Macmillan, Sydney, 1993)

Piesse, Ken, *Down at the Junction, There's a Cricket Ground, St Kilda CC, the First 150 Years* (St Kilda CC, Melbourne, 2005)

Piesse, Ken, *Football Legends of the Bush, Local Heroes & Big Leaguers* (Penguin/Viking, Melbourne, 2011)

Piesse, Ken, *Miracle Match, the Day David Downed Goliath, July 6, 1963, Brunswick St Oval* (cricketbooks.com.au, Mt Eliza, 2014)

Porter, Ashley, *Crows' Tales, Stories from the Dressing Room* (Harper Collins, Sydney, 1993)

Powers, John, *The Coach, a Season with Ron Barassi* (Sphere Books, Melbourne, 1978)

Ramsland, John and Christopher Mooney, *Remembering Aboriginal Heroes* (Brolga Publishing, Melbourne, 2006)

Richards, Lou with Stephen Phillips, *The Kiss of Death* (Hutchinson Australia, Melbourne, 1989)

Richardson, Matthew and Martin Flanagan, *Richo* (Random House, Sydney, 2010)

Ridley, Ian with John Ridley, *Urge to Merge* (Crown Content, Melbourne, 2002)

Roos, Paul, *Beyond 300, an Autobiography* (Random House Australia, Sydney, 1997)

Rose, Peter, *Rose Boys* (Text Publishing, Melbourne, 2001)

Schwarz, David with Adam McNichol, *All Bets are Off* (Hardie Grant Books, Melbourne, 2010)

Silvagni, Stephen and Tony de Bolfo, *Silvagni* (HarperSports, Sydney, 2002)

Spencer, Fay, *Stuey: My Life with Stuart Spencer* (cricketbooks. com.au, Mt Eliza, 2014)

St John, Joe, *Don't Be Where the Ball Ain't, Celebrating the Immortal Humour and Wisdom of Football Legend Jack Dyer* (New Holland, Sydney, 2012)

Strevens, Steve, *Bob Rose, a Dignified Life* (Allen & Unwin, Sydney, 2003)

Thorp Clark, Mavis, *The Boy from Cumeroogunga* (Hodder and Stoughton, Sydney, 1979)

Walker, Max with Neill Phillipson, *Tangles* (Garry Sparke & Associates, Melbourne, 1976)

Wanganeen, Gavin, *The Power to Win* (Pan MacMillan Australia, Sydney, 1998)

NEWSPAPERS & PUBLICATIONS

AFL Season Guide, various years (Slattery Media Group, Melbourne)

The Age (Fairfax Media, Melbourne)

The Football Record (Slattery Media Group, Melbourne)

The Sporting Globe (The Herald and Weekly Times, Melbourne)

The Sunday Herald Sun (The Herald and Weekly Times, Melbourne)

Sunday Observer (Peter Isaacson Publications, Prahran, Melbourne)

The Sunday Press (David Syme & Co., Melbourne)

Sunday Times (WA Newspapers, Perth)

WEBSITES

www.afl.com.au

www.australianfootball.com

www.footyalmanac.com.au

Index

Ablett, Gary snr   6, 8, 9, 10, 105,
    243, 260
    a warm-up lunch   86–7
Ablett, Kevin   165
Adams, Frank 'Bluey'   211, 221,
    279
Adamson, Lee   58
Alessio, Steve   15
Allan, Matt   258
Allen, George   116
Allen, Mel   266
Allford, Grant   166
Alves, Stan 'the Edithvale
    Flash'   115, 221–3, 241, 282
    cartwheels of joy after Grand
        Final   237
Alvin, Tommy   205
Andrew, Bruce   33–4
Angeloski, Spasa   191
Angwin, Andy   124, 254
Anstey, Chris   13
Archer, Glenn   13, 14–15, 19, 98,
    232, 242
    rejects Sydney's $145 000
        offer   260
Arthur, Graham 'Mort'   79
Ataata, Fatui   126
Atkinson, Darren   63, 64
Aylett, Dr Allen   100, 196, 270
Aylett, Marj   196
Ayres, Gary 'Conan'   7, 8, 136–7,
    223

Badcock, Jackie   178
Baggott, Ron   187
Bahen, Chris & John   28
Bailey, Jo   192
Baker, Barry   262
Baker, Phil 'Snake'   253

Baldock, Darrel 'Doc'   1, 62, 65, 97,
    136, 252, 265
Ball, Jason   202
Balme, Neil   250
Bamblett, Les 'Lally'   126
Banfield, Peter   264
Barassi, Cherryl   17
Barassi, Ron jnr 'Barass'   17, 30, 31,
    46–8, 56, 62, 66, 82, 92, 97, 112,
    113, 117, 140, 143, 146, 153, 237,
    249, 253, 272, 280
    a cross line at the '68 Grand
        Final   210
    coaches North to '75
        flag   207–8
    high opinion of Bruce
        Doull   248
    insists on no sex before
        finals   195
    king hits Don Furness   223–4
    six premierships as a player   279
    tagged in '58 Grand Final   217
    wears No. 2 in the '58 Grand
        Final   272
Barassi, Ron snr   187
Barker, Daryl   43
Barker, Trevor 'Barks'   6, 9, 115,
    143, 166
    dates Tommy Hafey's
        daughter   171
Barnett, Greg   209
Barrot, Bill   166
Barry, Leo   8
Bartel, Jimmy   240
Bartlett, Kevin 'KB'   119, 136, 168,
    172, 224, 235, 244, 251, 291
    400th game   137–8
Bayes, Mark   19
Bayliss, George   277

Beames, Percy   94, 155–6
  best afield in three Grand Finals
    in a row   274
Beard, Colin   285
Beck, Ken   26–27
Beckwith, John   270
Bedford, Peter 'Wheels'   210
Beers, Brian   101, 270–1
Beha, Jimmy   55
Beitzel, Harry 'H'   124, 211
  Harry Beitzel's Footy Show   237
Bell, Denis   77
Bell, Peter   185
Benetti, John   101
Bentley, Percy   154
Berenger, Mark   57
Bertrand, John & Raza   17
Bigelow, Doug 'Bigs'   237
Birt, John   144
Blackburn, Bill   274, 275
Blethyn, Geoff   210
Blew, Don   235
Blight, Malcolm   8, 85, 232, 243,
    245
  matchwinning long bomb at
    Princes Park 27–8
Bolger, Martin   190
Bolton, David 'Bolts'   291
Bond, Graeme   166
Boon, David   41
Border, Allan   14
Bortolotto, Mario   120
Bosustow, Peter   127
Bourke, Barry   84, 227
Bourke, David   244
Bourke, Francis   152, 235, 244, 250
Bourke, Graeme   69
Bowden, Michael   166
Box, Peter   141, 176–8
Boxall, Greg 'Bocka'   88
Boyd, John   237
Boyd, Ken   122–3
Boynton, Frank   278
Bradley, Craig   224–5
Bradman, Don   9, 96, 97, 229, 252
Bradmore, Phil   52
Brady, John   55
Bray, Jeff   255
Breen, Barry   264
Brereton, Dermott 'Kid'   4–5, 11,
    15, 137, 141, 151, 192, 204, 205,
    225, 237
  Cleo's Bachelor of the Year   260
  how he got his nickname   247

match-day superstition   291
Brereton, Dermott snr   5, 141
Brereton, Jean   5, 6, 141
Briedis, Arnold   225
Brittingham, Bill   286
Brophy, Ron   144
Brouin, Jim   57
Brown, Alf   179, 180, 212, 218,
    269
Brown, 'Bomber'   57
Brown, Campbell   152
Brown, Gavin   291
Brown, Jonathan   10, 12, 160, 161,
    239
Brown, Lloyd   30
Brown, Mal   152
Brownless, Billy   132–4, 243
Bruns, Neville   247
Buckenara, Gary   21, 41, 84, 244
Buckley, Jimmy   128, 137
Buckley, Nathan   19
Buhagiar, Tony 'Budgie'   165
Bull, Dennis   265
Bunton, Haydn snr   94, 185
Burgess, Reg   75–7
Burke, Nathan   244
Burns, John   64–6
Burns, Keith   272
Burns, Peter   273
Burt, Laurie   52–4
Bussell, Norm 'Dad'   210
Buttifant, David   130
Byrne, Ray   137

Cable, Barry   66, 207
Caesar, Julius   180
Cahill, John   280
Callander, Charlie   152, 287–8
Callander, Theresa   152
Cameron, Peter   204
Capper, Joanne   109
Capper, Warwick 'Wok'   107–9,
    244, 281
Cardwell, Jim   286
Carey, Wayne 'the King'   9, 10, 12,
    51, 153, 232, 242, 243
  recruited for a song 19–20
Carlson, Leigh   130
Carlyon, Gordon & Vivian   144–5
Carman, 'Fabulous Phil'   237
Carroll, Brian   212, 219
Carroll, Dennis   19
Carter, Rod   281
Carter, Wally   55, 56

Casey, Ron   224
Cassin, Jack jnr   248
Cerutty, Percy   171–2, 173
Cheatley, Barry   154
Chitty, Bob   273, 274
Chitty, Peter   274
Christian, Michael   109
Clancy, Johnny   72
Clark, Jimmy   230
Clark, Wally   212–19, 268
Clarke, George   150
Clarke, Jack   76, 119, 265
Clarke, Matthew   230
Clarke, Ron   252
Clarkson, Alastair   153
Clay, Dick   166
Clayden, George   218
Clegg, Ron 'Smokey'   234
Cleland, Ian 'Clelo'   113
Clements, Bryan   215–18, 225–6
Cloke, David   110–11, 128
Cloke, Travis   110
Coghlan, Kevin 'Skeeter'   101, 273
Cole, Ewan   57
Coleman, Glenn 'Galaxy'   40
Coleman, John   75, 229, 286
Collier, Albert 'Leeta'   156, 279
Collier, Harry   92, 218, 254, 279
Collins, Bill   120–1
Collins, Ian   63
Collins, Mike   55
Cook, Freddie   116, 179
Cook, Ron   17, 245, 250
Cooper, Graham   55
Cooper, Ian 'Humper'   249, 266
Cooper, Ron 'Socks'   33
Copeland, Ernie   188
Cordner, Denis   48, 197, 273
Cordner, Dr Don   187
Cornes, Graham   39–40
Couch, Paul   291
Courtney, Pat   45
Cousins, Ben   240, 243
Cousins, Bryan   240
Coventry, Gordon 'Nuts'   33
Coventry, Syd   218
Coward, Alan   274
Cowton, Gary   166
Crane, Gary   210
Croad, Trent   35
Crocker, Darren 'Crock'   130
Crompton, Neil 'Froggie'   267
Crosswell, Brent 'Tiger'   87, 112, 207, 232, 237, 249

Crouch, Jeff   144, 210
Crow, Max   234
Crowe, Neville   172, 233–4
Curcio, Frank   200
Curran, Matt   64
Curran, Peter   8, 244

D'Amico, Helen   237
Daffy, Geoff   212, 219
Daicos, Peter 'Daics'   38–9, 64
Dalton, Denis   267
Daniher, Neale   240, 241
Daniher, Terry   111, 135, 232
Danos family   167
Darcy, David & Luke   226
Davis, Barry   149, 250, 264, 269
Davis, Bob 'Woofa'   43–5, 97, 127, 153, 183, 253, 267–8
  recalls the '63 Grand Final   252
Davis, Craig   135
Davis, Ken 'KD'   179–80
Davis, Nick 'Davo'   135, 201–3
de Lacy, Hec   254, 273
Dean, Peter   139
Dear, Greg   204, 293
Dear, Harry   293
Dear, Paul   164, 292–3
Delaney, Brendan   57
Dempsey, Gary   179
Devonport, Craig 'Devo'   279
Di Pierdomenico, Robert
  'Dipper'   7, 25, 105, 126, 206–7, 243, 244
Dietrich, Marlene   126
Ditterich, Carl 'the Shadow'   1, 89–90, 115, 117, 126, 225, 227
  first-game memories   252
Dixon, Brian   31, 76, 117, 225, 267
Doherty, Chris   57
Doig, George   276
Donaldson, Graeme   31
Douge, Brian   21
Doull, Bruce 'the Flying
  Doormat'   120, 165, 209, 241, 246, 248
  ten different coaches   280
Downs, Barrie   39–40
Drake, Ian   246
Drinan, Keith   155
Duckworth, Billy   111
Dugdale, John 'Dugga'   90, 100
Dunn, Ray   127
Dunne, Emmett 'Plod'   149
Dunne, Ross 'Twiggy'   87

Dunstall, Jason 249
Dunstan, Ian 'Mocca' 22
Dwyer, Laurie 100
Dyer, Jack 'Captain Blood' 32, 92, 97, 120, 123, 125–8, 183, 186, 219, 253
   criticism of Glenn Elliott 262
   Hec De Lacy's high opinion 254
   how he got his nickname 226

Eade, Rodney 40–1
Edelsten, Dr Geoffrey 164
Edelsten, Leanne 109
Edmond, Jimmy 'Jock' 22
Edwards, Brendan 76, 101, 153, 270
Edwards, Jack 208
Egan, Micky 112
Eicke, Wells 92, 94
Elderfield, Shirley 78
Elliott, Glenn 262
Elliott, Herb 171, 172
Elliott, Jack 259–60
Epis, Alec 'the Kookaburra' 120, 267–8
Erwin, Mick 280

Falvo, Don 63–4
Famechon, Johnny 121
Fanning, Fred 84, 286
Farmer, Graham 'Polly' 153, 172, 175–6, 212, 215, 218, 235
Farrell, Freddie 266
Fellowes, Graeme 145
Fellowes, Wes 128
Fenton, Ronny 87–8
Ferguson, Neil 117
Fevola, Brendan 104–5, 162–3, 241
Filandia, Peter 15
Fink, Jack 144
Fitzgerald, Gerard 150
Flaherty, Pat 116
Flanagan, Fred 183
Fletcher, Dustin 13
Florence, Stewie 72
Flower, Robert 226–7
Foote, Les 2, 56
Fordham, Ted 267
Fothergill, Des 95–7
Foulds, Gary 'Vault' 141
Francis, Peter 280
Franklin, Lance 'Buddy' 35, 84

Franklin, Tony 280
Fraser, Don 'Mopsy' 32
Fraser, the Hon. Malcolm 124
Freer, Freddie 96
Fry, Ronny 216
Furness, Don 223–4
Furness, Jack 274

Gabelich, Ray 'Gabbo' 144, 145, 272
Gallagher, Adrian 'Gags' 63, 195–6
Galt, Rod 166
Gambetta, John 285
Gardiner, Michael 259
Gayfer, Mick 109
Gehrig, Fraser 'the G-train' 237
Gepp, Tim 21
Gerard, Ned 'the Moth' 151
Giansiracusa, Daniel 289
Gibbs, Phillip 32
Gill, Barry 76
Gill, John 76
Goggin, Billy 212, 218, 252
Gooch, Arthur 238
Goode, Bob 56
Goode, Frank 54–6
Goode, Ray 55
Goodes, Adam 201
Goodger, Eddie 101
Goold, John 'Ragsy' 144
Goosey, Simon 59
Gordon, Harry 120
Goss, Norm jnr 210
Gough, Stephen 109
Graham, Ben 258, 292
Graham, Mark 105–7, 227, 259
Grant, Chris 11
Grant, Peter 'Grub' 142
Green, Jack 71
Green, Michael 166
Greene, Russell 138, 292
Greeves, Edward 'Carji' 276–7
Greig, Keith 27
Guinane, Pat 'Paddy' 67, 234
Gumbleton, Frank 87
Gunstone, Jack 239

Hafey, Karen 171
Hafey, Maureen 170, 171, 174, 249
Hafey, Tommy 119, 141–2, 151, 153, 167–75, 217, 249, 253, 257, 280

Hall, Barry   202
Hamilton, Jack   99, 144, 151, 236
Hamilton, Paul   57
Hammond, Bob   280
Hammond, Harry 'Happy'   252
Hammond, Michael   67
Hammond, Tom   269
Hams, George   144, 236
Hands, Ken   74
Hanna, Mil   111
Hannan, Jimmy   20
Hansen, Brian   142
Harford, Daniel   227
Harley, Tom   103
Harmes, Wayne   166
Harper, Alan   116
Harris, Dickie 'Hungry'   92
Harris, George   23, 247
Harrison, Barry 'Hooker'   217
Hart, Eddie   101
Hart, Kevin   101
Hart, Royce   29, 65, 153, 172, 234,
    235, 253
    two Grand Finals in two
        weeks   282–3
    Kevin Bartlett's high
        opinion   251
Hartkopf, AEV 'Bert'   278
Harvey, Robert   92, 292
Haward, Johnny   291
Hawkins, Dougie   128, 194, 245,
    246
Hawkins, Tom   84
Hay, Phil   79
Hayes, John   218
Hayes, Lenny & Tara   191
Hayes, Ray   23, 24
Heal, Stan 'Pops'   282–3
Healy, Gerard   91–2, 164, 206
Healy, Greg   227–8
Healy, Lisa   91
Healy, Pat   63
Heathcote, John   123
Hegarty, Mark   166
Heywood, Doug   113, 237
Hickey, Pat & Tony   49–52
Hickey, Reg   154, 183, 275
Hill, Kevin 'KB'   148
Hird, James   153
Hobbs, Greg   17–18, 94, 177–8
Hocking, Steve   247
Hodge, Luke   12, 153, 241
Hogan, Neville   52
Hogan, Peter   77

Hoiles, John   226
Holmes, Merv 'Farmer'   54
Howard, Bruce   265
Howell, Verdun   1, 65
Hudson, John   101
Hudson, Peter 'Huddo'   58, 65, 81,
    82, 85, 250, 251
    goal of his life 82–4
Hughes, Frank 'Checker'   188–9,
    218, 251, 288
Hunt, Rex   29, 173, 257
Hutchison, Billy   75, 76

Icke, Steven   138
Iles, Geoff 'Chopper'   151
Irvine, Jack   190
Ishchenko, Alex   230

Jackson, Wayne   23–4
Jacobs, Bob   55
Jakovich, Glen   39
James, Bill   277
James, Ronnie   261
Jamieson, Ray   177
Jarman, Darren   164
Jarvis, Nathan   241
Jeans, Allan 'Yabbie'   1–8, 117, 181,
    205, 244, 247, 249, 252, 261
Jeans, Mary   1–4, 8
Jeans, Mrs   2
Jencke, Ray   227
Jenkin, Graeme 'Jerka'   265
Jesaulenko, Alex 'Jezza'   84, 85,
    98–9, 104, 253, 280
    criticism of his training
        demands   261–2
    mark of his life   265
Jess, Jim   166
Jewell, Nick   255
Jewell, Tony 'TJ'   7, 153, 168, 170,
    280
    waters Moorabbin Oval on
        match-eve   228–9
Jillard, John   62
Johnson, 'Big Bob'   267
Johnson, Brad   292
Johnson, Steve   157, 239
Johnston, Wayne   128
Jones, Dorothy & Geoff   196
Jones, Jack   229–30
Jones, Jan   195–6
Jones, Peter 'Perc'   23, 99, 143, 144,
    152, 195–6, 280
Jones, Warren 'Wow'   136

Jordon, Ray 'Slug'   132, 227, 246
Joseph, Ron   250
Joyce, Alan   55, 225, 243
Judkins, Noel   140
Judkins, Stan   187

Keane, Merv   27
Keddie, Bob   82
Keenan, Peter 'Crackers'   15, 116
Kekovich, Sam   46, 56, 80, 117–19,
    140, 252
Kellett, Peter   77
Kelly, Paul 'Kel'   105
Kennedy, John snr 'Kanga'   7, 26–7,
    80–1, 82, 85, 117, 208, 210, 217,
    228, 241, 243, 247, 248
    congratulates Don Scott 40 years
        on   129
    door-knocking at dawn   101–2
    non-selection of Peter
        Crimmins   99–100
    recommends a teenage Leigh
        Matthews   231
Kennedy, Pat   188
Kennedy, Rick   109, 112
Kennelly, Tadhg   201–4, 241, 289
Kenter, John   57
Kerley, Neil 'Knuckles'   23–4, 49,
    49, 154
Kernahan, Jenny   195
Kernahan, Stephen   109, 195, 246,
    292
Kidd, Barry   210
Kilby, John 'Killer'   207
Killigrew, Alan 'Killer'   31, 123,
    180, 252
Kilpatrick, John   7
King, Peter   238
Kirk, Brett   61
Knights, Peter   79
Koutoufides, Anthony & Susie
    191–2
Krakouer, Jimmy   90, 248
Kyne, Phonse   238

Lacy, Brendan   57
Lahiff, Tommy   124
Laidley, Dean   120
Landy, Peter   237
Lane, David   69
Lane, Greg & Joey   57–8
Lane, Tim   136
Langsworth, Graeme   68–9
Law, Ian 'Liberty'   79

League Teams   237
Lee, Bernie   269
Lee, Dick   289
Lee, Graeme 'Gypsy'   265
Lee, Mark 'the General'   120, 166,
    206
Leek, Geoff   268
Lenne, George   211
Leppitsch, Justin   160, 230
Lewis, Chris   204
Liberatore, Tom   11
Liberatore, Tony   11, 243
Lillee, Dennis   89
Lindsay, Jill   114
Lieschke, Billy   77
Ling, Cameron   161–2
Lloyd, John   62, 230
Lloyd, Matthew   62, 230, 239–40
Lockett, Tony 'Plugger'   9, 11, 86,
    105–7, 244
Loewe, Stewart   279
Lofts, Gary   52
Lofts, Wes   30, 31, 82, 229
Long, Brendon   57
Long, Michael   163
Longmire, Fred   243
Longmire, John 'Horse'   19, 20, 51,
    92, 232, 243
Lord, Alistair   64–5, 67, 69, 268–9
Lord, John   30, 31, 70, 211, 253
Lord, Normie   81
Lord, Stewart   67–9, 269
Lovelace, Linda   41
Ludlow, Johnny   226
Luke, Sir Kenneth   270
Lynch, Alastair   240
Lynch, Allen   215
Lyon, Garry   68, 203
Lyon, Peter   68
Lyons, Maurie   101

Mackenzie, Darrel 'Goose'   138
Mackenzie, Graeme   263
Maclure, Mark   166
Madden, Justin 'Harry'   15, 139,
    229, 246
Madden, Simon   12, 15, 164, 246
Madden, Thelma   246
Maher, Paul   57
Malthouse, Mick   245, 259
Mandie, David   165–7
Mann, Harold 'Hassa'   85
Mann, Neil   280
Mansell, Ken   185

Manton, Glenn   292
Marchesi, Gerald   54
Marcou, Alex   259
Marshall, Denis   45
Martello, Alan   25, 82
Matera, Phil   258
Matthews, Herbie snr   96
Matthews, 'Lethal Leigh'   25,
    79, 116–17, 120, 128, 152, 160,
    230–1, 247, 248, 280, 292
speech before 1990 Grand
    Final   163–4
McCabe, Luke   105
McCarthy, Gerry   41
McColl, Sharon 'Shazz'   109
McCormack, Basil   190
McCrabb, Austin   245
McDonald, Ian   212
McDonald, Normie   123–4
McGrath, Ash   85
McGregor, Ian   69
McGuane, Mick   38–9
McGuinness, Luke 'Spook'   58–60
McGuire, Eddie   239
McHale, Jock   33, 95, 145–6, 254
McKay, David   261–2
McKenna, Peter   70, 81, 82
McKenzie, Bob   272
McKenzie, Don   282
McKenzie, Keith   280
McKeon, Mark   38–9
McKeown, Ronny   128
McKernan, Corey   11–12, 19, 97,
    98, 232
McLeod, Andrew   158
McMahen, Noel   71
McPherson, Cam   101–2
McRae, Ian   66
McSporran, Kevin   23
Meagher, Des   82
Meaklim, Bill   175
Menzies, Sir Robert   30
Merrett, Roger   76, 77, 232
Merrett, Thorold   257
Michael, Mal   257–8
Miles, Mr   276
Millane, Darren 'Pants'   92
Miller, Greg   19–20, 51, 97, 264
Miller, Jim 'Frosty'   87–8
Miller, Keith 'Nugget'   93–4
Mitchell, Hughie   76
Mitchell, Percy   254
Mithen, Laurie   76
Modra, Tony   158, 244

Molloy, Jarrod   257–8
Moncrieff, Michael 'Gladys'   25
Monteath, Bruce   166
Mooney, Cameron, Jagger &
    Seona   103
Moore, Kelvin   142, 207
Moore, Rod   240
Moore, Roy   275
Moriarty, Jack   287
Morphett, Drew   113
Morris, Kevin   142–3, 161
Morris, Russell   5
Morrow, Brooke   192
Morwood, Shane   134–5, 231
Motley, Peter 'Mots'   224–5
Mueller, Elizabeth & Frank   94–5
Mueller, Jack 'Melba'   92, 94–5,
    97, 187
Mugavin, Noel   65
Mulvihill, Brian   117
Munro, Mrs   145
Murphy, John   249, 251
Murphy, Rob   239
Murray, Dan   231
Murray, Kevin   101, 138, 212, 216,
    224, 231, 249, 268
    North Melbourne
    approach   264

Nash, Allan   224
Nash, Laurie 'LJ'   92, 93–4
Nash, Phillip   52
Naitanui, Nick   12
Neagle, Merv   292
Neitz, David 'Neita'   37–8, 129–30,
    240
Newman, John 'Sam'   41–3,
    149–50
Nicholls, (Sir) Douglas   184–7
Nicholls, Dowie   184
Nicholls, John 'Big Nick'   28, 67,
    73, 122–3, 268, 280
Nicholson, Harvey   278
Nolan, Mary   149
Nolan, Mick 'the Galloping
    Gasometer'   72, 92, 120, 146–9
Nolan, Nettie   149
Nolan, Peter   149
Northey, John 'Swoop'   166, 203,
    280, 281
Notting, Tim   160

O'Brien, Frank   288
O'Brien, Leo   43

O'Brien, Mr   220
O'Callaghan, Denis   293
O'Donnell, Gary   264
O'Donnell, Simon 'Scuba'   231–2, 279
O'Loughlin, 'Mickey O'   202, 237
O'Neill, Kevin   187, 190
O'Neill, Pedro   50
O'Sullivan, Shane   35–7
O'Toole, Con   72
O'Toole, Jack   127
Oakey, Howard & Ron   55
Oakley, Ross   17–18
Olarenshaw, Ricky   13
Olsson, Elly   209
Olsson, Rod   150, 208–9
Ongarello, Tony   154
Oppy, Max   219–20

Pagan, Cheryl   93
Pagan, Denis   10, 14–15, 92–3, 97, 98, 103, 153, 232, 241, 253
Pagan, Don   232
Page, Percy   94–5, 187–90, 251
   Jack Dyer tribute   189–90
   one-off match for Tigers   287–8
Palmer, Scotty   9
Papley, Tim & Max   255
Parker, Dr Roy 'the University Midget'   277–8
Parkin, David 'Parko'   24–5, 35–7, 104, 129, 234, 255–6, 259, 280
   high opinion of Leigh Matthews   249
Patterson, Mark 'Patto'   151
Patterson, Mike 'the Swamp Fox'   144, 280
Pavlich, Matty & Stephen   163
Pavlou, Chris   166
Payne, Ernie   148
Pearson, Bill 'Soapy'   88
Pearson, Charles 'Commotion'   278
Peck, John   79, 84, 121–2, 144, 217
Peperkamp, Bert   69
Pert, Gary   38, 150, 205
Philippoussis, Mark   13
Pianto, Peter 'Pint'   183
Picken, Bill   253
Picione, Lance   158
Picken, Billy   161, 280
Piesse, KC 'Ken'   79, 155
Piesse, PAR 'Pat'   155
Pike, Martin   160, 240
Piltz, Brent   60–1

Platten, Johnny 'Rat'   7, 227
Pleydell, Bill, Chris & Jimmy   61–3
Ponsford, Bill 'Ponny'   89
Porter, Mick   26, 117
Potter, Trevor   69
Powell, Peter   99
Pratt, Bob   92, 94, 97, 275, 276, 287
Prentice, Jim   210
Price, Barry   81
Priestley, Charlie   166
Prince Charles   209
Prince Philip   216
Prior, Tom   120
Pullen, Rex   179
Purser, Andrew   41

Quade, Ricky   280
Queen Elizabeth II   216

Radziminski, Richard   126
Rantall, John   250, 264
Ratcliffe, Raelene   194
Ratten, Brett   139
Read, Jimmy   72
Reid, Dr Bruce   112
Rendell, Matt 'Bundi'   40, 138
Renfrey, Russ 'Hooker'   155
Renouf, Jim   57
Reynolds, Dick 'King Richard'   75, 76, 123–4, 219–20, 229, 253
Rhys-Jones, David   136–7, 246
Ricciuto, Mark   49
Richards, Edna   127
Richards, Lou 'Louie the Lip'   30, 97, 119–21, 125, 127–8, 146, 224, 232–3
Richards, Ron   232–3, 280
Richardson, Alan 'Bull'   68, 76, 154, 171
Richardson, Barry 'Bones'   166, 234
Richardson, Matty   68, 154, 292
Richardson, Max   87
Richardson, Richie   84
Richardson, Wayne   87, 145
Richmond, Graeme   67, 152, 168, 250, 251
Ridley, Ian   116
Riewoldt, Nick   12
Risk, Alex   218
Roach, Michael 'Disco'   142
Robbie, David   76

Roberts, Brian 'the Whale'   119,
   141–2, 151
Roberts, Michael   286
Roberts, Michael   143
Roberts, Neil 'Coconut'   270
Roberts, Neville   166
Rogers, Bernie & Evelyn   78
Romero, Jose   11
Ronaldson, John   172, 233–4
Ronaldson, Tony   234
Roos, Paul 'Roosy'   150, 193–4,
   201, 202
   abused by David Parkin   234
Roos, Tami   194–4
Rose, Bob   197, 209–10, 280
Rose, Elsie   197
Rose, Peter   210
Rose, Robert   209
Rosenow, Geoff 'Tex'   285
Roughead, Jarryd   292
Rudolph, George   183
Rumph, Peter 'Hughie'   151
Ryan, Denis 'Dinny'   254
Ryan, Reg 'Dodger'   236, 263

Salmon, Paul 'the Big Fish'   11–12,
   128–9, 241, 264
Sandilands, Laurie   179
Sarah, Paul 'Ferret'   176
Sawers, Rohan   137
Sawley, Brian   121–2
Schimmelbusch, Daryl   21–2
Schimmelbusch, Wayne   21–2
Schultz, John   285
Schwab, Alan   4, 17, 27, 250, 257
Schwab, Cameron   4
Schwarz, David   37-38, 203
Schwass, Wayne   19
Scott, Don   25, 79-80, 100, 129,
   235
   refuses to talk to his coach   261
   wins the Damn-low
      Medal   293–4
Serong, Bill   100, 101
Sessions, Bob   12
Sewell, Brad   239–40
Shanahan, Jamie   241
Shannon, Bernie   101
Sharp, Lerrel   144, 145
Sharrock, John 'Shadda'   43–6, 212,
   215
Sharrock, Wally   43–4
Shaw, Gary   281
Shaw, Tony   38, 131, 134–5,

259–60
Sheahan, Maurie   190
Sheahan, Mike   239, 240, 269
Sheedy, Kevin 'Sheeds'   35, 111,
   153, 167, 174, 235, 247, 280
Sheehan, Kevin   150, 161–3, 175–6
Sheldon, Ken 'Bomba'   241
Shelton, Ian 'Bluey'   74
Silvagni, Jack   17
Silvagni, Sergio   17, 72, 101, 242,
   280
Silvagni, Stephen   17, 192, 242
Sinclair, Cameron   285
Skilton, Bob   178, 234–5, 253, 265
Skilton, Marion   178
Slattery, Geoff   32
Smallhorn, Wilfred 'Chicken'   185,
   237
Smith, Gary   166
Smith, Greg 'the Bionic Man'   19,
   120
Smith, Jack   188
Smith, Len   1, 180–3, 224
Smith, Norm   31, 48, 88, 153, 178,
   181, 187, 189, 211, 212, 236
   rejects Stan Alves   222–3
Somerville, John   54
Southby, Geoff   165, 250
Spargo, Bob   259
Spencer, Fay   46–8, 197–200
Spencer, Stuart   46–8, 85, 97,
   197–200
Sproule, Paul   280
Stanton, Barry   234
Steer, Trevor   148
Stephen, Bill   22
Stephens, Brett   193
Stephens, Peter   69
Stevens, Steve   154
Stewart, Ian   1, 65, 235, 268–9,
   280, 285
   waters Moorabbin Oval on
      match-eve   228–9
Stockdale, David   122
Stone, George   5, 7
Stynes, Jim   92, 245
Swift, Fred   172–3, 252

Tafft, Craig   61
Tanner, Xavier   157
Taylor, Brian 'BT'   128
Taylor, Dick   200
Taylor, Kevin   262
Taylor, Mick   40

Teasdale, Noel   100, 236, 267–8
Teasdale, Graham   235–6
Templeton, Kelvin   281–2
Theobald, Paul   57
Thomas, Dale   289
Thomas, Hughie   33
Thomas, Ron   20
Thompson, Alan   241
Thompson, Mark   162
Thoms, George   89
Thorogood, Ian   25–6, 280
Timms, Daryl 'Daz'   10
Timms, Ken   121
Titus, Jack 'Skinny'254
Todd, John   205–6
Tolkien, JR   292
Toohey, Bernard   164
Tossol, Peter 'Toss'   151
Trainor, Tony   55
Travers, Mrs   95
Tresize, Neil 'Nipper'   183
Trott, Stuart   116–17
Tuck, Frank   144
Tuck, Michael 'Friar'   231, 260, 279
Tuddenham, Des   51, 70, 100, 249
    coaches against
        Collingwood   265
Turner, Mick   112, 241
Twomey, Bill   101, 144, 245
Twomey, Mick   76, 101, 144
Twomey, Pat   101, 144, 236

Vallence, Harry 'Soapy'   141
Vinar, Paul 'the Swede'   28
Voss, Michael   160

Wade, Doug   81-82, 207, 212, 264, 285
    on crossing to North
        Melbourne   250
Walkelin, Darryl & Shane   240
Walker, Max   236
Walker, Peter   172
Walker, Robbie   52–3
Walker, Taylor 'Tex'   189, 293
Wallace, Terry   41
Walls, Robert   14, 29, 40, 280
Walsh, Kevin   206–7
Warnie, Shane 'Warnie'   84
Watson, Tim   246
Watts, John   285
Wearmouth, Ronnie   143, 247–8
Weekes, Robbie   113

Weideman, Murray   77, 236–8, 280
Weissmuller, Johnny   153
Weightman, Dale 'the Flea'   238, 244
Weightman, Kent   238
Wells, Greg   112
Welsh, Peter   82–4
Wheildon, Darren 'Doc'   130
White, Allan   72–4
White, Darryl   14
Whitten, Ted 'EJ'   5, 15, 30, 32, 93, 113, 120, 179–80, 206, 237, 243
    four best and fairests in same
        year   285
    gamesmanship at the
        toss   234–5
    trials at North Melbourne   225
Willett, Ray   69–72
Williams, Fos   154
Williams, Greg 'Diesel'   90–1, 164, 244, 292
Williams, Mary   90–1
Williamson, Mike   253
Willis, Paul 'Whistle'   57
Wills, Tom   20
Wilson, Brian   98
Wise, John   166
Witcombe, Murray   281
Woods, Michael   63
Woods, Bervyn   274
Woolley, Roger   40–1
Worsfold, John 'Woosha'   158, 240
Wright, Kevin   101
Wright, Roy   178
Wynd, Scott   11

Yeates, Mark   6, 7
Yeats, Graeme   203
Young, Gary   45, 72
Young, George   166
Yze, Adem   289

BOXES
Catchphrases   253
Famous goals   84
Father and son 'mosts'   284
Jack Dyer's most famous
    one-liners   126
Len Smith's words of wisdom   182
Match day superstitions   291–2
Number 13: Most games &
    goals   290
Remarkable results   217–18